SILENCING THE GUNS IN HAITI

Silencing the Guns in Haiti

THE PROMISE OF DELIBERATIVE DEMOCRACY

Irwin P. Stotzky

The University of Chicago Press
Chicago and London

IRWIN P. STOTZKY is professor of law at the University of
Miami School of Law and has served as attorney and ad-
viser to Jean-Bertrand Aristide and as adviser to the René
Preval administration. For his representation of Haitian ref-
ugees before the U.S. Supreme Court, Stotzky has received
Human Rights Awards from the American Immigration
Lawyers Association and the Haitian Refugee Center. For
his work in investigating human rights abuses and his
scholarship, he has received the *Inter-American Law Review*'s
Lawyer of the Americas award.

The University of Chicago Press, Chicago 60637
The University of Chicago Press, Ltd., London
© 1997 by The University of Chicago
All rights reserved. Published 1997
Printed in the United States of America

06 05 04 03 02 01 00 99 98 97   1 2 3 4 5

ISBN: 0-226-77626-3

Title page illustration: Haitians celebrate the return of Jean-
Bertrand Aristide in front of the National Palace, Port-au-
Prince, October 15, 1994. Photograph © Chantal Regnault.

Library of Congress Cataloging-in-Publication Data

Stotzky, Irwin P.
    Silencing the guns in Haiti : the promise of deliberative
democracy / Irwin P. Stotzky.
        p.   cm.
    Includes index.
    ISBN 0-226-77626-3 (alk. paper)
    1. Haiti—Politics and government—1986– 2. De-
mocracy—Haiti. 3. Human rights—Haiti. I. Title.
JL1090.S76   1997
320.97294'09'049—dc21   97-19494
                                                    CIP

♾ The paper used in this publication meets the minimum
requirements of the American National Standard for
Information Sciences—Permanence of Paper for Printed
Library Materials, ANSI Z39.48-1984.

To Audrey, for her love and support,

and

to the memory of Soia Mentschikoff, Carlos Nino, and Michael Katz, who, each in a unique way, spent their lives fighting for justice.

Contents

Preface

The last two decades of the twentieth century have witnessed many Latin American and Eastern European nations become involved in a remarkable political experiment. Their historically ubiquitous authoritarian regimes, typically in the form of military juntas and dictatorships, have gradually been replaced by constitutional democracies. This process—usually referred to as the transition from authoritarianism to democracy—is, however, far from complete.

One of the best examples of the promises and pitfalls of such an undertaking is Haiti. The October 15, 1994, reinstatement of Jean-Bertrand Aristide as president of Haiti was a historic moment, for it marked the first time a democratically elected president replaced the very military officers who had deposed him. It opens the possibility that Haiti, which has never had a functioning democracy, may make the transition to democracy. If this potential is to be realized—if Haiti is not to slide back to dictatorship and repression—there are severe problems to overcome.

Indeed, the economic, political, and social challenges posed by Haiti's odyssey from the Duvaliér era to one of democracy are as difficult as those faced by any nation in the world undergoing a transition process. While the international community, specifically the United States and the Multi-National Force (MNF)—a smattering of troops from other countries—has helped to secure a measure of stability by successfully reinstating President Aristide to office and providing the necessary security to allow the second democratically elected president in the history of Haiti, René Preval, to assume his office, that stability is fragile at best.

It remains unclear whether the international effort to restore the democratically elected government and to help create the necessary conditions for a democracy will again founder on the intransigence of the most powerful forces in Haiti—the economic elites and the military and paramilitary forces. Even assuming that these powerful corporativist influences can be brought under democratic control, the difficulties of creating the infrastructure for a viable economy and a functioning governmental institutional framework remain formidable. Unfortunately, this is not all. Another crucial task is changing the conditions of social interaction between the various socioeconomic groups, particularly those between the urban poor, the rural peasants, and the economic elites. Perhaps even more urgent for the development of a democracy is the need to inculcate in the minds of the people of Haiti respect for the rule of law, which, of course, must undergird all of these factors. The question of whether to investigate and prosecute those who have committed serious human rights violations played a key role in the events leading up to the September 1991 coup. It continued to be a significant factor in the negotiations for President Aristide's return, and is now a major issue in the consolidation of the democratic government. Dealing with past transgressions is crucial to opening up new possibilities for establishing and securing the rule of law in the public institutions and private enterprises of Haiti, and in the minds and actions of the Haitian people. In sum, the challenge of creating a democracy in Haiti is daunting.

This book analyzes these problems, within the context of Haiti's history, and suggests solutions to them based on a particular justificatory theory of democracy. Part 1 discusses the origins of dictatorship in Haiti; the exile of President Aristide; and the negotiations, conflicts, and courses of action between the Aristide government, the U.S. government, the international community, and the de facto regime during the period of Aristide's exile (1991–94).

Part 2 moves to an analysis of theories of democracy and the specific theory that I champion, which suggests a justification for democracy quite different from most other theories. It also analyzes the critiques of my theory. Talking generally about the term "democracy" without analyzing its possible meanings or justifying the reasons for creating such a polity is dangerous in that it may help to legitimate the very evils that a real democracy is meant to alleviate. The term is open to limitless interpretation and could therefore be used as a means to sanction almost any political and social system, even a totalitarian one. In this study, failure to delineate adequately the meaning of democracy as applied to the lives of the real people of Haiti, and further to justify its choice as the preferred system of government, could legitimate a return to state-initiated violence and terror instead of a step toward freedom.

Parts 1 and 2 are complementary in that the historical background information is necessary to an understanding of how to go about the delicate task of institution building and how to create the social, political, and economic conditions that are so crucial to the creation of a viable democracy. A justificatory basis for a stable democratic government, in turn, is itself essential to the development of the very conditions needed to perpetuate a democracy.

Part 3 tackles the thorny issues associated with the transition from dictatorship to democracy. First I look at the problems that the Haitian people face—on a macro- and micropolitical level, as well as on a theoretical and practical level—and suggest and analyze possible solutions through an application of my theory of democracy. I next address the question of what to do, if anything, with those who have committed massive human rights violations. I examine this question—which is intertwined with all of the obstacles facing Haiti in its transition to democracy—from a moral, political, and legal perspective.

Part 4 analyzes the attempts made by the Aristide and Preval governments to change Haitian society. I discuss the positive and negative aspects of the changes, including the role that the international community, particularly the United States, has played in creating problems and the possible solutions to them.

Acknowledgments

This book began as a collection of notes about my approximately nineteen years of legal work on behalf of Haitian refugees. I intended to turn these notes into a wide-ranging discussion of justice, or the lack of it, in the American legal system. Events intruded on those plans, however, and in 1991, the focus of the book changed. In September, the military and paramilitary forces of Haiti staged a coup d'état and overthrew the first democratically elected government in Haitian history. President Jean-Bertrand Aristide began his exile and struggle to return to power. Soon after his ouster, I held a conference in Miami on the transition to democracy in Latin America. It was here that I met President Aristide and became one of his advisers. During his three-year exile, I worked with him and his government on a broad range of issues. In 1994, when the MNF reinstated President Aristide to office, I began to work for his government in helping to investigate and prosecute those who were responsible for the close to five thousand murders, countless tortures, and other unspeakable human rights violations that took place under the de facto regime from 1991 to 1994. The idea for this book came from those experiences. I originally planned to incorporate my work on Haitian refugee litigation with the issues involved in creating a democracy in Haiti, but that task proved simply too broad. I decided instead to write a book on democratic theory and its application to the transition to democracy in Haiti. The book on the Haitian refugee litigation will come later.

The investigations and other work on the transition process, as well as the actual writing of the book, were experiences of personal transformation. Like all intense academic endeavors, the book is a product of many special people and circumstances. Indeed, there are so many persons who were involved in this work of scholarship to whom I am indebted and grateful that it would be difficult to acknowledge adequately all those who have helped. Moreover, many people who provided useful information must remain publicly anonymous because of security and other concerns. Nevertheless, I shall attempt to acknowledge those persons who have been most helpful and who can be recognized without fear of either physical harm or social or political revenge.

I am especially indebted to Ira J. Kurzban for all of his support, knowledge, and helpful comments on drafts of the manuscript. His dedication to the struggle of the Haitian people is unparalleled. Michael Ratner, Richard Harvey, Katie Orenstein, and Reed Brody did much of the hard work in investigating and in working with Haitian police, prosecutors, and judges. I owe them special thanks. Moreover, I wish to thank Richard Harvey for his wonderful description of the Zimbabwe trial. Jean-Jean Pierre was critical to the completion of the manuscript. I am specially grateful to him. We worked hand-in-hand in the investigations. His knowledge, intelligence, and never-ending sources of information were invaluable. His friendship and inspiration were incalculable.

I owe a special debt to Jean-Bertrand Aristide for asking me to work with the Haitian people to help create the conditions for democracy. His intelligence, courage, and skill in protecting the Haitian people and attempting to create a democratic ethic in governmental institutions and a moral consciousness in the citizenry are truly heroic deeds. Mildred Trouillot Aristide's work in Haiti and encouragement of the project also deserve special attention. Yvon Neptune, Laura Flynn, Michael Levy, and the liaison staff provided important help and information. Many other Haitian government officials were extremely helpful, as were officials from the United Nations and the United States. The identities of these people, however, must remain unmentioned.

I am particularly grateful to Chantal Regnault for permission to use her wonderful photographs. She is an artist of exceptional merit. Her haunting photographs make the discussion of Haitian life come alive.

I am deeply grateful to Owen Fiss for first introducing me to the ideas involved in the transition to democracy and for all of his encouragement and support over the years as a teacher and friend. His moral commitment to democracy and intellectual integrity make him truly unique. I am also profoundly grateful to the late Carlos S. Nino for all of his support, friendship, and intellectual work on democratic theory. Stanley Katz played an indispensable role in the project. His astute analysis of my manuscript and his editorial insight were extraordinary. His example of living life as a moral individual, intellectual integrity, friendship, and support are truly appreciated. John Hart Ely's comments on the manuscript, friendship, and support of the project were specially beneficial. Jules Coleman's comments on the manuscript and support of the enterprise were also very useful. Jaime Malamud-Goti's work in this area and his comments on my manuscript were invaluable. David Feingold's insights on the themes of the book, friendship, and support of the project were very helpful.

Susan Bennett played an especially important role in the completion of the project. She worked extremely hard and with great skill in finding source material, editing, cite checking, and proofreading. Her intelligence and insight proved invaluable. She never wavered, even in the face of impossible deadlines and unreasonable demands. She deserves special praise.

Brooks Fudenberg's organizational comments were insightful and intelligent. Vivien Toomey-Montz's comments on the manuscript and her encouragement of the project were equally valuable. Ann St. Peter-Griffith's cite checking and editing were also extremely helpful. Therese Lambert's encouragement of the project and critical comments on some of the themes of the book proved invaluable. I am equally grateful to Sue Cobb for her editorial comments and support of the project.

The lectures I gave at Princeton University in 1993, 1994, and 1995 were invaluable in forcing me to concentrate on this project. I am especially grateful to Léon-François Hoffmann for his encouragement of the project, friendship, and vast knowledge of the history and culture of Haiti, which he shared with me. I am also grateful to participants in a 1994 conference at the Yale Law School dedicated to the work of Carlos Nino on Democracy and Human Rights. Their insights were very helpful in getting me to focus my analysis. The papers I delivered at a conference held at Dartmouth in 1994 on the future of democracy in Haiti allowed me to test my ideas to a very knowledgeable group of scholars. I am indebted to Martin Sherwin for this opportunity. The lectures I delivered at Hebrew University and Tel Aviv University in 1995 allowed me to present my ideas on democratic theory to an international audience. I am grateful to scholars at those schools, especially Alex Stein, for the opportunity. I am also grateful to participants of the Legal Theory Seminar at the University of Miami School of Law and to the Ethics Program participants at the University of Arkansas at Little Rock. Their comments were very stimulating and helped me to fine-tune some of my analysis.

The library staff of the University of Miami School of Law was always supportive. In particular, I am indebted to Clare Donnelly Membiela, whose research was invaluable. Nora de la Garza, Anne Klinefelter, Virginia Templeton, and Brian Williams also provided important research help. I am deeply grateful to all of the library's staff.

There were many students whose energy and talent eased my research and proofreading burdens as the work progressed. I am especially grateful to Deanna Allen, Thierry Desmet, Lucy Hahn, Allison Hift, Lisa Joyner, Marni Lennon, and Raquel Libman.

I also wish to thank the secretaries who helped me by typing various parts of the innumerable drafts of the manuscript: Sue Ellen Cypkin and Cynthia Lyons. Cary Garcia did an excellent job of typing and formatting. Andrea Calow deserves special mention. She combined intelligence with competence and hard work and almost single-handedly typed several drafts of the book. She also made helpful suggestions concerning format and style. Her work was truly first-rate.

The production aspects of the book have been much more pleasant than I imagined. I would particularly like to thank my editor at the University of Chicago Press, John Tryneski, for all of his helpful editorial suggestions, intelligence, support, and insight. He helped make this book as good as it could be. I also wish to thank my production editor at Chicago, Leslie Keros, for her ideas, editing, energy, and efficiency; my copyeditor, Louise Cameron Maynard, for her excellent editorial suggestions and insights; and my promotions manager, Erin Hogan, for her ideas, wise counsel, and suggestions about the book's title.

Finally, although she will undoubtedly consider this unnecessary, I would like to thank my partner and soon-to-be wife, Audrey R. Goldman, for her suggestions and support, and for making me so very happy during these past several years.

Prologue

October 15, 1994, was an extraordinary day. After three years of forced exile, President Jean-Bertrand Aristide was scheduled to return to Haiti from Washington, D.C. Aristide—the first democratically elected president in the nearly 200-year history of Haiti, who had been overthrown by a military coup in September 1991, approximately eight months after his election—represented the last and best hope of the Haitian people for the creation of a meaningful democracy.

The weather in the D.C. area that day was brisk, the sky clear. I remember thinking to myself that it was fitting for the situation. President Aristide was about to become the only democratically elected leader ever to be returned to office during his term and was to replace the very de facto military coup regime that overthrew him. The weather seemed to be the harbinger of a new beginning. This beautiful day promised an end to tyranny, senseless large-scale genocide, and dire poverty; it held out the promise of a democratic society. To put it another way, Aristide's return signaled the start of a journey for the Haitian people, as he often states, "from misery [tyranny] to poverty with dignity."

When I left my hotel in Alexandria, Virginia, for Andrews Air Force Base, my mind was racing. Had it actually been almost eighteen years since the Haitian refugee litigation began? Was it possible that President Aristide would return to Haiti and be able to regenerate a dying nation? I thought that the possibility of making such a change was quite problematic at best.

When I arrived at the main gate at Andrews, the two very serious military guards examined my "official" documents, an invitation from the Aristide government, and gave me directions to the terminal. It was 5 A.M. I was relieved to get onto the grounds of the base because I had inadvertently left my passport at home in Miami. I

1

prayed that the invitation would be sufficient to allow me to accompany President Aristide on his return to Haiti.

It was a long ride from the gate to the terminal. As I approached, the weather suddenly changed, and, in what seemed like a split second, the sky clouded over. Inside the terminal was an interesting mixture of people, all of whom had played a significant role in keeping alive the hope that Haiti would be freed from the bonds of tyranny, and democracy restored (or, more accurately, created). Joseph Kennedy, Jonathan Demme, Dante Caputo, Michael Barnes, Eric Trouillot, Steven Forester, Cathy Maternowska, Leslie Voltaire, Amy Wilentz, Michael Ratner, and Taylor Branch, among many others, scurried about talking and drinking coffee with high-ranking U.S. and Haitian government officials. Everyone was elated.

Hernan Pantino Mayer, Argentina's ambassador to the Organization of American States, commented: "For the first time in the history of the Americas, a toppled president is being returned to his country because of pressure from the international community, and is displacing the very same dictators who overthrew him." Even Dante Caputo, the former United Nations (UN) special envoy for Haiti, who had resigned in alleged dismay when U.S. troops invaded Haiti in September, grumbled an upbeat message. The restoration of Aristide, even at gunpoint, he said, demonstrates "a new sort of doctrine about regional democratic security, which isn't bad."

Finally, forty-five minutes late, Secretary of State Warren Christopher's sleek, black limousine pulled onto the tarmac. Out stepped Aristide, with the secretary and William Gray, President Clinton's special adviser for Haiti. Christopher triumphantly announced: "Haiti will resume its rightful place in the community of democratic nations. . . . The time for struggle and resistance is past and the time for governance has begun." Aristide responded by saying, "On behalf of my nation, I would like to share my sincere thanks with you, to President Clinton, to all of you for your support. . . . Let's continue this celebration . . . a wonderful day of peace, democracy, respect." At that moment the sun cracked through the clouds for his departure. Aristide led the entourage up the red-carpeted steps, clasped his hands together like a prizefighter, and stepped onto the plane.

The arrangements for the flight to Haiti were intriguing. Three planes carrying different categories of people were scheduled to fly to Haiti, each one leaving at a different time because the airport in Port-au-Prince could accommodate only one of these aircraft at a time and, of course, because of serious security concerns. Two were official U.S. Air Force planes, with the appropriate logos. One of these carried President Aristide, Haitian government officials, and high-ranking U.S. officials. Among its passengers were Warren Christopher, William Gray, Samuel Berger, deputy assistant to the president for national security affairs, and influential senators and congresspersons interested in Haiti, such as Senator Christopher Dodd of Connecticut. Political celebrities, such as Jesse Jackson, also traveled on this plane. The other U.S. Air Force plane carried additional Haitian government officials and high-ranking U.S. government officials. The Haitian government had leased the third plane from Carnival Airlines. It carried an assortment of Haitians and Americans—the not-so-famous or infamous. I, of course, left on this plane. A large number of journalists and broadcast media representatives also traveled on each of these three planes.

The atmosphere on the third plane during the four-hour flight to Haiti was charged with anticipation. Everyone walked up and down the aisles chatting and laughing.[1] Throughout the trip, three large Haitian women, dressed in wonderfully vibrant, bright-colored Haitian clothes and head gear, sang Haitian songs a cappella, in preparation for the state ceremony. They were wonderful. Everyone bustled about, clapping rhythmically to their singing. The Academy Award–winning director, Jonathan Demme, ran up and down the aisles, videotaping the scene.

We landed at approximately 10:50 A.M. It seemed to take forever to exit the plane. As I stepped off the plane, I was struck by the full force of the bright sun, which at first blinded me. When I regained my focus, I was stunned at the scene that confronted me. American troops in tanks and humvees and on foot surrounded not only the plane but the entire airport. It looked as if every one of the 21,000 American troops stationed in Haiti had come out to greet us. The scene around the perimeter was even more compelling. Literally thousands of Haitians surrounded the airport, cheering wildly at our arrival. The slightest gesture from any of us to the crowd gave rise to deafening cheers. A wave or smile to the Haitian people symbolically represented their liberation. It meant hope. Our arrival was a fulfillment of their most sacred hopes for freedom. The scene was almost surreal.

As we exited the plane, we were greeted formally by William Swing, the U.S. ambassador to Haiti, and Stanley Schrager, another U.S. embassy official. We then boarded buses to go to the National Palace, where President Aristide and his guests were to meet for his reinstatement ceremony and banquet. The buses were old, rickety, and broken down, yet brightly colored. The heat inside them was stifling. It took us over fifty minutes to travel the roughly three miles to the National Palace. We made slow progress along potholed streets, which were lined with dense crowds of cheering people. The noise was so loud that I could not hear myself speaking to other people on the bus. Waving to the Haitian crowds raised the decibel level substantially. Revelers jumped on the bumpers and shook our outstretched hands. There was an incredible feeling of joy and a wonderful sense of collective optimism.

We eventually reached the National Palace, where we waited for President Aristide.[2] Arriving at Port-au-Prince at midday, he boarded a U.S. helicopter, which would deliver him to the enormous crowd awaiting him at the palace. As his helicopter took off, an ecstatic crowd at the airport began running toward the palace. There, thousands of onlookers pressed up against the wrought-iron fence that surrounded and marked off the palace grounds. Thousands of other Haitians danced and sang in an endless series of processions that moved by the compound, and every time an airplane flew overhead, the crowd erupted in cheers. When Aristide's helicopter landed, and he stepped out of it, wearing a black suit and the colorful presidential sash, a big red and blue, gold-fringed sash of office, the throng cheered wildly. They waved tree branches, handkerchiefs, and portraits of Aristide, and periodically shouted, "Titid," the affectionate diminutive of his name.

Several of us had toured the palace while waiting for Aristide to arrive. It is a very beautiful, very large structure with countless rooms, and it was clear that the Haitian people had worked like demons in preparation for the president's return, meticulously cleaning and painting.

There had also been a spate of cleaning and decorating beyond the palace grounds that amounted to an all-out shakeup of some of the country's almost totally depleted infrastructure. Shovel-and-broom brigades had literally attacked massive piles of festering garbage. Even the streets in the slum known as Cité Soleil were spotless. There were decorations everywhere. "What a beautiful day to be here again," read a freshly painted sign on a cinderblock wall near Cité Soleil, followed by "We thank Clinton, we wish him good luck in his life." All along the roads, trees, guard rails, and posts had been painted red and blue. There were pictures of a rooster—an important symbol of Aristide's movement—and portraits of Aristide. Crowds of people had arranged painted stones on newly raked dirt by the roads, with messages like "Thank you Jesus—Welcome Aristide" and "Viva Democracy."

It was only a surface clean, however. The structure of the National Palace appeared sound, for example, but much of the interior, particularly the living quarters, was in shambles, purposely trashed by the de facto regime—the military coup leaders and their soldiers—before they fled.[3] There was no electricity, no running water, and no modern communications system, such as telephones or fax machines, all of which was symbolic of the condition of the country's infrastructure, and it portended the serious difficulties that lay ahead. On October 15, 1994, however, what was more intensely significant, of course, was the return of Aristide, the restoration of democracy, and the replacement of despair with hope.

We anxiously awaited Aristide's speech, many observers fearing that, if it did not stress the themes of reconciliation and forgiveness, his followers would seek violent revenge on the military and its allies. We hoped that it would set the proper tone and be viewed as the first step down the unknown path to democracy. We were not disappointed.

After walking about the palace and greeting people for approximately an hour, President Aristide was ready to speak. He first blew kisses to the crowd, took a seat in a gilded ceremonial chair, and released a white dove. He then rose and walked down the palace steps, where he stood behind a triptych of bulletproof glass. "Honor. Respect," he said, smiling, using the greeting that rural people give in Haiti's villages and mountains. Then, he delivered the message that he would repeat in four languages—Creole, English, French, and Spanish: "No to violence. No to vengeance. Yes to reconciliation." The security was massive and intense. U.S. troops in full combat regalia stood guard on the lawn and surrounding rooftops. U.S. combat helicopters flew overhead, and international police monitors wearing their well-recognized yellow caps stood guard near the outer gates.

In his speech, Aristide consciously set a tone strongly opposed to the taking of street vengeance against the gunmen who had killed approximately five thousand people, tortured and severely injured tens of thousands of other people, and pillaged the countryside since the 1991 coup: "Never, never, never, never again will one more drop of blood flow. Let us live in peace. All the guns must be silent." But his speech did not focus solely on reconciliation. President Aristide also stressed the competing theme of ensuring justice for the Haitian people. We all marveled at his fluency, his use of metaphors,[4] and his rhetorical skills. He often used a favored technique of eliciting responses from the crowd, coaxing louder and louder calls of "No to vengeance!" and "Yes to reconciliation!" President Aristide's speech had clearly worked up the huge crowd.

President Aristide profusely praised the American forces who had, in effect, delivered the government back from the Haitian generals.[5] "If you see an attaché with his gun, bring him to the American military, who will give you security," the president said. The word "security" was one he used often as he spoke in this land of brutal political murders. "There will be security in the morning, security at noon, security at night. Days come and days go, but what a beautiful day this, October 15, 1994, is." He continued to develop this theme. "To all those who question their dreams, remember October 15. October 15 affirms the strength of solidarity, the fortitude of conviction, the power of dreams." He ended with his traditional campaign slogan, with which he had once ended all of his speeches and which he used when he led the popular movement, known as Lavalas, that put him in power: "Sèl nou feb. Ansanm nou fò. Ansanm, ansanm, nou se lavalas" (Alone, we are weak. Together, we are strong. Altogether, we are Lavalas).[6] It was a crowning moment.

I watched the scene in utter amazement. Who could have predicted that Aristide would be restored to office? It suddenly struck me that this was the first time Aristide had set foot in the National Palace since September 29, 1991, the day before the military and economic elites of the nation carried out a bloody coup that forced him into thirty-seven months of exile, first in Venezuela, then in Washington. By all rights, Aristide never should have survived the coup.

The night of the takeover, soldiers loyal to the Port-au-Prince police chief, Lieutenant Colonel Michel François, arrested Aristide in his home. They tied his hands behind his back and took him to the army headquarters, where he met army commander Lieutenant General Raul Cédras, who apparently saved him from being killed by angry soldiers. Aristide's three-year exile began.

After two years of efforts, largely consisting of the international community placing the nation under a series of economic embargoes, President Clinton amassed U.S. soldiers and a small number of troops from other nations to invade Haiti and force the military leaders to resign. In the face of this threat, and after a last-ditch diplomatic effort by former President Jimmy Carter, Senator Sam Nunn, and General Colin Powell, the de facto coup leaders—François, Cédras, and Cédras's chief aide, Brigadier General Philippe Biamby—agreed to leave the country. They all left Haiti in early October, just before Aristide's triumphant return.

Nevertheless, upon his return, President Aristide extended an olive branch to the military that overthrew him, murdered and tortured thousands of innocent Haitians, and plundered the national treasury. Aristide stated that he would walk "hand in hand" with them to "rebuild the nation." He shook hands with Major General Jean-Claude Duperval, interim commander of the Haitian army, and the two men reviewed a nine-man army honor guard—an unlikely scene and a moment of high drama.

After the public reinstatement ceremony, most of the massive crowd stayed in front of the palace, celebrating by dancing and singing. President Aristide appeared in a balcony window, waving and blowing kisses to the cheering crowd. He then greeted his guests. A multitude of people from the United States and other foreign nations waited to meet him, somewhat impatiently, in a long line. I entered the line, but, when I saw how long it was taking to greet President Aristide, I decided not to wait. I hoped to see him privately later in the day. At that moment, Jean Casimir, Aristide's ambassador to the United States, pulled me to the front of the line. President Aristide hugged me, told me that I was a brother to him and the Haitian people, and thanked me profusely for my help. He also told me that I would be needed in the near future to help Haiti become a democracy. I was honored, embarrassed, and elated. I thanked him for the opportunity to work with him and the Haitian people for democratic change, congratulated him, and pledged my future support.[7] I was particularly happy about his peaceful return and the effect it had on the Haitian people. Approximately an hour later, the greetings ended, and we all joined together in a grand banquet to celebrate the occasion. I returned to the United States that evening, my mind racing through all the improbable events that had occurred during the trip.

Several months later, on January 11, 1995, as I returned from another trip to Haiti, this time to work with the Aristide government on the question of what to do with those who had committed massive violations of human rights, my mind returned to the themes Aristide raised in his reinstatement address. The great and perhaps insurmountable task that confronted him during the remainder of his reinstated term, which officially ended on February 7, 1996, and that now confronts the new democratically elected president, René Preval, is leading Haiti through the difficult transition period to a stable democracy that can endure once the UN peace-keeping forces have left the country.[8] In order to do that, President Aristide focused his presidency on what he often calls the "twin issues" of reconciliation and justice. "We shall prepare the coffee of reconciliation through the filter of justice," he said before his return, in one of his characteristically aphoristic proverbs that usually leave U.S. officials scratching their heads. For him, reconciliation means not seeking revenge against those who supported and financed the coup against him or against the military regime of the three years he spent in exile (1991–94); it means working with them. Justice, on the other hand, means seeking legal action against those who committed crimes against the Haitian people during that three-year period.

Unfortunately, the twin themes may ultimately prove to be incompatible in Haiti. Some of the supporters of the coup with whom Aristide sought reconciliation, and with whom Preval is now attempting to seek reconciliation, are perpetrators of gross human rights abuses for which the Haitian people are seeking justice. With as many as 250,000 guns still in the hands of Haiti's former army troops, paramilitary groups, and other individuals, any political conflict could turn bloody.

In Haiti, people appear to juggle a sense of impending doom with one of optimism. There has certainly been more cause for optimism in Haiti under Aristide and Preval than there was under the de facto military regime. People who used to shop at almost-bare markets and then rush home before dark are now out on the streets until all hours of the night. The markets, much fuller now that the trade embargo against Haiti has ended, are vibrant with the sights and sounds of life. In the shantytowns, domino games and other social activities go on until the early morning hours, and some of the *borlettes*[9] are lit up past midnight. Women no longer live in fear of being abducted by some paramilitary attaché who is too powerful to be refused, or that their male companions will be beaten or killed for merely walking past the police headquarters. Parents can now fall asleep without worrying that their children will be shot through the walls of their tin-and-cardboard shacks. Human rights organizations, political parties, and, in almost all parts of the country,[10] peasant groups can now hold open meetings that are not overshadowed by the terror of paramilitary violence.

All of these advances notwithstanding, a mind-boggling assortment of problems, not the least of which is security, remains to be addressed. To begin with, security is a necessary precondition for the transition to democracy, but it is an extremely fragile notion in Haiti. During Aristide's term, foreign troop strength was reduced by more than two-thirds; as Aristide left office, fewer than 6,000 troops remained in Haiti. As of May 1996, that number had dropped to 2,000;

and as of July 1, 1996, only 1,300 UN peace-keeping forces and Canadian troops remained there. The MNF, and UN peace-keeping and Canadian forces have recovered only approximately 20,000 weapons, most of which came from the Haitian army. If international estimates are correct, and 250,000 weapons remain in the hands of Haiti's paramilitary forces, then a return to rampant political violence is a real possibility.[11]

It is not that the people and government of Haiti are unaware of the problem. Rather, it is a question of what they can do about it. Presidents Aristide and Preval are painfully aware of the potential for violence. When Aristide was president, for example, he had the desk in his formal office moved away from any windows, and instead of sitting behind the desk with his back to the window, which was protected by bulletproof plastic, he sat with his back to a corner of the room, and his desk rested at an angle. The reason he moved the desk was not an aesthetic one. It simply made him nervous to work at night with his back facing the window.

The Haiti to which Aristide returned on October 15, 1994, was not the same country that he so hurriedly left on the night of the September 30, 1991, coup. Arriving back as president, Aristide simply was not free to move around Haiti without strict security. He could never be left unprotected. As president, on all of his trips, even those trips he made from the palace to his private home, he had to take American transportation, very often a helicopter. He was surrounded at every moment by private security guards and by an American team of professionals originally contracted by the U.S. government. Even now, as a private citizen, his life remains severely restricted and in constant jeopardy. At his private residence in Tabarre, for example, he is not allowed to keep the door open for more than fifteen seconds as he says goodbye to guests; he is not allowed to stand by the window at night with the lights on.

This state of affairs has certainly not been helped by the failure of the American forces to arrest and secure most of the paramilitary forces and confiscate their huge weapons caches. Simply because the U.S. Army, MNF, and UN peace-keeping force refused to take these actions, there was little the Aristide government could do, and there is little that the Preval government can now do, to create a society of people who do not fear for their lives and do not take law and justice into their own hands. The method that the Haitian people have traditionally used to respond to the paramilitary forces, when the power shifts away from dictatorship and they have the opportunity to do so, is what the they call *déchoukaj* (uprooting).

People go into the streets to search for those whom they consider to be agents of the fallen regime's evil acts. Usually carried out by a crowd, *déchoukaj* takes the form of lynching, looting, and burning.

To prevent these kinds of incidents from occurring, the international effort must concentrate on security. The American incursion into Haiti in mid-September 1994 destroyed the military regime and sent its leaders into exile. The mere presence of American troops calmed the streets both in Port-au-Prince and in the provinces. But the intervention has been a mixed blessing and may ultimately work against the establishment of democracy in Haiti. Though the United States took the big step of a military intervention, it refused to take the smaller steps that would create a secure Haiti over the long term. At first, under intense pressure from the Aristide government, the American forces incarcerated the paramilitary thugs taken into custody by Haitian crowds and then chased down arms caches, but that action did not last long. Indeed, very soon after the intervention, U.S. policy changed to avoiding disarmament, and releasing detained thugs.

While he was president, Aristide, of course, took steps toward serving justice. Most significantly, this included making changes in the military and police forces. Under Aristide, the military (the Forces Armées d'Haïti, or FAD'H) was slowly but effectively vetted and purged of those who had committed gross human rights violations, and the groundwork was laid for a new police force.[12] According to the Aristide government's original plan, which continued into President Preval's term, when all the vetting, purging, recruitment, and training were finished, the new Haitian army was to consist of approximately fifteen hundred men and women. This plan has been even more successful than was originally thought possible. The Haitian army has been totally disbanded, and ultimately the police force will stand at approximately five thousand to six thousand people, all either retrained or newly recruited and trained. The soldiers who were purged and who believe that they can safely remain in Haiti are to be retrained for other jobs.

As Aristide attempted to downsize the army and send corrupt or dangerous officers to posts in foreign embassies, the Haitian people's desire for justice intensified, and killings that took place during the military regime's reign of terror—specifically the murders of Antoine Izméry, Aristide's major financial backer; Guy Malary, his justice minister; Jean-Claude Museau, a student activist; and Father Jean-Marie Vincent, his lifelong friend—will be test cases for the new Haitian judicial system, which exists on paper but barely in practice.[13] A new Supreme Court has been named, but many inferior judicial posts are yet to be filled. The rural section-chief system, which Aristide declared to be abolished, still retains significant authority and must be demobilized. Prisons need to be modernized, and new lawyers and judges have to be trained. There is, in effect, no functioning system of justice.

At this point, little has been done to reconstitute the judicial system, mainly because human and material resources are extremely scarce. Indeed, there are very few trained lawyers in Haiti willing to work on this reform. Nevertheless, Aristide appointed a National Truth and Justice Commission, headed by Françoise Bouchard, to investigate the human rights abuses and to issue a report. That report was supposed to have been completed and turned over to the Aristide government for possible prosecutions before the expiration of Aristide's term in February 1996. As of November 1996, however, the report remained unfinished. It is not clear whether the report will ever be issued. At the same time, an international group of human rights lawyers is helping the government investigate the massive human rights abuses and bring to justice those responsible for the crimes. These actions, of course, will create a dilemma. Proceeding with the prosecutions will certainly be seen by the corporativist powers in Haiti—the economic elites, the hierarchy of the Catholic Church, and the military and paramilitary forces—both as a direct threat to their power and as a profound contradiction to Aristide's, and now Preval's, plea for reconciliation.

As the drama in Haiti continues to unfold, another one—directly related to the U.S. government's involvement in the Haitian crisis—is also being played out. One of the main catalysts for U.S. intervention in Haiti was the influx of a vast number of Haitian refugees who were seeking asylum in the United States. (The inflow of refugees increasingly became a politically sensitive issue, and it was in response to domestic political pressure to take action to stem the tide of boat people that the U.S. government lent its support to an internationally sponsored intervention in Haiti.) The U.S. government's handling of those refugees continues to raise significant questions about U.S. policy in the treatment of asylum-seekers in general and about the strength of the U.S. government's commitment to establishing a true democracy in Haiti in particular. The government seems to be operating on several conflicting levels. It is pushing the Haitian government to live up to the most stringent requirements of democracy while at the same time undermining such efforts. Simultaneously it is violating one of the most fundamental tenets of democracy—the rule of law—in its treatment of Haitian refugees while publicly championing the virtues of democratic governance and human rights at home.

As a result of the 1991 military coup and President Aristide's ouster from power, thousands of Haitians seeking asylum departed Haiti by boat and attempted to reach the United States. Between May 1992 and June 1994, the U.S. Coast Guard interdicted Haitians bound for the United States on the high seas and returned them directly to Haiti. This action was taken in violation of an agreement between the Haitian and U.S. governments, and in violation of international law. On any sound reading of domestic law, it also violates the laws of the United States.

In June 1994, the government abruptly changed its policy and began processing some of the refugees for asylum in the United States. In July 1994, the government again changed its position, and began offering "safe haven" to the Haitian refugees, housing them at the Guantanamo Bay Naval Base.[14] The government stopped allowing the Haitian refugees to enter the United States, but also stopped returning them directly to Haiti. At the peak of emigration in 1994, over 16,800 Haitian boat people were simultaneously housed together at the Guantanamo Bay Naval Base. After President Aristide's reinstatement to office, some Haitians in "safe haven" volunteered to repatriate to Haiti. Nevertheless, thousands feared persecution and refused to return. Indeed, the situation in the countryside remained unstable, at least through Aristide's term and into the early months of Preval's.

The U.S. government did not stop there, however, and it tried to lure the Haitians into "voluntary repatriation." On December 29, 1994, the U.S. government announced its offer of a carrot—approximately $80—to each Haitian asylum-seeker who "volunteered" to return to Haiti by January 5, 1995. But the government also used the stick: it informed the Haitians that, if they failed to "volunteer" to return to Haiti, they would not receive any compensation and would be involuntarily repatriated beginning on January 5, 1995. True to their word, government officials began the involuntary repatriation process on that date. In response, the Haitian Refugee Center (HRC) and two individual Haitian refugees at Guantanamo Bay Naval Base initiated suit in the Southern District of Florida, requesting a temporary restraining order to prevent the involuntary repatriation of Haitian refugees scheduled to begin that evening.[15] During the evening of January 5, the district court heard oral arguments regarding HRC's and the individual Haitian refugees' claims that the defendants-appellees (the "government") were violating the Haitian refugees' putative equal protection and due process rights by repatriating them without their consent. After a two-hour hearing, the district court orally converted HRC's and the individual Haitian refugees' request for a temporary restraining order into a request for preliminary injunctive relief so that appeal could be taken. The district court then orally denied injunctive relief to HRC and the individual Haitian refugees. On January 9, 1995, HRC and the two individual Haitian refugees moved in the U.S. Court of Appeals for the Eleventh Circuit for summary reversal of the district court's denial of injunctive relief or, in the alternative, an expedited briefing schedule for appeal on the merits. On January 18, 1995, the Eleventh Circuit found that the district court did not abuse its discretion and affirmed the district court's denial of injunctive relief.[16]

The illegal treatment of Haitian refugees by the U.S. government has, of course, been an ongoing process since at least the late 1970s. Haitians have been discriminated against in every aspect of their treatment—from initial interviews, which have consistently not conformed to legal requirements, to the processing of asylum claims, to the incarceration of Haitians in detention facilities pending determination of their claims. No other group of refugees has ever been treated in such a blatantly illegal manner since the founding of this nation. This action reflects not only an invidious discriminatory intent against Haitian refugees, but also a national confusion about immigrants and immigration, the application of immigration policy and laws, and the role of the rule of law in a democracy. It suggests a strong racist bias against Haitians, the first substantial wave of black refugees ever to attempt to seek asylum in the United States. Such treatment is also indicative of a serious problem in U.S. foreign policy toward Haiti, and the judiciary's role in that process.[17]

PART ONE

Democracy in Haiti

A HISTORICAL VISION

Top: Family members of murdered Aristide supporter grieve in Cité Soleil, Port-au-Prince, May 1994. Photograph © Chantal Regnault. *Bottom:* Delmas Go, Port-au-Prince, April 1994. Photograph © Chantal Regnault.

CHAPTER ONE

A Democratic Vision for Haiti

In part 1 of this book, I begin with a short discussion of Haitian history. I analyze the dominant themes of that history, including the structure of Haitian society that helped create the conditions for dictatorship. This analysis is important, of course, because it suggests the conditions that must be changed for democracy to flourish.

Following this analysis, I discuss the more recent history of Haiti. Specifically, I look at the election, overthrow, exile, and reinstatement of President Aristide, the negotiations and conflicts leading to those circumstances, and the role of the United States and the international community in these activities.

This background information sets the scene for considering and understanding the difficulties of attempting to make the transition from authoritarianism to democracy in the special circumstances of Haiti. It also suggests broader themes inherent in any transition to democracy. Similarly, the information is a necessary precondition for an analysis and discussion of democratic theory and how such theory is essential to the process of transition. Indeed, democratic change must necessarily be grounded in the real conditions—economic, political, and social—of a society.

A HISTORICAL VISION: THE ORIGINS OF DICTATORSHIP

The history of Haiti is a tragic tale of political corruption and military violence. With the singular exception of one regime that governed between 1818 and 1843, Haiti has been plagued by ceaseless coups, assassinations, massive violations of human rights, and ongoing hostilities with its neighbor, the Dominican Republic.[1] The only period of relative stability[2] since then was between 1915 and 1934, when the U.S. Marines occupied the country in order to ensure U.S. commercial privileges.³ When the troops were finally removed, the conventional antagonism between Haiti and the Dominican Republic resumed.⁴

The history of Haiti is also one of sharply opposed interests, starkly competing visions of state and nation, and a rigid class structure. If "the Haitian mind"⁵ or attitude is meant to signify the political, economic, and social positions of the majority, Haitians have been of one attitude only twice in their history. Their first coming together as a people was in the period 1791–1804, when they bravely united against slavery and French colonialism.⁶ The second was in 1990, when a majority of at least 67 percent elected Jean-Bertrand Aristide to the presidency in the country's first democratic and free elections. The events that have occurred since that election, however, reflect the deep divisions that developed in this society between these two defining moments. Class structure, not merely income, and historical tides, not simply the immediate past, are at the root of Haiti's modern crisis.⁷ Indeed, a positive resolution of this crisis is impossible unless these cultural and historical issues are understood and confronted.⁸

Haiti is the product of a revolution against slavery and colonialism. It emerged as a nation in 1804, from the destruction of the French colony of Saint-Domingue. By the late eighteenth century (around 1790), Saint-Domingue was reputed to be the most profitable colony of the Western world. Indeed, it established world production records for coffee and sugar.⁹ It was, however, also the worst place in the world to be a black African slave. The French colonialists imported many more enslaved Africans than almost any other plantation society in the Americas, including the United States. Unfortunately, they also killed off these slaves at a much more rapid rate, through general mistreatment and harsh labor conditions.

Finally, in August 1791, the slaves of Saint-Domingue revolted. Under the successive leadership of two figures who later became Haiti's national heroes—Toussaint Louverture and Jean-Jacques Dessalines—they defeated Napoleon's army, allegedly the strongest in the world, after twelve years of brutal, protracted struggle. This was an incredible victory for the Haitian people. Indeed, during this period, it was almost impossible to believe that such a guerilla force could defeat the most powerful army in the world. This first large-scale successful slave revolt in the Americas helped create one of the first independent states of the Americas and, not incidentally, the first black state of the Americas. The revolution was, on one level, both a revolution for social justice in Haiti and a victory against

French colonialism. It was also significant for broader reasons. It foreshadowed the independence of Latin America in general, and the destruction of African-American slavery.

The European powers and the United States did not easily accept the success of the revolt, however, and they ostracized Haiti diplomatically. Even though they continued to trade with Haiti, they did so only on harsh terms of their choosing. The reasons for this were clear. In 1791, European powers controlled Caribbean colonies and freely and happily accepted African slavery; and representatives of southern states in the U.S. Congress, of course, argued vehemently against the recognition of Haitian independence, fearing that it would encourage black slaves in the United States to revolt. In fact, the United States did not recognize Haitian independence until 1862, when the Civil War brought an unexpected need for cotton and destroyed southern power and influence in Washington.

The revolution failed for perhaps an even more significant and insidious reason. Internal forces in Haiti worked against the progress of the revolution. Almost immediately after independence, the Haitian elites attempted to recreate the plantation economy, treating the rural masses in much the same way as the old colonial aggressors. The former slaves, however, despised plantation labor, and they simply refused to return to a state of slavery. Instead, they settled as small peasants on land bought or reconquered from the state, or abandoned by large landowners.

The urban elites then devised a complicated but effective strategy to counter this problem.[10] The first part of this attack was economic. The elites used the fiscal and marketing systems of the country to create wealth-producing mechanisms for themselves, which, in turn, allowed the elites to steal the productive labor capacities of the rural peasants. The elites became traders, politicians, and state employees. They prospered by living off the peasants' labor. Taxes collected by the import-export bourgeoisie at the urban markets and customhouses—paid by the peasants—provided almost the entire source of government revenue. In 1842, for example, perhaps 90 percent of government revenue was collected at the customhouses. In 1891, more than 90 percent of state income came from the heavy hand of import and export taxes.[11]

Coffee, Haiti's main agricultural export, became the central focus of the elites' fiscal policy, and they taxed this product almost beyond its limits. Indeed, the coffee crop accounted for 60–90 percent of government revenue from the late nineteenth century to the first half of the twentieth century. Until recently, charges on coffee amounted to a 40 percent tax on personal income. After almost two hundred years of independence, however, the government has yet to collect income taxes from most merchants, civil servants, or middle-class employees.[12] In addition to coffee, successive Haitian governments heavily taxed food and other necessities, such as flour, oil, candles, kerosene, and matches. When coffee exports fell, taxes on the necessities rose to offset this shortage. Luxury items for the elites, not surprisingly, entered the country free of any tariffs.

This economic response of the elites posed a serious threat to the creation of any form of democratic government in Haiti. They made sure that they received their wealth, even if it meant killing the nation. The state reproduced itself by living off the peasants and abusing them; the urban classes reproduced themselves by taking over the state and, therefore, the wealth of the peasantry. This strategy inevitably led to the needless death of innumerable people— through harsh labor conditions, starvation, disease, and repression—the destruction of any progressive social and political movements, and, of course, political instability.[13]

It was to limit these problems of political and social instability, that the second part of the elites' strategy was implemented. The idea was to isolate the peasantry on its small mountain plots, thus keeping them away from politics. It was a brilliant but corrupt tactic. The very peasants who unknowingly subsidized the elites and the state would have no input whatsoever in how the state was to be run. This was achieved "legally" and illegally through manipulation of election laws and harsh repression. For example, before the twentieth century, it is highly unlikely that any elected politician ever received as many as a thousand legitimate votes.[14] Before the Duvaliér dictatorship, many peasants could not even name the president. The peasants encountered the state mainly through the *preseptè* (market tax collectors), and through the *chèf seksyon* (section chief), a member of the army who acted as the sole representative of all three branches of government in the rural parts of the country. It is not an exaggeration to claim that the rural areas of Haiti comprised a colony of the urban elites. Even today many of these rural areas retain this status.

Haiti continues to be a society of stark socioeconomic contrasts, which, although initially born out of the country's colonial economy, were artificially perpetuated by greedy elites unwilling to relinquish status and wealth (and therefore power) in post-independence Haiti. These divisions have worked to exacerbate cultural rifts— manifested in language, religious practices, and attitudes toward skin color—which can only make more difficult the transition to democracy that the Haitian government is now trying to effect. These rifts, too, have been fabricated to some degree. In many cases, the underlying cultural repertoire is the same for peasants and elites alike, but subtleties of labeling and practice give the appearance of significant disparities and work to impose barriers.

Variation in the use of language is one manifestation of cultural division.[15] All Haitians speak Haitian Creole to one degree of fluency or another; 8–10 percent of the population (the elites) speak French well enough to claim fluency; however, only a tiny minority within the elites is truly bilingual in both French and Creole. More important than the fact of bilingualism are the number of times elite children are told that it is unacceptable for members of their class to speak Creole. Until Aristide's reinstatement to office, French was the official language in schools and in the court systems.[16] In this way, language is effectively used as a social barrier and one that denies majority participation in certain state institutions—90 percent of Haitians are thus excluded from power. Furthermore, there are subtle nuances of meaning within Haitian Creole that illustrate cultural prejudices and cynicism. For example, the word *leta* in Creole means both "the state" and "bully." The urban people, in turn, refer to the rural peasants as *mounn andewò*, which means "outsiders."

Religious convictions and their representation also work to divide Haitians culturally. The elites proclaim their adherence to Christianity. A large number of the peasants, too, claim to be Roman Catholic Christians—indeed, they practice it and follow the annual cycle of Roman Catholic events—but they also refer to themselves as "servants of the gods," members of the major Haitian folk religion Vodoun. Publicly, the elites associate this folk religion with evil, and successive Haitian governments have persecuted many individuals who openly practice Vodoun. Yet there is widespread evidence that many of the elites themselves consistently practice aspects of it behind closed doors. They thus claim for themselves a sense of cultural superiority based on adherence to Christianity and rejection of Vodoun (they have even accepted the encouragement and support of the Roman Catholic hierarchy in the persecution of Vodoun believers), while continuing to practice Vodoun in private.

Variation in skin color is perhaps the most "real" of the agents of cultural strife: there exists in Haiti a historical tension between the older "mulatto" elites and the "black" middle class. This is a complex issue, however; no aspect of Haitian history is more confusing than the physical appearance of its people. Haiti is said to be divided by color, but that is a gross simplification. It is closer to the truth to say that consciousness of color varies between social classes and also within each class, and that for many people light skin is symbolically important. But this statement merely skims the surface. The skin color of people must be seen as part of a perceptual whole that includes hair type, nose type, lip type, eye color, ear size, and other features, such as amount of body and facial hair, and body type. It also includes such factors as the appearance of one's siblings and their in-laws. For men in particular, the color and appearance of one's wife and her family is extremely relevant. As important as color is to Haitians, however, it is not clear that it determined the emergence of a ruling class so much as did education, military record, and personal connections. Thus, while color is a significant cultural issue, it was not at the birth of the nation, nor is it today, so neatly defining a marker that social groups can safely be described in color terms.

That is not to say that a long-standing tension regarding color does not exist. Indeed, according to the noted scholar Léon-François Hoffmann, this tension has survived down to the present. It is, in fact, based upon opposing ideologies concerning the form of government best suited to the country. As he puts it:

> The black slave leader Makandal, for example, is celebrated in history textbooks. But at the time that he was conducting what we today would call terrorist activities against slave owners, at least one-third of the slaves belonged to mulatto planters, who were no doubt as relieved as their white colleagues when the rebel was caught and burned at the stake. Jean-Baptiste Chavannes and Vincent Ogé, agitators broken on the wheel by the colonial authorities in early 1791, are also textbook heroes, but in point of fact only for the mulatto elite: they died for the rights of the freedmen of color, not for those of the black slaves, whom they explicitly declared should be kept in bondage. Even after the abolition of slavery, Toussaint had to fight a ferocious war for supremacy against the mulatto freedmen commanded by Rigaud. After independence, to be sure, black and mulatto leaders joined in assassinating Emperor Jean-Jacques Dessalines, whom they suspected of wanting to protect the downtrodden peasantry against the depr[e]dations of the new ruling class. But the country was then partitioned for almost fifteen years into the Kingdom of Haiti, ruled by King Christophe, a black man, and the Republic of Haiti, under the mulatto president Alexandre Pétion. These two leaders had very different ideas regarding the form of government that Haiti should adopt. Christophe believed in an authoritarian, centralized form of government; Pétion favored a parliamentary system and laissez-faire economics.[17]

Apparently, the tensions between the older mulatto elite, who tended to perpetuate the ideology of Pétion, and the black middle class, who favored Christophe's, have survived down to the present. As Hoffmann states:

> "Black" and "mulatto" governments succeed each other and political rivalries add to the generally unspoken undercurrent of mistrust and resentment that separates the two ethnic groups. Under the rule of militant black presidents, such as Saloman (1879–89), Estimé (1946–50) or François Duvaliér (1957–71), mulattos were persecuted or discriminated against, and the celebration of Dessalines and Christophe, who in their time had also proclaimed a *noiriste* ideology (even though the latter had conspired to assassinate the former), took on special relevance. Conversely, when mulattos come to power, as during the presidency of Elie Lescot (1941–46) for example, special honor is paid to the memory of Ogé and Pétion. The founding fathers are thus at the same time undifferentiated national heroes, remote mythical pillars propping up national pride, and familiar points of reference in the daily game of domestic politics and color discrimination.[18]

There is a further complication. All Haitians sincerely consider themselves members of the African race and claim bonds of brotherhood with black Africans. Nevertheless, educated Haitians have always shared the Europeans' paternalistic disparagement of things African. Indeed, historically, not only did Haitians consider themselves intellectually superior to their African cousins, but more aesthetically pleasing too. The Haitian mulatto elite and the black middle class were also satisfied to adopt Western intellectual and aesthetic norms and to distance themselves from their African origins. This did not bode well for the black middle class. While internalizing these mulatto attitudes, this group did not have any biological ties to Europeans. The problem ran deeper still in that the majority of important positions in government, public administration, and diplomacy were long monopolized by light-skinned Haitians, whose social clubs refused admission to those with undesirable skin color. This color discrimination pervaded all aspects of social life, including the selection of partners. As Hoffmann tells us:

> Marriage partners were valued in exact relation to their phenotype, the ideal being to "marry lighter" than oneself and thereby "improve the race" (*améliorer la race*). Mulatto girls were thus encouraged to marry foreign whites, and only if they belonged to rich or powerful families could young black women aspire to a mulatto husband. While this internalization of anti-black racialism is far from unknown in the

rest of the Caribbean, it is especially shocking and paradoxical in the country which has always defined itself as the Black Republic.[19]

Thus, Haitians are acutely aware that, while they risk discrimination by Western nations based on their color, they exercise, or are the victims of, the same discrimination in their own country.

Two major aspects of Haitian life emerge from this sketch. First, the same elite groups that have traditionally exercised political and economic control of Haiti, have totally rejected and ostracized the present majority. Second, the elites have coopted the state and used it as the key mechanism of control and rejection. Stated otherwise, the elites believed, and continue to believe, their lifestyle to be more important than the survival of the majority. That choice meant using the state to expropriate the economic output of the majority and simultaneously repressing it culturally by establishing as superior in some way (real or fabricated by nuance) their own particular cultural signatures. As Michel Rolph-Trouillot has so eloquently argued, the Haitian state is predatory; it has always operated against the nation it claims to represent.[20]

The 1915–34 U.S. occupation of Haiti did not alleviate, but instead exacerbated, this situation. It left the country with a weaker civil society and a solidified state apparatus. First, the U.S. Marines reinforced the fiscal and economic power of Port-au-Prince. They did this most obviously by centralizing the customhouses. Second, and more significantly, they consciously contributed to the centralization of political power in Port-au-Prince by "pacifying" the countryside. This took the form of "modernizing" the so-called rural police (*chèfs de sections*), and by creating a new Haitian army, the very army that the Aristide and Preval governments have since attempted to dismantle and contain. The first Haitian army, born of the war against France, could legitimately claim a patriotic mission. The Haitian *Garde*, however, was created specifically to keep the Haitians in line. Indeed, this force has never fought anyone but Haitians. In contrast to the first, whose allegiances were primarily regional, this army created by the Marines was heavily centralized.

Centralization meant that power could be more efficiently organized. Thus, it became easier for would-be dictators to control the state.[21] For example, the cadets of the Military School set up by the U.S. Marines took part in the overthrow of President Elie Lescot (1941–46), and in the nomination and overthrow of his successor, Dumarsais Estimé (1946–50). They then placed one of their own, Paul Magloire (1950–56), in the presidency. By the time Magloire left office, the army had become the power behind the throne, the determining factor of Haitian politics.[22]

Any notion of stability from that point meant dictatorship. First, it was the regime of François ("Papa Doc") Duvaliér, who ruled with an iron fist between 1957 and his death in 1971 with the aid of a maniacal private security force known as the Tonton Macoutes.[23] Papa Doc consolidated his power quickly and ruthlessly, eviscerating individual liberties and political opposition with equal dispatch.[24] Indeed, over forty thousand Haitians reportedly lost their lives as the victims of official brutality during his presidency.[25] Duvaliér stole over $500 million in foreign aid and taxes and deposited the money in personal accounts in Haiti and abroad.[26] Officials at all levels of government, taking their cue from Duvaliér, took part in similar acts of corruption.[27]

Papa Doc Duvaliér certainly learned the lessons of Haiti's military well. He gradually discharged most senior officers in the army and then relied heavily on their successors to build the most centralized power in the history of the nation. Then, he closed the Military School. By employing the full powers of the centralized state, Duvaliér formalized a system of absolute individual power. He created an all-powerful and intensely personalized executive branch that created and controlled all state activities, from family life to military training. The state even controlled the writing of national school exams. Its apparatus also attacked all the groupings and institutions of civil society—from athletic teams to trade unions. Haiti became an authoritarian state.

Papa Doc remained in power for over fourteen years, and, in order to ensure a legacy of Duvaliér control over the country, organized a referendum on January 31, 1971, in which voters approved his nineteen-year-old son, Jean-Claude ("Baby Doc"), as his successor.[28] When his father died, Jean-Claude became "President for Life." His rule was almost as repressive as his father's. In 1986, however, when the economic disparities and political corruption in Haiti reached ungovernable proportions, Baby Doc fled for exile in France.[29]

The senior Duvaliér achieved his aim only because of the role played by the state in Haitian history since independence. Duvaliér was a very clever dictator, but he did not succeed simply because of his intelligence. Duvaliérism invented few formulas of power. Instead, it systematically codified historical practices of the Haitian state. For example, the methods of the Tonton Macoutes are almost identical to those developed and refined by the death squads in earlier Haitian history. Similarly, the Duvaliér state systematized and multiplied the practice and power of the state to extract money from the average rural peasant and urban citizen. For example, the Duvaliér government centralized the management of coffee exports and, simultaneously, dramatically increased taxes. The executive and its favored elites took complete control of the basic commodities, such as oil, flour, and tobacco. They even determined the import and distribution policies of these commodities. These forces simply raided the treasury. Indeed, they made their personal fortunes the very *raison d'être* of state revenue.

This systematizing of the extractive and repressive power of the state significantly worsened the plight of the Haitian nation. Decisions that made almost everyone worse off, such as predatory price policies, geometrically increased the speed of environmental degradation. Impoverished peasants rushed to urban centers. Baby Doc Duvaliér tried to take advantage of this increased urban labor force to create an economic reversal, but the rapid spread of what are often termed "light-assembly industries" had the opposite effect. These assembly industries, subcontracted to U.S. firms, only reinforced polarization. This contributed to an increase in the already huge gap between the economic and social elites and the poverty-stricken peasants, and to the urban civil uprisings in the mid-1980s. This forced Jean-Claude Duvaliér into exile in February 1986. He left behind a much poorer country, an almost totally depleted economy, and an even more desperate underclass of peasants.

The conversion to a non-Duvaliérist regime is only one of the transitions Haiti must face. The other is the internalization in the hearts and minds of the people of the rule of law and its everyday practice in both the public and private spheres. But there is a strange cycle that seems to operate in Haiti. If Duvaliérism impedes the creation of the rule of law, the weakness of democratic institutions keeps Duvaliérism alive. The Haitian "problem" is not merely political. It resides in the rigid class structure, in the military organization of a nation that seems to be at war with itself, in an economic system that tends to discourage production and investment, and in sociocultural elitism.

Legitimacy of the state requires the participation of Haiti's majority in deciding the fate of the country. It requires the recognition by all sections of Haitian society—particularly the urban elites and their foreign partners—that Haiti is fundamentally a nation of extremely poor rural peasants who must somehow be incorporated into the life of Haiti as equal partners. To put it another way, Haitian democracy will have to develop in the rural areas and in the city ghettos, or it will simply not be able to develop at all.[30]

THE FIRST STEPS TOWARD DEMOCRACY

Following the Duvaliérs came a series of political regimes[31] that owed their survival to a large military caste that operated with the indefatigable support of a small upper class.[32] None of these regimes had the support of the majority of the Haitian people. Each ruled through the power of the gun.[33]

Nonetheless, the fall of the Duvaliérs raised expectations that some of the military and security forces, including the Duvaliér-associated Tonton Macoutes, would be brought to justice. In the weeks after Duvaliér was ousted, mobs killed a number of known Macoutes. After crowds looted the home of former secret police chief Luc Desir and prevented him from leaving the country, the Namphy government promised to arrest and bring to justice the persons suspected of committing serious crimes during the twenty-eight years of Duvaliér rule.[34]

Spurred by large demonstrations demanding justice, the government did prosecute several low-ranking army officers, and three Macoutes were tried and convicted of killing political prisoners. However, the regime also allowed a number of high-ranking officers, including the head of the Macoutes and the former army intelligence chief, to leave the country; others known to have committed crimes were freed after army courts found insufficient evidence to convict them. According to human rights activists, intimidation of witnesses and jurors made bringing such cases to trial extremely difficult.[35] Whatever small advances were made initially soon became buried under a new wave of army shootings, repeated coups, and instability.

The popular will was finally expressed in December 1990, when the Haitian people elected Jean-Bertrand Aristide to the office of president in the first fully democratic election to take place in Haiti in the nearly two hundred years of Haitian history.[36] Popular support for Aristide was astonishing: he received two-thirds of the vote, giving him an unprecedented mandate for reform.[37] Equally impressive was the election process. It represented the culmination of an extraordinary international effort to launch Haiti on the path to democracy. Both the Organization of American States (OAS) and the UN actively participated in helping Haitian officials assure the security and dignity of the election process.[38] Voter turnout was remarkably high: 75 percent of the eligible voters—approximately 2.7 million out of the 3.2 million registered voters—turned out despite extremely difficult logistical problems.[39] The dirt roads and mountain paths of rural Haiti, where around 75–85 percent of the population lives, made the distribution of election materials particularly difficult. The high illiteracy rate of Haitians compounded the challenge of registering and voting.[40] Despite these problems, virtually all observers who monitored the voting claimed that the elections were fair and that voters experienced no intimidation.[41] In addition, the military helped ensure that violence would not occur.[42]

This peaceful, positive election, however, soon gave way to violence. Even before Aristide took his oath of office, the military and paramilitary forces, with the encouragement and even the outright participation of other corporativist forces, challenged his legitimacy in an unsuccessful coup, and coup attempts continued throughout his tenure.[43] The September 1991 coup was not only successful, it also resulted in a widely publicized reign of terror in Haiti.[44]

Nevertheless, during its short tenure, the Aristide government took important steps to improve the rule of law in Haiti.[45] In one of his first official acts,[46] President Aristide announced the retirement of senior military officials who had either been involved in past human rights violations or had failed to punish persons responsible for such abuses.[47] He also appointed several new public prosecutors and removed corrupt officials linked to the military.[48] At the same time, Aristide announced the creation of a human rights commission charged with investigating some of the most notorious human rights abuses that had been committed in the past.[49] The new president also closed down Fort Dimanche, known as a torture center, and drafted detailed plans to create and dedicate a museum to its victims on the site. In addition, the Aristide government arrested a number of people believed to have been involved in a 1987 massacre, along with other people alleged to have directed killings and torture under past regimes. Unfortunately, Aristide was overthrown before these individuals could come to trial.[50]

The most significant step Aristide took to improve respect for the rule of law was the dissolution of the institution of rural section chiefs who were accountable solely to the military authorities.[51] These section chiefs had unfettered control over the lives of the peasants in rural areas. This unchecked power led to systematic disregard of human rights with complete impunity.[52] The Aristide government replaced the section-chief system with a rural police force made up of individuals untainted by the abuses of the old system, which came under the jurisdiction of the Ministry of Justice. It appointed a completely new corps of rural agents.[53]

These reforms, however, did not last long. The overthrow of the Aristide government has resulted in the deaths and torture of thousands of innocent people, which continues even to the present day.[54] The military and its paramilitary allies did not stop with violence. Directly after the overthrow of Aristide, the de facto regime rapidly took steps to consolidate power. It named a civilian government, including an interim president, to complicate the return of President Aristide.[55] It reversed the systemic changes made by the Aristide government. First, the military fired or hunted down many of the prosecution and judicial officials who had been appointed by Aristide.[56] Next, it released prisoners who had been convicted of human rights violations during Aristide's presidency, including Tonton Macoutes.[57] The military also restored the old section-chief structure, thus returning to power individuals who were known to have committed massive human rights abuses.[58] These section chiefs, in turn, enlisted their old private armies, formerly known as the Tonton Macoutes, but now referred to as attachés, and reasserted their control over the countryside.[59]

CHAPTER TWO

International Efforts to Restore Aristide to the Presidency

THE PRELIMINARY EFFORTS TO NEGOTIATE A PEACEFUL SETTLEMENT

During the first two years after Aristide's overthrow (1991–93), the international community made serious efforts to help restore Aristide to power and to support the nascent democratic movement in Haiti.[1] Each attempt at a negotiated settlement, however, was met by the intransigence and duplicity of the military coup leaders. They attempted to placate the international community by pretending to negotiate in good faith, all the while hoping to prolong the return of Aristide until his official term in office had ended. The de facto leaders simply refused to believe that either the United States or three of the other four "friends of Haiti"—Canada, France, and Venezuela—would ever take serious military action to restore Aristide. The issue was complicated by the fact that certain forces of the U.S. government, including members of Congress and defense establishment figures, most notably the Central Intelligence Agency (CIA), continued to assure the de facto government that the United States actually supported the coup leaders and not the democratically elected government. These forces orchestrated a campaign to smear Aristide's public image.[2]

Nevertheless, the diplomatic reaction of the OAS and the UN to the coup was vigorous and forceful. Immediately after the coup, an OAS-led delegation demanded that the military relinquish power.[3] The military bluntly refused, and the member states of the OAS responded by freezing the assets of Haiti and imposing a trade embargo on the country.[4] There followed a round of negotiations, under UN and OAS auspices, that stretched out over the next two and a half years.

The first major negotiated agreement came in February 1992. On February 23, Aristide and representatives of the Haitian Parliament signed the so-called Protocol of Washington.[5] The agreement called for Aristide's eventual reinstatement as president, but a specific date for his return was notably absent.[6] The agreement also called for a new prime minister to run the country during Aristide's absence,[7] and a broad general amnesty for common criminals.[8] From the beginning, military intransigence doomed the agreement to failure. On March 6, 1992, the military illegitimately appointed Joseph Nerette to be president of Haiti, and declared the Protocol of Washington illegal.[9] Following Nerette's lead, the Haitian Parliament failed to approve the agreement.[10] Soon afterward, the Haitian Supreme Court dealt the agreement a fatal blow by declaring it unconstitutional.[11]

The Haitian Parliament's alternative to the Protocol of Washington was the Villa d'Acceuil Tripartite Agreement.[12] Its most striking feature was that it failed to provide for Aristide's return. Other significant features of the agreement included a call for Nerette's resignation, with the presidency to remain open,[13] and a provision that Marc Bazin, a former World Bank economist and finance minister under Duvaliér, become prime minister.[14]

The OAS foreign ministers immediately declared their rejection of the Tripartite Agreement[15] and attempted to stiffen sanctions by urging member states to close their port facilities to any vessel that did not abide by the embargo.[16] As the negotiations bogged down, the United States resorted to more aggressive political pressure to force a resolution. Specifically, the Bush administration pushed Aristide to negotiate with Bazin,[17] threatening to lift the embargo if the two did not reach an agreement.[18] A similar desire for speedy resolution also led the OAS to pressure Aristide in the same way.[19] In response to these pressures, Aristide initiated negotiations, mediated by the OAS, between a panel of his supporters and representatives of Bazin.[20] These negotiations resulted in an agreement to send eighteen OAS democracy monitors to Haiti in September of 1992.[21]

The monitors proved ineffective, largely because they were limited to Port-au-Prince. The UN and OAS also appointed a special joint envoy, Dante Caputo, to facilitate an agreement between the Aristide government and the coup leaders,[22] but the military continued to frustrate the negotiations. For example, on January 18, 1993, the military conducted an election for the Senate under the auspices of the Electoral Council. Aristide's supporters, realizing the election was a sham, boycotted it.[23] Thirteen new members opposed to Aristide were nevertheless elected to Parliament.

The Clinton administration, apparently now inclined to exert a greater degree of pressure on the de facto government, sent a Marine Corps general to Haiti in January 1993 to warn the Haitian military that Aristide had to be allowed to return.[24] In February 1993, forty UN human rights observers arrived in Haiti.[25] Finally, in March 1993, President Clinton appointed Lawrence Pezzullo as a special adviser on Haiti.[26] As a direct result of these actions, negotiations appeared to be leading to a settlement. In the end, however, the military remained opposed to giving up any power. Indeed, when the joint envoy presented the plan on April 14, 1993, the military simply rejected it.[27]

THE GOVERNORS ISLAND AGREEMENT

By April 1993, the outlines of a settlement were becoming increasingly visible. The sticking point turned out to be amnesty for the military's past human rights violations. As part of the price for Aristide's reinstatement, the military demanded a complete amnesty. In February 1993, Aristide agreed to a general amnesty for political crimes, but refused to extend the amnesty to "common criminals." He argued that the Haitian Constitution forbade such an amnesty, adding that he believed the killings and torture by army leaders would subject the latter to prosecution as "common criminals." Intense negotiations took place in March and April. The U.S. and UN negotiators made no secret of their belief that a full amnesty was necessary and that Aristide was being unrealistic as well as intransigent. Aristide supporters, for their part, accused the UN and the Clinton administration of exerting enormous pressure on Aristide to accept an illegal amnesty. That is to say, they were making the cost of a settlement prohibitively high in order to blame the exiled president if the talks collapsed.[28] Finally, Aristide apparently gave in to the increasing pressure to settle, agreeing to guarantee the military freedom from criminal prosecutions and not to oppose future parliamentary efforts to preclude civil suits against its members. In exchange, the settlement was to include the creation of a "Truth Commission" to investigate the most serious human rights abuses.[29] The military rejected this deal, however, and, as a result, the international community imposed even stricter sanctions, including an oil embargo.[30]

Nevertheless, negotiations between these opposing forces continued to take place. The culmination of these was the July 1993 Governors Island Agreement,[31] in which President Aristide agreed to appoint a prime minister, who would be subject to confirmation by

Parliament,[32] after which the embargo would be suspended. The agreement further provided that the UN and OAS sanctions would be suspended at the initiative of the respective secretaries-general of the two organizations immediately after the new prime minister "is confirmed and assumes office."[33] President Aristide would return to Haiti on October 30, 1993.[34] Shortly before his return, Cédras would retire from the high command in favor of an Aristide appointee, who would then name new members to the high command "in accordance with the constitution."[35] Other coup participants would be allowed to remain in the military, but they would be posted outside Haiti.[36] The agreement also gave Aristide the right to appoint a new chief of police to head a reorganized police force for Port-au-Prince, which would no longer be part of the military.[37] An international police force would be stationed in Haiti, and other steps would be taken to "modernize" the army.[38] Moreover, in connection with the agreement, an international aid program amounting to $1 billion over five years would be instituted. Finally, there would be international cooperation in matters of technical and financial development aid, and assistance for administrative and judicial reform.[39]

The Governors Island Agreement provided for the president granting full amnesty to the coup leaders and supporters within the framework of Article 147 of the Constitution of the Republic of Haiti, and "implementation of other instruments which may be adopted by the Parliament."[40] Article 147 allows a presidential amnesty only for political matters "as stipulated by law." Thus, the amnesty would have covered the military's human rights violations only if Parliament defined those violations as "political." Although Aristide's government agreed to the amnesty, violence and intimidation, as well as the total abrogation of the Governors Island Agreement by the military, kept Parliament from meeting to debate and define the issue.

The Governors Island Agreement was a total failure. Neither Cédras nor François resigned. Instead, Cédras violated every part of the brokered deal. It mattered little that Aristide, as well as the United States and the UN, meticulously complied with the agreement's terms.

Aristide and the Haitian Parliament took the first steps toward implementing the Governors Island Agreement by signing the so-called New York Pact, which called for an end to human rights violations, the immediate release of all political prisoners, and the establishment of a Compensation Commission for victims of the coup.[41] It also called for implementation of other parts of the Governors

Island Agreement, including the nomination of a new prime minister, the passage of laws to create a civilian police force, and amnesty for members of the coup.[42] Less than two weeks after the pact was signed, the new prime minister, Robert Malval, was sworn in.[43]

Soon afterward, the UN Security Council voted to send an aid mission to Haiti.[44] This was to consist of 1,200–1,300 individuals, including 567 police trainers from France, Canada, and the Caribbean.[45] Justice Minister Guy Malary would control the police after Lieutenant Colonel François had been forced out.[46] The United States would contribute about 60 military advisers to retrain the Haitian army in road building and other civil engineering endeavors.[47] Despite Aristide's and the international community's show of good faith in implementing the Governors Island Agreement, the Haitian military employed every kind of delay while their paramilitary subordinates, known as attachés, terrorized the population.[48]

Indeed, this latest campaign of terror was simply a continuation of the one that began with Aristide's overthrow. After seizing power, the coup regime began a relentless program of murder, torture, and intimidation of persons who supported the return of democratic rule in Haiti. The repression was carried out by Haiti's 7,000-strong military and security forces with the cooperation of thousands of others, including the 560 section chiefs (with dozens, and sometimes hundreds, of "deputies") and thousands of civilian paramilitary troops—the infamous attachés. Reminiscent of the notorious Tonton Macoutes of the Duvaliér era, attachés freely roamed the streets of Port-au-Prince and other areas of the nation, committing murder and other acts of violence to intimidate opponents of the coup regime. Attachés sometimes operated in loosely organized criminal groups known as *zenglendos*.

In the second half of 1993, a group of attachés formed a quasi-political organization known as the Front for the Advancement and Progress in Haiti (FRAPH). FRAPH, the name of which (in Creole) is a homonym for the French and Creole word for "hit," staged a number of violent demonstrations with the support of the Haitian military. Their terror knew no bounds. They assassinated Aristide's largest financial backer, Antoine Izméry, pulling him from a church in broad daylight and shooting him in the streets. They also assassinated the minister of justice, Guy Malary. Those Haitians who could, fled the capital, hoping the countryside would be safer. Like the attachés, the men at the top—the military and economic elites—were determined not to lose the power they had amassed since the coup. Indeed, they had made huge amounts of money from control of the ports and taxation, and some shared in the illicit drug trade that moved through Haiti at a rapid clip.[49]

As the military's defiance heightened, the collapse of the Governors Island Agreement became clear. In a single day, members of the UN/OAS human rights observer team were stopped at gunpoint outside Port-au-Prince,[50] and a mob organized by the army prevented the USS *Harlan County* from docking at Port-au-Prince. The ship was attempting to bring the second installment of 200 U.S. troops and twenty-five Canadian military trainers to Haiti.[51] The Security Council warned the Haitian military that sanctions could be renewed if the UN troops were not permitted to land,[52] but the coup leaders remained unyielding, and the USS *Harlan County* left Haitian waters.[53] Three days later, Cédras failed to resign as had been stipulated in the Governors Island Agreement, and soon afterward he announced the agreement was at a dead end.[54]

POST–GOVERNORS ISLAND ACTIVITY

When Cédras reneged on the agreement, the UN slapped a new embargo on oil and arms shipments, and U.S. and allied warships encircled the nation.[55] The new sanctions included freezing all assets in the United States owned by Haitians residing in their homeland. This last action was the Clinton administration's attempt to show the powerful Haitian elites that they would not be allowed to escape the consequences of their support for an illegitimate and illegal government.[56] The UN also imposed tighter, but more limited, sanctions than those imposed by the United States.[57] These sanctions did not adversely affect the military coup leaders. The almost free flow of contraband goods, especially gasoline, across the Dominican Republic border substantially weakened the effectiveness of the sanctions.[58]

Immediately after Aristide failed to return on October 30, 1993, as planned, the joint envoy scheduled a new round of talks.[59] But the futility of those negotiation efforts became clear when no military representative bothered to show up for a scheduled meeting.[60] Negotiation efforts continued as Prime Minister Malval planned to hold a conference in Haiti attended by the military, the Aristide government, and other groups, but the plan was never executed because, in December of 1993, Malval resigned as prime minister and canceled the conference.[61] The United States quickly reacted to the failure of the Malval talks by publicly blaming Aristide.[62] President Clinton then went on record to state that Aristide's prospects were clouded and that the United States would have to reassess its approach to Haiti.[63]

Shortly thereafter, Aristide announced that he would hold his own conference in Miami, in January of 1994, to address the Haitian refugee problem.[64] Mounting political pressure, however, soon forced him to revise the conference focus from that of resolving the refugee crisis to that of building a political coalition aimed at coercing Haiti's military to give up power.[65] The original intent was that representatives of the Haitian military, members of Parliament, and labor and refugee groups would attend. In the end, once again, no one from the military showed up.[66]

The tensions harbored by the conference participants came to a boiling point during supposedly open discussions. A bitter rift developed between Aristide loyalists in Miami, who affected a more conciliatory tone toward the military, and the hard-liner constituency, dominated by Miami exiles and Aristide's U.S.-based advisers. Haitians criticized President Clinton for associating with drug-dealing authorities in Port-au-Prince. To make matters worse, Michael Kozak, a senior U.S. administration policy maker for Haiti, angrily stalked out after Aristide supporters denounced the refugee treaty for causing grievous harm to the Haitian people.[67] The conference ended inconclusively, with many conflicting proposals,[68] including the recommendation of termination of the 1981 agreement between the United States and Haiti that formed the basis of the U.S. interdiction program, and the endorsement of either international military intervention or the training of a Haitian expatriate army.[69]

In February of 1994, Aristide was presented with a new plan, backed by the U.S./OAS envoy.[70] It was purportedly drafted by both pro-military and pro-Aristide political leaders in Haiti.[71] Although it called for Cédras to retire,[72] and for a new prime minister, it also contained provisions less favorable to Aristide. Specifically, the plan provided for Parliament to enact an amnesty law, but it failed to specify a date for Aristide's return to the presidency, and it proposed leaving the military largely intact.[73] Although the UN pressured Aristide to accept the plan,[74] after meeting with the Haitian politicians backing it, he rejected it.[75] Once again, the United States blamed him, calling him intransigent and stating that the plan was his best hope for returning to power.[76]

In March of 1994, in response to pressure by the Congressional

Black Caucus, the State Department modified an earlier plan to provide that, in a single day, amnesty for the military officers would be declared, Cédras would resign, and a new prime minister would be confirmed.[77] Because the plan did not specify a date for Aristide's return, he rejected it.[78]

Even underscored by an ever-tightening embargo, the negotiation efforts proved futile. Although sanctions hurt, they were clearly not enough. The reality was that impoverished Haitians suffered severe deprivation under an on-again, off-again embargo, while the military bosses prospered from rising prices and trade in smuggled goods.[79] Thus, it was clear that, although the embargo could push Cédras into negotiations, it was not enough to secure the ouster of Haiti's de facto government or oppressive military. So how could the United States and the international community successfully fulfill its pledge not just to restore President Aristide to office but also to ensure the creation and growth of a democratic nation?

The United States, of course, has recently been particularly concerned with this question. Historically, there has been only one way for Haiti to make its problems matter in the United States—or elsewhere internationally, for that matter: by having thousands of desperate asylum-seeking refugees attempt the hazardous 600-mile journey by sea to Miami. Indeed, Haitian boat people are a large concern to President Clinton, who initially continued the Bush policy of returning them to Haiti without hearings on their asylum claims, in flagrant violation of international law.

During the summer of 1994, the Clinton administration, under intense political pressure from many members of Congress, especially the Congressional Black Caucus, and human rights groups, changed its policy of forcibly returning Haitians stopped at sea.[80] Instead, the administration agreed to hold interviews on-board vessels docked at third countries and to take those found to have a well-founded fear of persecution to the United States for further processing of their asylum claims.[81] Because of this change in policy and increased acts of violence against the Haitian people by the Haitian military, thousands of Haitians fled Haiti in boats.[82] Historically unwelcome on U.S. shores, the surge of refugees, in turn, imparted new urgency to the Clinton administration's efforts to reinstate Haiti's rightful government,[83] and correspondingly increased the likelihood of a U.S. invasion.[84]

Military invasion was a disputed issue both within the United States and abroad.[85] Yet the Haitian military coup's three-year history of intransigence and duplicity indicated that a credible threat of force would be necessary to remove the illegitimate regime. To further complicate matters, Cédras doubted that the United States would commit troops to a military operation in Haiti, and, as a result, he boldly abandoned any pretense to a negotiated return of Aristide.[86] In response, President Clinton stepped up economic and diplomatic pressures, leaving invasion as a serious, and even likely, option.[87]

Throughout the summer of 1994, President Clinton vacillated between diplomacy and military intervention.[88] His indecision not only allowed Cédras to remain politically obstinate, but also served as a springboard for the Haitian military and its supporters to step up human rights violations.[89]

Despite the Haitian military's aggressive stance, the political and economic pressures finally took effect and soon began to expose a rift within the Haitian military.[90] The meager advances made by the diplomatic efforts and sanctions were, however, quickly drowned out by the flood of refugees and its inherent problems.[91] On July 5, 1994, in the wake of American Independence Day celebrations symbolic of democracy and liberty, the Clinton administration changed its policy once again, announcing that Haitians interdicted at sea would no longer be resettled in the United States.[92] Instead of allowing those refugees with a well-founded fear of persecution to come to the United States for processing, President Clinton's new policy required sending those Haitians to third countries.[93] For the Clinton administration, this policy change satisfactorily stemmed the tide of freedom-seeking refugees.

Slowing down the flow of refugees gave the Clinton administration sufficient time to obtain international support for an invasion, and, in late July 1994, it sought UN approval for the use of military force in Haiti.[94] The UN gave its backing for the use of force on July 31. The Security Council, by a 12 to 0 vote, authorized a U.S. invasion and occupation of Haiti if the international sanctions and embargo failed to remove the illegitimate military regime.[95]

By summer's end, the prelude to U.S. military intervention seemed complete. Already suffering from economic isolation, Haiti had its air links to the rest of the world severed as a total ban on commercial flights to and from Haiti took effect on July 31.[96] One day later, the de facto Haitian government declared a state of siege, suspending constitutional guarantees and transferring governmental authority to the Haitian military.[97] Military and paramilitary abuse of Haitian civilians continued undaunted, if not catalyzed, by the threat of a U.S. invasion.[98]

THE CARTER NEGOTIATIONS AND THE
RETURN OF ARISTIDE

After years of serious but frustratingly unsuccessful international efforts to negotiate the restoration of the democratically elected Aristide government, President Clinton made a televised address bluntly informing the Haitian military that it must relinquish power or be forced out.[99] In a last-ditch effort to avoid an invasion, he asked former President Jimmy Carter, Senator Sam Nunn, and General Colin Powell to go to Haiti to negotiate the peaceful departure of the military.[100] On September 18, 1994, the Carter delegation reached an agreement with the Haitian military leaders, which provided that U.S. forces would enter Haiti with the "close cooperation" of the Haitian military and police, under conditions of "mutual respect."[101] In addition, high-ranking military officers were to retire upon the enactment by Parliament of "a general amnesty . . . , or [by] Oct. 15, whichever is earlier."[102] Finally, sanctions were to be "lifted" without delay in accordance with relevant UN resolutions.[103]

Haitians interested in restoring democracy to Haiti correctly responded angrily to this agreement. In contradiction to the U.S. government's claims, they believed that the agreement did not restore Aristide to power, but instead almost ruined any chances for his return. First, the agreement provided for "certain military officers" to retire honorably, without leaving Haiti, thereby allowing the junta to remain in Haiti. This would clearly have undermined the transition to democracy. The agreement also called for a "general amnesty" to be voted by the Parliament, which would presumably have covered all acts by all wrongdoers against government agents and civilians. Finally, the agreement was signed by the de facto president, Emile Jonassaint, thus recognizing and legitimizing an illegal regime. The agreement made no mention whatsoever of President Aristide and included no stipulation about his return to Haiti.

Conceivably, then, the Carter Agreement allowed for President Aristide's return to Haiti with the military junta and its thugs still at large, enjoying amnesty for the thousands of murders, rapes, and tortures committed against Haitians, and still either maintaining security in Haiti or receiving government pensions paid by the Aristide government, whichever they preferred. Moreover, it undermined prior accords, including the Governors Island Agreement. It was obvious that the Aristide government could not return under such conditions.[104]

In any event, on September 19, 1994, the day after the Carter delegation reached an agreement with the Haitian military, approximately two thousand U.S. troops entered Haiti.[105] By the second week of October, approximately twenty thousand U.S. troops had arrived.[106] Nevertheless, the U.S. assertion of power during the transition period between September 19 and October 15 was very uncertain and frustratingly incremental. The United States had pledged to cooperate closely with the Haitian military, but, by doing so, it failed to take effective actions to bring the army and its allies under control. In at least two instances, for example, the U.S. forces passively observed as attachés murdered pro-Aristide demonstrators.[107] They did take some steps to disarm the military, particularly of its heavy weaponry,[108] but its efforts to disarm the paramilitary forces were never serious. The reasons appeared to be the fear that possible American casualties would produce a political backlash in the United States,[109] and the U.S. commitment under the September 18 agreement to cooperate with, rather than supersede, the Haitian military and police.[110]

The United States acted decisively in late September to bar the members of Parliament elected in the January 1993 sham elections from taking part in the legislative deliberations over amnesty.[111] This action paved the way for Haiti's Parliament to approve a bill on October 7, 1994, giving Aristide the power to grant amnesty for political crimes but apparently not for human rights violations. This was, of course, Aristide's position all along on the question of amnesty.[112] On October 10, 1994, General Cédras retired,[113] and, three days later, he left for exile in Panama.[114]

The U.S. occupation gave the Haitian masses new-found feelings of hope and empowerment mixed with deeply imbedded rage toward the military and elites. These mixed emotions initially threatened wide-scale vigilante justice.[115] Amid this atmosphere of hope lingered reminders of the harshness of daily life in Haiti. In the cities, the Haitian military and its paramilitary affiliates continued to abuse Aristide supporters when the opportunity presented itself.[116] Hunger abounded and literally compelled Haitians to loot a food warehouse.[117] The rural areas were devoid of the political and administrative infrastructure needed to restore, with any degree of efficiency, basic services such as water, electricity, and schools.[118] Concerned about growing disorder and unrest in Haitian cities, the Pentagon announced plans to add to the existing 19,600 U.S. troops.[119]

As Cédras departed Haiti for exile in Panama, on October 13, 1994,[120] befittingly, the Haitian civilians enthusiastically gave Port-au-Prince a complete makeover, cleaning the streets and painting city buildings in expectation of Aristide's return.[121] Indeed, Haitians welcomed Aristide's return with cheers, singing, and dancing.[122]

On October 15, Aristide triumphantly returned to Haiti, after three years of forced exile.[123] His peaceful return marked a victory for the United States and the international community.[124] It promised an end to tyranny and represented an important step toward the creation of a lasting democracy. All in all, it was a magnificent day for the Haitian masses.

CHAPTER THREE

Haiti since Aristide's Return

A Preliminary View

Aristide's reinstatement was a dream come true for 95 percent of the Haitian people, and a nightmare for the remainder.[1] Indeed, all the hatred that festered between the social classes was only fueled by the euphoria surrounding Aristide's return.[2] Appropriately, his reinstatement speech focused on creating a peaceful democratic society through what he called the "twin themes" of reconciliation and justice,[3] and, indeed, Aristide's restoration to power and the formation of his government did bring cautious but definite advances to the Haitian people. There were clear signs that Haiti's infrastructure was beginning to improve,[4] and Haitian civilians, of course, began to enjoy exponentially greater social and economic freedoms than they had under the de facto government.[5]

Nevertheless, difficulties persisted, and the warm embrace surrounding Aristide's arrival belied a morass of problems that to this day has had a strangling effect on democracy.[6] The Aristide government and, now, the Preval government have faced a multitude of seemingly intractable obstacles: an abused and neglected populace, many of whom viewed Aristide as more of a deity than a mortal and formed their expectations accordingly;[7] a complete lack of infrastructure due in large part to military and elite pilfering; the devastating effects of the embargo; a completely dysfunctional justice system;[8] an incredibly rough topography that impedes the ability to travel and communicate, and thus hampers progress in the rural areas;[9] and deeply imbedded cross-class hatred.[10]

To complicate matters further, many of Haiti's problems are intertwined, making rapid change impossible. Indeed, unrealistically high expectations and lack of infrastructure resulted in a growing

42

frustration at the slow pace of fundamental change following Aristide's return.[11] Furthermore, Aristide's desire to pacify the more powerful Haitian groups that previously opposed him[12] slowed him in filling key posts in his administration and resulted in early criticism from his supporters.[13] To make matters worse, one month after Aristide arrived home, hundreds were left dead when Tropical Storm Gordon hit. Hampered by unregulated construction and poor infrastructure, Haitians were unable to cope.[14]

Haiti's inherent problems have been even further compounded by the contradictory U.S. military intervention. Although the United States made a major commitment to military intercession, it did not follow through with additional smaller commitments needed for Haiti's long-term political and social stability.

Specifically, the U.S. force resisted policing Haiti—due partly to a fear of violent conflict[15]—and that task was left to the existing Haitian police force. That plan was fundamentally flawed, of course, because the Haitian police force was notorious for its oppression and was therefore feared and hated by the general population. Furthermore, most of the crime that occurred during the early stages of the occupation was committed by paramilitary troops (attachés) against Aristide supporters, and the Haitian police showed an unwillingness to intervene against its former auxiliaries on the behalf of civilians.[16] These obvious flaws in the U.S. plan led to its swift failure as the Haitian police force's lack of morale and well-placed fear of the Haitian masses led to desertion and insurrection.[17] By the end of October, about 70 percent of the three thousand police had deserted,[18] and the U.S. troops seemingly had no choice but to play an increasingly heavy role in maintaining order.[19]

On March 31, 1995, however, the United States formally relinquished responsibility for securing Haiti, and transferred responsibility to a UN peace-keeping force.[20] The UN troops that replaced the U.S. troops numbered over six thousand, and represented more than thirty countries.[21] Approximately twenty-four hundred U.S. troops remained in Haiti as part of the UN peace-keeping force.[22] U.S. troops formally left Haiti on February 7, 1994, at the termination of President Aristide's term. A small contingent of UN forces—approximately fifteen hundred troops—were then scheduled to remain in Haiti until November 30, 1996.[23]

During their seven-month tenure, U.S. forces attempted to fill the gaps left by the fleeing Haitian police by recruiting volunteers for

Haiti's new "professional" police force.[24] If government plans work out, this force will eventually number between 5,000 and 6,000 men and women,[25] and will be under the authority of the Justice Ministry, as opposed to the military.[26] Critics of the professional police concept, however, believe that it increases the potential for a post-occupation coup, claiming that the same high-tech equipment used to establish a "professional" police force—squad cars, two-way radios, record-keeping systems, and modern command control—could be used to transform that force into the front line of the next despotic regime.[27] Perhaps even more important, the Haitian police force will not be fully established until some time late in 1997 or, perhaps, 1998.[28] Thus, it is unlikely that it could be a viable opposition to either anarchy or military insurgence at any time in the near future, and certainly not until some time after Preval has served a substantial part of his presidential term. Furthermore, although the UN peace-keeping force is in place, there is concern regarding its ability to ensure order in the event of a widespread paramilitary uprising.[29] Indeed, the UN voted to extend the June 30, 1996, date of departure of the peace-keeping force to November 30, 1996, and then extended that date to July 31, 1997, for fear that Haiti would again confront violence on a large scale.

Unfortunately for the Haitian people, a paramilitary uprising is a distinct possibility. Although the Haitian military was quickly disarmed after Aristide's return, divesting the paramilitary troops of their arms has been much more difficult: neither the U.S. troops nor the UN peace-keeping force ever committed to a full-fledged disarmament of the paramilitaries,[30] and even the sporadic attempts to recover paramilitary weapons are hampered because most of the paramilitary members—rumored to have obtained heavy weaponry just prior to the U.S. occupation—have blended into the civilian population.[31] They have now had the time and opportunity to hide their arms.

Former Aristide government officials estimate that only 30 percent of paramilitary members have been disarmed.[32] Many of these officials fear that thugs are patiently waiting to reinstate their oppressive rule now that the UN peace-keeping force has replaced the U.S. troops and it may leave Haiti by the end of November.[33] Indeed, paramilitaries have already tested the boundaries of the UN peace-keeping force's role, as well as the strength of Haiti's emerging democracy. As the U.S. troops withdrew, violence in Haiti correspondingly increased.[34] Not only did the traditional political violence continue,[35] but random crime, a new phenomenon in Haiti, appeared on the scene.[36] Paramilitaries were inciting street violence in an effort to undermine social order with the hope of creating political chaos.[37]

Maintaining the political and social stability necessary to build a democracy in Haiti has been like walking a tightrope. The U.S. and MNF troop withdrawal, as well as the possible UN peacekeeping force withdrawal, may be just enough to throw the democratically elected Haitian government off-balance, while simultaneously pulling out the safety net. In addition, neither Aristide, in his role as private citizen, nor Preval, as president, can be sure of post-occupation support from the United States. Despite formal words of support, the United States has shown a lack of clear resolve throughout its Haiti mission and wavered in its commitment to Aristide as Haiti's leader. Although the United States was the major participant in Aristide's return to Haiti, tensions between him and American policy makers were evident throughout his presidency. While perhaps not as severe, there are similar tensions between U.S. officials and President Preval.

Before and during his exile, U.S. officials repeatedly attempted to undermine Aristide as Haiti's rightful president. To varying degrees, this treatment was either promoted or passively accepted by the Bush and Clinton administrations,[38] as well as by the CIA.[39] Some of the most frequent efforts to sabotage Aristide's reputation involved allegations that not only painted him as a promoter of human rights violations and mob violence, but also portrayed him as an impediment to successful negotiations with the Haitian military.[40]

Within a week of the 1991 coup, characterizations of Aristide as a human rights violator began to emerge.[41] American news media widely publicized these charges, which were lent credence when the Bush administration promoted reports that Aristide had ordered the murder of one of his political enemies, Roger Lafontant, during the coup.[42] This charge is almost impossible to believe given that Aristide was under the control of the coup leaders at the time Lafontant was killed and, therefore, had no authority to order a murder. Moreover, the military had reason to want Lafontant dead, as he had a substantial following from right-wing military and paramilitary forces.[43] Despite the substantial doubts surrounding this charge, the Clinton administration, whose support for Aristide has been shaky at best, also bought into the accusations.[44] Furthermore, U.S.

officials under Clinton stated that they believe Aristide was involved in a cover-up of the killing of five youths by a pro-Aristide policeman.[45]

Aristide was also frequently accused of sanctioning mob violence through "necklacing" (*p'ere lebrun,* the practice of putting a tire around the victim's neck and shoulders, and then setting it on fire). It seems that the charges hinged on a series of misinterpretations, in which Aristide is said to have vowed to "turn the streets red," using the apparently well-known protest mechanism of lighting bonfires in tires. If he did make that statement, it was misunderstood as a threat to make the streets red with blood.[46] Furthermore, when Aristide refused to renounce popular self-defense against the military, insightfully observing that violence is more likely if peaceful change is continually frustrated,[47] he was represented—incorrectly—as endorsing mob violence.[48]

There are several other incidents used as proof that, in the past, Aristide sanctioned violence. The first is the trial of Roger Lafontant and his accomplices, which took place on July 29, 1991, under intimidating conditions. Crowds surrounded the courtroom and courthouse, calling for conviction and death, jeering at the defendants. Several of the demonstrators carried tires and threatened to "necklace" the defendants. In a speech to students on August 4, President Aristide failed to condemn their organized dissent. Rather, he suggested that the sustained demonstration helped obtain the jury's decision to sentence Lafontant to life imprisonment, even though the maximum legal sentence for his crime was fifteen years. The second example used against Aristide is his failure, in August 1991, to condemn crowds armed with tires who surrounded the National Assembly and threatened lawmakers who had passed legislation in opposition to that introduced by his government. In both instances, Aristide supported organized demonstrations but never violent physical assaults against anyone.

To the same end, it has been alleged that President Aristide has made several public statements actually condoning mob violence. For example, toward the end of 1991, on his return from New York, where he gave a speech to the United Nations General Assembly, he is said to have declared:

> Your tool is in your hand. Your instrument is in your hand. Your Constitution is in your hand. Don't neglect to give him what he deserves.

. . . Your equipment is in your hand. Your trowel is in your hand.
Your pencil is in your hand. Your Constitution is in your hand. Don't
neglect to give him what he deserves. . . . Throughout the four corners
of the country, we are watching, we are praying, we are watching,
we are praying—when we catch one of them, don't neglect to give
him what he deserves. What a beautiful tool! What a beautiful instrument! What a beautiful appliance! It's beautiful, it's beautiful, it's
pretty, it looks sharp! It's fashionable, it smells good and wherever
you go you want to smell it.[49]

Immediately after this passage came the observation: "It is provided
for by the Constitution, which bans Macoutes from political activity."

The speech employs metaphor, humor, and vivid rhetoric. Its
meaning, like much of the Creole language, therefore, is not crys-
tal clear. On the face of it, the speech characterizes the Haitian
Constitution as a tool and strongly suggests using constitutional
means to fight members of the former Haitian regime. However,
it could be, and has been, read as a confirmation of the appropriate-
ness of vigilante justice in some circumstances. Some Haiti observers have stated that, in fact, at the time of the speech, President
Aristide knew that the military was planning a coup and he was
simply warning his followers of the impending crisis. In any
event, there is no point in the speech where Aristide explicitly
promotes "necklacing" or other methods of violence. Furthermore, it is not even certain that the speech has been accurately
translated.

All such charges fail to explain the many public speeches that
Aristide made before the coup that praised the rule of law and urged
his followers to turn over suspected criminals to the police. His actions since his reinstatement prove decisively that he believes
strongly in following the rule of law. In all of the years that I have
known him, I have never heard him condone violence. Neither have
his advisers, with whom I had intimate talks in gathering the information for this book. He has always condemned violence in the
strongest terms.

Even if false, the charges did succeed in tainting the public perception of Aristide, thereby inhibiting support for military intervention
to restore him to power,[50] and legitimizing the U.S. threat to aban-
don support for him. The threat of abandonment, in turn, was used
as a bargaining tool to pressure Aristide to make changes in his amnesty policy.[51]

On the eve of the U.S. military occupation, tensions persisted between the United States and Aristide, indicating that President Clinton's and President Aristide's agendas were not in complete alignment. Aristide refused the Clinton administration's requests to ask Haitians to stop the mass exodus during the refugee crisis.[52] The National Security Agency was suspected of eavesdropping on Aristide's phone calls.[53] Immediately before he dispatched the Carter delegation to negotiate the Haitian military leaders' relinquishment of power, President Clinton implicitly indicated that long-term interests in democracy in Haiti were expendable when, in an attempt to win congressional support, he announced that the invasion would be limited to little more than the restoration of Aristide.[54] Moreover, just prior to the U.S. occupation of Haiti, the House Intelligence Committee held a closed-door briefing during which transcripts of Aristide were used to question whether the Americans should advance the interests of an individual who apparently held the United States in such contempt.[55] For example, Aristide had discussed the possibility that the United States masterminded the coup that ousted him from power. Emmanuel Constant, the leader of FRAPH, one of Haiti's most infamous paramilitary groups, was revealed to be on the CIA payroll. The CIA admitted paying Constant for information but denied assisting him in the formation of FRAPH.[56]

This negative sentiment filtered into Aristide's reinstated administration. U.S. officials suspected Brigadier General Mondesir Beaubrun, Aristide's interior minister, of plotting the murder of Mireille Durocher de Bertin, a prominent Aristide opponent and supporter of the military coup.[57] However, in approximately seven months of intensive investigations in Haiti, the FBI failed to determine who may have killed her.[58] Many Aristide government officials vehemently deny that Beaubrun was involved in any way with this incident. Senate Foreign Relations Committee chairman Jesse Helms accused Aristide of being antidemocratic, and establishing "vigilance committees" to keep an eye on political opponents.[59] In reality, of course, almost all of the recent political violence in Haiti has been directed at Aristide supporters.[60]

Underlying the continuing tensions between Aristide and the United States is the view held by many U.S. officials that Aristide is a dangerous radical.[61] Aristide has publicly criticized the United States for creating and perpetuating much of Haiti's economic decline.[62] Many U.S. officials disagree with what they understand to be his economic policy. Much of the American government's alleged concern is unwarranted. The United States obviously favors a "free-market" economy, and, after his election, Aristide took steps to mix conventional and more radical approaches. He agreed to the appointment of a pro-business prime minister, Robert Malval, signaling his willingness to accommodate members of the business community who were willing to break ties with the military.[63] While calling for free markets and a secured community for investors, Aristide also emphasized the injustice of the stark economic inequality between the vast majority of Haitians and the very small number of economic elites, arguing that rural cooperatives would be a good means of empowering peasants. Furthermore, he emphasized the importance of increased agricultural production, environmental awareness, and slowed migration to the cities.[64] What he refused to do was to privatize completely the major government-owned enterprises.[65]

In the months after his return, Aristide worked to improve conditions in his beleaguered country under the constant threat of a paramilitary insurrection and under the shadow of U.S. misgivings about his character and policies. He was faced with an almost insurmountable task in the rebuilding of Haiti and was furthermore expected to accomplish it within what can only be described as a hostile environment. The forces responsible for ousting him in the first place continued to exercise considerable influence in Haiti; the forces behind returning him to power were, at best, inconstant in their support of him—personally and politically.

He was also under pressure from his own support base: beyond the urgent need for economic, political, and social reform, he had at some point to face head-on the issue of serving justice to those responsible for the countless human rights violations that were perpetrated in his absence. Indeed, as Haiti began to rebuild its economic and political infrastructure, the call for justice from the people intensified. Although the Haitian masses now enjoyed greater freedoms, they still yearned for judicial vindication of prior military abuses. To the Haitian people, the concept of democracy in Haiti was completely incongruous with the idea of absolution for human rights violations committed during military rule.[66] At first, Aristide attempted to reconcile the elite oppressors' desire for amnesty and the masses' desire for justice through moderation, but his efforts left the public disillusioned.[67] The amnesty issue was quickly becoming a primary fuse in Haiti's emotional time bomb, and in December of 1994 Aristide ordered an investigation into the murders of thousands of Haitians committed during the military reign.[68]

After consultations with international advisers, he appointed a National Truth and Justice Commission[69] to investigate human rights abuses committed during the military regime and to write a report. He also asked an international group of human rights lawyers to assist the Haitian government in prosecuting those involved in these acts.[70] These efforts continue under the Preval administration.

Haitian civilians have also initiated actions in search of legal vindication for past abuses.[71] So far, their efforts have been mostly symbolic because many courts are either afraid of, or politically adverse to, prosecuting military and paramilitary leaders,[72] or simply incompetent.

As Haiti started on the long and perilous road to democracy, the United States continued to massage its refugee policy. For a brief two-month period during Aristide's exile, the Clinton administration had changed its refugee policy of immediate repatriation and had begun asylum processing for refugees with a legitimate fear of persecution in Haiti.[73] But because of the violence and fear of persecution in Haiti, the resultant flood of refugees was, of course, overwhelming, and in response the U.S. government shifted its policy again, this time offering Haitian refugees "safe haven" at the Guantanamo Bay Naval Base in Cuba.

The U.S. occupation and Aristide's return had a chilling effect on the refugee crisis. Nevertheless, months after Aristide's reinstatement, thousands of the original Haitian refugees were still being housed at the Guantanamo Bay Naval Base. Ninety percent of those remaining there in early January 1995 rejected the U.S. offer of temporary jobs and three months' pay in exchange for their voluntary return.[74] U.S. officials then began holding immigration interviews with the purpose of clearing the camp and returning almost all of the Haitian asylum-seekers to Haiti.[75] At the end of February 1995, the United States stepped up its program to forcibly repatriate refugees housed at Guantanamo on the grounds that Haiti is much safer since Aristide's reinstatement to power.[76] By April, almost all of the Haitian refugees had been returned to Haiti.

These actions are not altogether surprising, as there were early indications that the Clinton administration would revert to its initial policy of immediate repatriation. For example, shortly after Aristide's return, the INS ordered the end of the moratorium for deporting illegal Haitian residents. Although the INS immediately rescinded the order, calling it a mistake,[77] the original order held ominous significance. Even more disturbing to refugee advocates, a federal judge's order that approximately 230 Haitian orphans at Guantanamo be released into the United States[78] proved to be short-lived when an appellate court reversed that order.[79]

PART TWO

Human
Rights and
Democratic
Theory

Jean-Bertrand Aristide receives members of popular
organizations at the National Palace, November 1994.
Photograph © Chantal Regnault.

CHAPTER FOUR

Searching for Democratic Alternatives in Support of Human Rights

In part 2, I discuss various justificatory theories of democracy, and the specific justificatory theory that I believe is best suited for a nation that seeks to travel the difficult, if not almost impossible, journey from dictatorship to democracy. More specifically, I believe that a particular type of democracy—what many scholars refer to as "deliberative democracy"—is the most powerful justification for democracy. Moreover, it is the only sound theory that has a chance of working to help stabilize, consolidate, and preserve democracy under the very difficult conditions that face the Haitian people. Indeed, the murders of approximately five thousand people during the de facto military regime's rule, from 1991 to 1994, are likely to be repeated in the future unless the Haitian people inculcate democratic values into their polity. This task requires institutional restructuring on a macrolevel, and the internalization of certain values—a moral consciousness about the importance of treating people with dignity and all that may mean—on a microlevel.

I proceed by describing the concept, ethics, and difficulties of human rights. This discussion demonstrates not only the significance of human rights to a democracy, but also the difficulty of establishing and perpetuating such rights. I then analyze various justificatory theories of democracy. Finally, I describe the strengths and critiques of the specific theory that I endorse.

All of this is necessary for quite pragmatic, as well as for intellectually demanding, reasons. Merely discussing democracy in general, without an analysis of its various normative meanings and applications, may lead to the very evils that democracy is meant to prevent, including mass murders and other massive violations of human rights. Thus, failing to justify the meaning of democracy is a dangerous enterprise. It jeopardizes the fate of the Haitian people. Indeed, a failure to justify adequately the transition to democracy may legitimate the reinstatement of state-initiated violence.

The discussion of democratic theory is also important for other substantial reasons. In this analysis, I hope to demonstrate the importance of viewing democratic theory and practice as indispensable to one another. Stated otherwise, I hope to show that any dichotomy between theory and practice—the application of theory to the lives of real people—is simply a false one.

HUMAN RIGHTS

The concept of human rights is a confusing one. Scholars, political actors, and lay persons refer to human rights in a variety of often contradictory ways. Perhaps even more confusing and unclear is the relationship between human rights and democracy. I therefore begin this part of the book with an introductory sketch of the concept and its importance to a deliberative democracy.

The recognition and protection of human rights are perhaps the most significant aspects of economic, political, and social life in a democratic society. Indeed, human rights constitute an indispensable instrument that sovereign nations and the international community employ to avoid social catastrophes that threaten the lives of large numbers of people. This instrument is especially important in the transition from dictatorship to democracy, precisely because that is such a long and arduous process, and one fraught with the potential for human atrocities. Haiti is a case in point.

The transition to democracy in Haiti is proving to be a particularly hazardous enterprise. The death, disappearance, torture, and unjustified imprisonment of thousands of Haitians during the coup period make it acutely clear that fundamental structural reforms and changes in interpersonal relationships are absolutely necessary. Indeed, as the transitional democratic regimes emerge and develop, they necessarily inherit the unwelcome legacy of repression that has caused such widespread suffering. The fundamental question is how these successive governments can use human rights to help the Haitian people come to terms with their history of impunity and suffering, so that they can avoid repeating the same atrocities in the future.

Haitians will have to recognize the wrongs done *as* wrongs and gain an understanding of why and how they happen. The misery and violence occur not simply because there is a scarcity of resources, but because many of the corporativist groups use their fellow humans *as* resources, either for their own benefit or to realize a peculiar vision of what they believe to be the good or the right. This practice of using human beings as mere instruments is even more pernicious since it is carried out by powerful and amoral people who also have access to weapons or other means of control and thus are able to subject the majority of people to their will on a broad-based scale. The only viable remedy that seems to help neutralize this kind of scourge is precisely that constituted by the recognition of human rights.

The historical underpinnings of human rights are not confined to one nation. There are precedents that acknowledge their value that are as remote as the Spanish *fueros*,[1] the English charters,[2] and the North American declarations.[3] Nevertheless, it was the Declaration of the Rights of Man and of the Citizen of 1789[4] that made explicit the two most fundamental principles that give intellectual and substantive content to human rights as an enduring concept. The first principle is that the will of the most powerful is not, and cannot be, the final and valid justification for actions that affect the vital interests of individuals. The second is that the mere fact of being human is sufficient in and of itself to allow claims for particular goods that are basic for a life of dignity and autonomy. These principles are the bedrock upon which human rights expanded.

The mechanism for expansion and acceptance of human rights has been the affirmation of these principles through the constitutions of almost all nation-states and through international norms, such as the Universal Declaration of Human Rights enacted by the UN in 1948, including the subsequent covenants about civil, political, economic, social, and cultural rights.[5] This, however, was just a start. It did not prevent unprecedented genocides, sinister purges, cruel massacres and persecutions, bloody interventions of the great powers in the lives of other peoples, avoidable misery, disease and illiteracy in the third-world regions, the permanent threat of nuclear warfare, and other unspeakable horrors.

At the same time, these terrible facts should not obscure the slow, if insecure, progress that has taken place in this area since World War II: large-scale slavery has almost disappeared from the face of the earth; the process of decolonization has been substantially advanced; increasingly more nations adhere to the rule of law; international tribunals have been established to protect human rights; and people are increasingly alert to atrocities even beyond their own borders. Unfortunately, it is not possible to evade the question of why these manifestations of progress are not more substantial, more widespread, and faster developing, or why there are lapses and renewed acts of massive human rights violations—Haiti being a sad example.

One of the major factors that weakens the quest to promote human rights is the perception that, once legally recognized, these rights are forever secured. Although legal recognition is important because it makes it possible either to stop or alleviate certain kinds of rights violations carried out by the state, it is not enough. It is insufficient because those who have a monopoly on power and the tools for repression may, in turn, employ the state machinery to carry out the most brutal and devastating violations of rights—in effect, in the name of the state.[6] Haiti is, of course, a particularly harsh example of this problem. The Haitian Constitution provides for every right a civilized Western nation with a liberal political economy can imagine; the brutal dictatorship simply disregarded that fact.

Recognizing this limitation, action in the field of promoting human rights concentrates increasingly on the establishment of international covenants that define rights and institute external sanctions for their violation, as well as regional courts and other monitoring procedures. This has been a decisive step because it makes human rights relatively independent of the internal contingencies of each country; but these covenants do have their limits. Ideological divergence among governing powers in different nations leads to the acceptance of only a limited set of undisputed rights, and notions of sovereignty restrict international obligations, including outside intervention in aid of the investigation and punishment of violations.

Connected to the fact that legal recognition alone cannot fully protect human rights is another barrier to their continued viability—totally self-centered and self-interested groups, such as the corporativist Haitian elites, who simply disregard legal obligations. Ironically, they may do this in the name of an ideology: some attacks on human rights are born out of ideologies actually based on concepts unfriendly to, or even contemptuous of, the notion of human dignity for all.

Because legal recognition alone does not ensure promotion or protection of rights, some have suggested additional strategies. Perhaps the most intriguing of these is the argument that one must look beyond the legal affirmation of human rights to the creation of a moral consciousness of humanity. The hope is that certain types of governmental structures and policies will increase popular participation in public life and thus help to foster a moral consciousness—a belief in the transcendent value of human rights and a commitment to fight against any actions that violate them. If this consciousness becomes commonplace, it should act as the strongest defense to large-scale violations of human rights. It should, in turn, act as a catalyst for the creation of institutions that will promote respect for human dignity and thus ensure autonomy rather than slavery.

This, of course, raises the question of how to create, develop, and perpetuate a moral consciousness in people and in nations. There are two possible methods: the direct use of propaganda, and the fostering of rational discussion or dialogue. Within the framework of a democratic conception, propagandizing may be more efficacious in the short term. Experience shows, however, that propaganda is considerably more problematic than dialogue because it conditions the mind to a type of response that may well adapt itself to the opposite stimulus and thus lead to the creation of an authoritarian regime. Moreover, the use of propaganda implies an elitist attitude, because it assumes that those who produce the propaganda are convinced of the veracity of their positions, not on the basis of the propaganda itself but for reasons that are out of reach of their audience. Moreover, this method is pragmatically inconsistent with, and even averse to, the defense of the very human rights it is meant to be aimed at promoting here.

The scope of rational discussion or dialogue is clearly much broader. Even the most shameless tyrants feel obliged to offer some justification for their acts. That attempt at justification, hypocritical though it may be, can often lead to illuminating discussion. At a minimum, this presents an opportunity for opponents to open a debate, and, at best, it has the potential for providing individuals who were previously excluded from any self-determining participation in society with information relevant to their lives.

There is, however, a caveat to offer. Sometimes the powerful decision makers refuse to allow those who are most affected by the resolutions of these disputes to engage in the dialogue. Even some defenders of human rights would rather argue on behalf of the rights of the majority than extend the net of participation in discussion to include that majority. Sometimes individuals are unable to participate because they cannot gain access to the information required, or they do not have the opportunity to develop the skills necessary, for the discussion.

At other times, however, people simply adopt hardened philosophical positions that are opposed to any dialogue. Unfortunately, some philosophers openly defend these positions, and many lay persons have accepted their validity. Indeed, it often happens that the most fervent defenders of human rights are those who attempt to avoid rational discussion or simply refuse to engage in any dialogue on important questions, such as the scope of a particular right. Apparently, they assume that it is possible to take a position in favor of the practical protection of human rights without having to face the troublesome question of the reasons that morally justify that protection. This can also be true for those who fervently support democracy.

The first philosophical position that bars dialogue is a morally dogmatic one. According to this theory, there are self-evident moral truths, or truths apprehended by an act of faith or by an intuition, which cannot be intersubjectively corroborated. For a defender of this position, this makes the attempt to offer supporting reasons of such beliefs superfluous. The second is skeptical in nature. Those who hold this position believe that it is impossible to proffer reasons in support of any conception that legitimizes such concepts as human rights because the adoption of such a conception would always be determined by decisions or emotions that are not subject to rational discourse.

Many of the staunchest defenders of human rights and democracy in Haiti adopt either or both of these stances. They argue that the protection of human rights is simply a self-evident requirement of democracy. This is dangerous and self-defeating. Any commitment to human rights and democracy is necessarily a moral one. If this position cannot be, or is not, justified on the basis of reason, one remains defenseless before those who reject it. Stated otherwise, it is not as simple as choosing between a credo that recognizes human rights and another that disregards them. One has to determine which rights should be protected and what degree of protection should be assigned to them. Any theory that suggests answers to these questions must be based on normative ideas and requires resolution through dialogue by all concerned parties—the very basis of a deliberative democracy.

It is clear, therefore, that the expansion and adoption of these philosophical, or metaethical, conceptions is one of the greatest obstacles to the creation and spreading of a moral consciousness that could act as a barrier against the broad-scale attacks on the dignity and autonomy of human beings. It is therefore necessary to confront the question of which type of a political, social, and economic system may be best suited to help overcome these powerful obstacles.[7] The question is a difficult one, and the answers are not clear-cut. The search, however, must begin with an analysis of justificatory theories of democracy.

CHAPTER FIVE

A Democratic Vision

In this chapter I will analyze somewhat tentatively the basis of a view of democracy that differs substantially from most established conceptions of that system of government. I believe that this interpretation is the best justification for democracy and coincides quite well with my analysis of the problems associated with the creation of a democracy in Haiti. The view I endorse is a derivation of a theory suggested by the Argentine philosopher Carlos Nino,[1] with whom I have worked extensively on a variety of projects.[2]

I wish to make clear the eclectic nature of my work in this chapter and, indeed, in the remainder of the book. I believe that the compartmentalization of academic disciplines is simply the product of corporate interests. There are no valid scientific or intellectual necessities or practical reasons for their isolation from one another. Thus, I intend to incorporate philosophical, political, sociological, historical, cultural, and economic ideas and theories into my analysis of what the theory and practice of a functioning democracy may mean and require in Haiti. I hope to demonstrate my strongly held belief that intellectual and political work should not be separated, and that political action has a substantially greater opportunity of being correct if preceded by rational discourse. To put it another way, I believe that the theoretical and practical are intimately intertwined in the transition from dictatorship to democracy, and that this symbiosis is essential to minimizing the threat of physical violence and terror for large numbers of people.

DELIBERATIVE DEMOCRACY

The process of stabilizing and consolidating the newly created Haitian democracy has attracted many international lawyers, political actors, and common citizens. Most of these participants are well intentioned, quite able, and highly motivated. They possess the necessary skills and dedication to help make the dream of moving from dictatorship to a functioning democracy a reality. At the same time, however, many of those who have become intimately involved in the transition process approach it in a narrow manner. They are essentially concerned with stabilizing the democracy, but largely uninterested in justifying it. They simply assume that it is the best political system and do not see the need for articulating its normative bases. This is dangerous because democracy is itself a normative concept and cannot be preserved without analyzing the values that justify its institutions. The factors that make democracy the best political system are relevant in determining the best means for its preservation. We simply cannot identify which institutions and which policies are essential, and which are not, in relation to democracy without a moral theory justifying the concept.

Fortunately, there exists a plethora of writings on the concept of democracy. Not only political philosophers and political scientists, but also constitutional lawyers have for many years attempted to articulate convincing conceptions of this system of government.[3] Moreover, the wave of democratization that swept over Latin America in the 1980s, and that has also been sweeping over Eastern Europe in the 1990s, has revived the study of these theories and conceptions. Hunger for a convincing set of reasons for creating and perpetuating democracies has prompted the academy to respond with new writings and reviews of older works on the subject.

There has been renewed interest in authors such as Joseph Schumpeter, who, by contrasting an elitist conception of democracy with the classical one, has given various explanations for the U.S. political system.[4] In a similar way, Robert Dahl gives explanatory prominence to the conception of democracy as a "poliarchy" over the populist and Madisonian models of democracy.[5] In another view, Anthony Downs describes an economic theory.[6] As opposed to these, which I will generally label "pluralist" views, scholars such as C. B. MacPherson argue for a model of participatory democracy.[7] In this camp, Jürgen Habermas defends a democratic system that takes as its model a process of ideal communication.[8] Cass Sunstein favors a Republican vision of democracy, or at least a conception that mixes elements of it with others coming from the opposite, "pluralist" conception.[9] In a slightly different guise, Bruce Ackerman seeks to put forth a unique outlook, which he labels "dualist," placing it in opposition to two other views of democracy that he terms "monist" and "fundamentalist."[10]

To generalize, the literature on democratic theory suggests two quite different, even incompatible, approaches to justifying democracy. The first employs theories that attempt to create a separate category for the operation of politics in general, and democratic politics more particularly, in which moral issues are left uncontested or moral evaluation is suspended a priori because of a presupposition of the value of the political process. In this view ethics and politics must remain separated from one another or dangerous results will occur to the polity.[11] The democratic process accepts without reservation the interests and preferences of people, even when they are totally self-interested or morally unacceptable. That process also accepts as unassailable the political actions of people and groups on the basis of those preferences. Democracy is seen as generating such a dynamic of collective action, that it produces morally acceptable results. Thus, there is no necessity to modify the preferences of people in a morally virtuous direction. In fact, such an attempt would be dangerous to the democracy.

This approach, of course, starts from a rather pessimistic view of human nature. Proponents of this school of thought are similarly pessimistic about the possibility of changing the self-interested motivations of people. They attempt to present democracy as a system of collective interactions that makes the best of those self-interested motivations. This view is also extended to the formation of factions and corporations. Although accepting the position that associations of people on the basis of their self-interest may be a threat to the rights of individuals, proponents of this approach argue that the virtue of democracy lies in neutralizing, but not dissolving, the power of these factions or corporations through a series of mechanisms that force results that respect the rights of individuals.

In addition, champions of this approach frequently assume a skeptical or relativistic metaethical stand that demonstrates serious doubt about the possibility of the existence of objective reasons for the determination that some people's preferences are immoral and therefore should be disqualified from consideration. They also claim that the process of discovering these so-called objective reasons generally leads to authoritarian political regimes and, ultimately, to unacceptable intrusions into people's private spheres of life. Thus, in this model, democracy is valuable precisely because the dynamics of the system work toward the accommodation of everyone's preferences without judging their moral content. The result of this so-called normatively neutral process is seen as morally valuable.

The second approach to justifying democracy is radically different.

Here, democracy is meant as a normative process to transform the preferences and inclinations of people. Unlike the theories used to support the first approach, those used here require that the democratic process must necessarily be part of the moral realm. What democracy is cannot be separated from what it should be. To proponents of this approach, the virtue of democracy lies precisely in the creation and use of various institutional devices to promote the transformation of people's original motivations, from self-interested ones into more altruistic and impartial ones. Democracy not only produces morally acceptable results, but does so by improving people's motivations. Some even go so far as to argue that democracy should turn people into moral beings. This vision of democracy implies a generous and optimistic view of human nature. It suggests that human nature is malleable; it can be molded through social mechanisms that reflect a morally positive value system.

Its view of factions and corporations is also radically different. Indeed, the ambition of this vision of democracy is that it may be able to dissolve groupings of individuals on the basis of their self-interest. If this dissolution cannot be accomplished, however, a democracy may nevertheless attenuate to a large extent the power of these groups in favor of that of the isolated citizen, or of associations of citizens, on the basis of altruistic inclinations or at least impersonal values and ideologies.[12]

There are other differences between these competing theories of democracy. This second approach is not, in general, relativistic or skeptical in metaethics. Unlike the first, it accepts the position that there may be a possibility of giving objective reasons for the moral correctness of certain outcomes. It goes so far as to argue that the democratic process itself helps to determine the morally correct result or at least the knowledge needed to reach that result. In some manner, this approach also attempts to rebut the criticism that this view of democracy may lead to morally unacceptable, even authoritarian, positions, and to models of democracy that are unconcerned with, violate, or refuse to recognize, the significance of liberal rights.

These two sets of justifications for democracy differ precisely in their views of the relationship between democracy and liberalism, and, thus, from at least one of the other dimensions of constitutionalism.[13] One dimension of constitutionalism is the requirement, which is part of the notion of the rule of law, that the positive or historical constitution and the legal system that flows from it be meticulously observed, even when they restrain the operation of the democratic process, and even when they are not completely legitimized by it. A second dimension of constitutionalism is the ideal dimension of individual rights.

The first approach to justifying democracy, as outlined above, appears to be so sympathetic to the recognition of liberal rights, through its insistence that democracy should not interfere with the sphere of morality that these rights help to create and sustain, that its proponents have named the system "liberal democracy." This system is also sometimes referred to as "constitutional democracy" or "representative democracy." Whatever its name, such a system is often envisioned as a separate and distinctive form of government from other conceptions of democratic government. According to the advocates of this first set of democratic theories, this is the only theory and form of democracy that acknowledges the weight that certain other dimensions of constitutionalism—the ones described above—exert upon democracy.

In contrast, the second approach is seen, almost always by its opponents and sometimes by its very advocates, as antiliberal or at least nonliberal. Sometimes, the system born of this second approach is called "populist democracy," "social democracy," or "participatory democracy." In addition, its defenders will oftentimes agree with the argument that their approach helps to reduce or even eliminate the counterweight of the other dimensions of constitutionalism to democracy.

The view that I wish to defend, which broadly fits within the second set of theories, is a derivation of a view championed by Carlos Nino. While considering aspects of all of these theories, it is markedly different from all of them, particularly in its specific justifications for a democratic system of government. Precisely because such a theory is most likely to resolve some of the tensions in the competing visions of democracy, and because it is most likely to help create a positive moral consciousness in the citizens of Haiti, and thus an enduring barrier against violations of human rights, I believe that this theory represents the most defensible justificatory basis for democracy.

A MORE SPECIFIC VISION OF DEMOCRACY

Some philosophers, lawyers, and political actors—most notably, Carlos Nino—have endorsed a derivation of a unique and specific theory that assigns value to democracy based on a processing of preferences and puts the greatest emphasis on the practice of rational deliberation. Stated otherwise, this view relies on the virtue of democracy to transform people's interests and preferences.

This view contrasts sharply with those that I believe may accurately and generally be labeled "pluralistic."[14] Pluralism, quite broadly defined, argues that the value of democracy is neither tied to the transformation of the self-centered interests or preferences of people nor meant to discourage the association of people in different groups or corporations in order to further their self-interested goals in the political sphere. Rather, for the pluralist position, that value lies in providing mechanisms to ensure that the extant preferences and interests of individuals and their groups work for what is conceived as the common good. This may, for example, mean protecting the liberty of people by stopping any of these associations from monopolizing power. The value of democracy is essentially negative. Its value lies in guarding against and stopping tyranny and anarchy.

In contrast to the pluralist position, the particular view of democracy that Carlos Nino champions assumes that the method of turning people's selfish preferences into the more impartial ones is collective deliberation—dialogue. Further, and most significant, Nino argues that collective deliberation has value in itself because it provides reasons for believing that the solution endorsed by that consensus agrees with what is prescribed by valid moral principles, which, in turn, provide us with autonomous reasons to act.

Nino's theory is an epistemic one, particularly with regard to social morality. He argues that, if certain strictures are met, democracy is the most reliable procedure for gaining access to the knowledge of moral principles. Thus, to Nino, intersubjective discussion and decision form the most reliable method for gaining access to moral truth. Dialogue, the exchange of ideas and the requirement that one must justify one's position against others, broadens one's knowledge and reveals defects in logic and reasoning. Rational discussion helps to satisfy the requirement of impartial attention to the interests of everyone concerned. It helps all participants understand the positions of the others. Impartiality is a state in which each person is required to look at an entire situation from the "God's-eye" point of view—from the point of view that considers the best interests of everyone else—rather than from the point of view of any one person or group, with special interests and special desires that do not coincide with those of other persons or groups. While this may be an impossible state to achieve in a polity, in this theory of democracy it is important to get as close as possible to this ideal state. Each person should have the maximum freedom of decision that is compatible with the equal freedom of everyone else.

This dialogue process suggests which policies are more likely to be the correct ones in a given situation, and which decisions are the crucial ones. When democracy is conceived of in this way, there is clearly an intrinsic relationship between democratic politics, the law that results, and morality. However, there is a defect in this process—it must at some point be conceded that the democratic process is almost always an imperfect substitute for the practice of moral discussion.

To make this claim, of course, requires an explanation of the value of moral discourse. Importantly, Carlos Nino argues powerfully that the practice of moral discourse has epistemic value for discovering correct moral solutions to intersubjective issues. In point of fact, the validity of interpersonal moral principles, which evaluate actions on the bases of their effects on the interests of people other than the agent, rests on a viewpoint of impartiality, rationality, and knowledge of the relevant facts. Moreover, the discussion and interplay of ideas, when they conclude in a unanimous consensus, are important factors in the achievement of impartial, rational, and knowledgeable moral intersubjective solutions. Because Nino's argument assumes that each person is the best judge of his or her own interests, unanimity is seen as the functional equivalent of impartiality when it results from discussion among all the concerned parties.

This immediately begs the question of how democracy fits into this vision. Democracy, as a system in which the majoritarian opinion is binding to the degree that all the people concerned have participated in both discussions and collective decisions, is the natural substitute, or surrogate, for the mechanism of informal discussion and unanimous consensus. Furthermore, this system allows for the adoption of new decisions at specific times. Without this allowance for changing circumstances, the status quo would prevail, even if it were favored by only a tiny minority. Nevertheless, majority rule presents its own problems. It is simply not the functional equivalent of impartiality. For example, the majority, for morally invalid reasons, may be unequivocally and openly opposed to any action that will help a particular minority. This does not, however, necessarily destroy the epistemic value of democracy. To put it another way, when all of the people concerned freely, openly, and equally participate in the process of deliberation and decision, democracy preserves some of the epistemic value inherent in the process of informal discussion and unanimous consensus. Indeed, in this epistemic view, democracy, based upon this process of collective deliberation, includes a dynamic of collective action and tends toward the creation and adoption of impartial solutions.

This is not to say, of course, that democratic solutions are always correct. That conclusion would be absurd. It means only that these democratic solutions are more likely to be right than solutions adopted by any other procedure. To Nino, and other proponents of the epistemic view, the democratic method of collective decision making is more reliable than the procedure of isolated individual reflection in reaching morally correct solutions to intersubjective moral issues. However wise and well-intentioned an individual may be, it is unlikely that he or she could represent the real interests of others better than they could by participating in the process of discussion and decision themselves.

Further, the epistemic value of democracy varies with the degree to which its underlying conditions are satisfied. Those conditions depend upon the openness of the debate and the degree to which people equally participate in, and support, the final decision. There is, of course, a threshold at the lowest degree of satisfaction of those conditions beyond which the epistemic value of the process is so weak, that it begins to be outweighed by the value of the process of individual reflection.

Indeed, there are a multitude of areas in which one may be absolutely certain that the majoritarian opinion is wrong, and that the result of our individual reflections is closer to the requirements of impartiality, rationality, and knowledge of the relevant facts. Nino argues that this is not the case in general and in the long run, however, and that the democratic process is more reliable than individual reflection. This leads him to conclude that there is a powerful derivative reason for following the results of the democratic process even when they are wrong. If we do not do so, individual reflection could always be viewed as the correct process for reaching morally correct decisions, and the democratic process would become superfluous. This conclusion, of course, would contradict Nino's conception and assumption that individual reflection is less reliable than the democratic process. Thus, according to this epistemic theory, for the democratic system to be operative, one must rely on it even in those cases in which we are sure that it is incorrect, unless the underlying conditions that determine its epistemic value are not fulfilled.

In addition, democratically enacted rules provide the epistemic reasons for adopting the actions they prescribe. This view leads to a possible valid solution to the paradox of the moral superfluousness of law. If proponents of this view are correct in their assumptions that law is not self-justificatory, but only provides reasons for actions when it is endorsed by autonomously accepted moral principles, why not rely specifically on those principles in order to justify decisions and actions? In this vision of democracy, the epistemic value of democracy provides the answer.

One simply cannot determine which valid intersubjective principles are the bases for action until they are expressed in legal rules that are adopted after a process of collective deliberation and decision. It is, therefore, certainly valid to claim that legal rules are not original reasons for action. Instead, they must be seen as reasons for discovering the reasons for action.

Furthermore, if one adopts this theory of democracy, then a necessary corollary is that any conception of human rights must conclude that they are of a basic and central moral nature, and that their legal recognition must be considered a precondition for the justification of legal norms and decisions. This democratic theory, and its corresponding conception of human rights, leads ineluctably to the conclusion that "it is the function of effectively guaranteeing basic individual rights that provides the primary moral justification for the existence of any legal order or government."[15]

This set of moral principles provides moral justification for the legal order. Furthermore, it leads one who accepts and follows a similar vision of democracy to consider several problems. First, what type of government is least likely to dictate ethically unacceptable norms? Second, is there an obligation to obey the law even when it is morally wrong? Finally, how can one solve the apparent paradox of the moral irrelevance of law and government?

OBJECTIONS

Objections to such an epistemic view of democracy are possible along several lines. As Carlos Nino himself has recognized, perhaps the strongest ones are grounded in the realities of political life and practice.[16] To put it another way, if it is true that the democratic process has an inherent tendency toward reaching just solutions to difficult problems, and that one can rely on its enactments in the process of justificatory reasoning, how can one explain the unjust distribution of resources that the democratic process often produces? What explains the existence of widespread poverty and profound inequalities in resource allocation and distribution within democratic nations? Why do certain portions of the populace in democratic constitutional societies appear to enjoy an almost unlimited freedom to pursue their interests at the expense of those who do not have enough resources to satisfy even their most basic material and psychological needs?

One logical response to this powerful critique of the epistemic value of democracy is to suggest an ideal model of society that is almost certainly impossible to meet, and thence to work back with a list of actual situations placed in order according to their relative distance from satisfying the requirements of the ideal. Thus, all actual situations that do not meet the demands of the model are not necessarily equal. The closer to the ideal, the better the chance of meeting the demands of the model. In the case of the epistemic theory of deliberative democracy, that order depends on the degree of fulfillment of the conditions that grant the democratic process its epistemic value. This depends, in turn, on institutional arrangements, which provide for different degrees of satisfaction of those conditions.

Thus, a proponent of this view of democracy must claim that challenges grounded in "real politic" may be met by showing a correlation between the order of real situations that present different institutional arrangements and provide different degrees of satisfaction of the conditions underlying the epistemic value of democracy, and an order of political units achieving different degrees of satisfaction of the needs of the citizenry. But there are serious difficulties with this analysis. Determining the possible correlations between these orders is a complicated task with its own set of extremely difficult conceptual and empirical problems. Moreover, this last order—the arrangement of political units and the satisfaction of the citizens' needs—is extremely complicated. It involves numerous variables related both to productivity and to the allocation and distribution of resources. Further, the same institutional arrangements applied to different societies, for example, may satisfy to quite different degrees the conditions underlying the epistemic value of democracy because of the impact of other types of conditions. These difficulties are exacerbated by other factors. It is clear that the complex of historical, cultural, physical, and psychological factors of each particular polity has differential impacts on those conditions. In addition, as anyone who champions an epistemic view of democracy must recognize, the very definition of human needs is a subject of great controversy, involving a variety of different norms and assumptions. Unfortunately, this is not the only set of problems that presents itself. For example, the question of how one values different balances between the goods provided to people in each polity is itself controversial.

Combined, these problems are not only staggering but perhaps even insoluble. It may be that any conclusion on these questions remains open to serious intellectual work and significant changes in human behavior. There is, however, perhaps an even more significant challenge to the epistemic theory. This is the argument that, because of the realities of modern societies, there is simply no possible set of institutional arrangements in existence that satisfies the underlying conditions of the epistemic value of democracy. If this is so, then the epistemic democratic position is open to a charge that it is merely an illegitimate utopian ideal. This problem, however, is not necessarily irresolvable. Imperfect as current democracies are, some of them strongly display the features of open and free discussion and popular participation that are necessary to show their epistemic quality. This is not all. At a minimum, the degree to which they have these features appears to be incomparably greater than any other existing system of government. It is also correct to claim that, though the existing democracies remain distant from the ideal democratic system that closely resembles the original practice of moral discourse, the epistemic view of democracy helps to explain the actual shortcomings of these existing systems through an explanation of the deficiencies of particular institutional arrangements. If this is correct, it may serve as some proof that this type of vision of democracy does not necessarily represent an invalid utopianism.

Yet a warning is in order. In turning to the specific case of Haiti, a country in the midst of transformation to a democratic system of government, this particular problem is exacerbated. The history of Haiti reveals that the institutions of government have never operated successfully, and that the underlying conditions do not even come close to creating the appropriate conditions for creating a democracy. Positive change—the consolidation and stabilization of the fledgling democracy—however, is unlikely without this theoretical perspective. The epistemic theory provides a method for thinking about the problems associated with the transition to and consolidation of a democracy, and their solutions. It suggests institutional structures and plans of action and it allows a basis for judgment about the actions taken to meet the democratic goals.

In the remainder of the book, I wish to analyze and employ some of the wonderful insights developed by those who champion democracy through their academic and theoretical writings and practices— philosophers (particularly Carlos Nino), social scientists, lawyers, and lay people—by looking at some of the breathtaking difficulties of moving from dictatorship and authoritarianism to democracy in

Haiti. I will describe and analyze the extremely difficult problems of making such a transition in the real conditions that confront the Haitian people. Finally, I suggest some institutional structures that may allow democratic processes to come closer to producing morally acceptable results in Haiti.

A MORE FOCUSED CONCEPTION OF DEMOCRACY

The democratic conception that I have in mind for Haiti is an extremely broad one indeed. It is explicitly a conception of a political, economic, and social order.[17] It is a conception of a social system in which public debate over the direction of social life is not only expected, but actively encouraged. I view democracy, in part, as a public forum for moral discourse, where principles, rather than special interests, prevail. I believe that the best means for countering the overpowering influence of special interests is to create a polity governed by universal and impersonal principles where individual citizens, who preserve the ability to adopt new interests and are not necessarily identified with any special interest, make choices in a process of public justification and dialogue.[18] This process, in turn, has epistemic value. Implicit in this conception of democracy is the realization that the removal of existing barriers to free deliberation would not necessarily eliminate all grounds for political, social, and economic disagreement. Indeed, democracy can never be a utopian conception simply dedicated to an ideal of a perfectly harmonious community. That would, in any event, be an illegitimate utopian conception of democracy. The task of a democratic conception, therefore, is not to describe a social order in which all disputes would be trivial or indicative of a failure to realize the principles of the order. Rather, the burden is to outline a political, social, and economic order in which disagreements over the direction of that order can be socially addressed through a process of free, equal, and collective deliberation. This means, of course, that everyone concerned with the outcome of a decision must be allowed into the dialogue.

In view of these considerations, it follows that the democratic order must satisfy several major requirements. The principles of that order must be clarified by describing the justification or principle of democratic legitimacy. Some description and explanation must then be given of a set of institutional requirements rooted in those fundamental principles. Finally, an account must be offered of the motivations that might lead people to support and maintain such institutions over time.

I have already suggested the requirements of the first condition. A democratic society is an ongoing order characterized in the first instance by a certain principle of justification—a principle that recognizes the legitimacy of democracy. This principle requires that sovereign individuals be free and equal in determining the conditions of their own association. It also requires that the participants in the order, who are presumed to be educated on the issues confronting society and thus have the ability to form rational judgments about the ends of social life, continuously exercise that sovereignty. In addition, the democracy must ensure that the citizens are constrained in making those judgments only by the conditions necessary to preserve reasoned public deliberation, and that nothing actually determines the ends of social life other than the judgments arrived at by the members of the order. Moreover, the views of each member of the democracy must carry equal weight in public deliberation. This means that people must be allowed to acquire the tools needed to engage in the dialogue, and that their ideas must be understood and respected. Further, the principles of democratic legitimacy must not be prey to the intrusion of private power. Thus, material inequalities in resource allocations and control must be changed.[19] How such changes should occur, of course, must be resolved through a process of collective deliberation. Allowing a small group of elites simply to decide to reallocate and redistribute resources, without the validity of collective deliberation, clearly violates the principles of this democratic conception. Means and ends are integrally related to the validity of collective action.

The satisfaction of this justificatory principle must be manifest or clearly visible to participants in the order, in the actual workings of its institutions. This, in turn, provides one of the foundations for the stability of the democratic order over time. In addition, this general conception of democracy has consequences for the sorts of claims that members of a democratic order can make on one another and on the society as a whole. There are certainly many such claims that can be made by free and equal participants in the exercise of sovereignty. The claim of autonomy, however, is of particular importance. Autonomy consists of the exercise of self-governing capacities, such as the capacities of understanding, imagining, reasoning, valuing, and desiring. Free persons have, and are recognized as having, such capacities. In a political order dedicated to securing the conditions of free deliberation for its members, those members can legitimately expect of that order that it not only permit, but also encourage, the exercise of such capacities—that it permit and encourage autonomy. Further, to claim autonomy for oneself is to recognize the reciprocal and equally legitimate claims for autonomy by others.

In sum, the principle of legitimacy requires an ongoing order of mutually assured and encouraged autonomy in which political, social, and economic decisions are always based on the judgments of the members who are free and equal persons. It requires that the expression of self-governing capacities operate both within the formal institutions of government and in the affairs of daily life. Finally, it requires that the democratic order stably satisfy the conditions of equal freedom and autonomy that give it definition. Because the absence of material deprivation is a prerequisite for free and unconstrained deliberation, a basic level of material satisfaction, which would be more precisely specified through a free process of collective deliberation, should be provided for all members of the political order.

These conditions provide the basis for considering the more specific institutional arrangements and requirements of a democratic order. But elaborating these requirements is not an easy task. It cannot be done in any absolute sense. The institutional structure for a visionary democracy that justifies itself in the way I have elaborated can proceed only in general outline. It must necessarily be experimental. Like any epistemic conception of democracy, this democratic conception assumes a broad framework of social cooperation. How that framework will be expressed institutionally must necessarily vary under different cultural, psychological, and historical conditions.

Thus, in describing the institutional requirements of a democratic political order, my discussion must remain somewhat provisional and abstract. I cannot necessarily anticipate the variety of conditions under which democratic institutions might arise. There are other complications. In describing these requirements within a structure that includes the real conditions of Haiti, the intricacies become even more complex and the discussion even more problematic. Nevertheless, it is worth emphasizing that the various institutional requirements do comprise a unitary whole. To put it another way, these various institutional requirements within a democratic conception comprise a system—a set of constraints and conditions that are intimately interrelated and that define a distinct social structure of coordination and power.

PART THREE

The Transition from Dictatorship to Democracy

FRAPH members demonstrate in front of La Normandie, a bar in Port-au-Prince, November 1993. Photograph © Chantal Regnault.

CHAPTER SIX

The Difficulties of the Transition

Before one can judge the potential for a democratic transition in Haiti that justifies itself through its epistemic value, one must be clear about the problems that Haiti is currently facing. The epistemic conception is helpful in suggesting criteria by which the distance between an ideal democracy and the Haitian reality can be judged. It also helps one make reasoned judgments about which institutions are necessary, and which are contingent, to the transition process. Different conceptions of democracy suggest different institutional designs and help us weigh diverse policies and strategies. Since democracy is not simply a descriptive concept, but rather a normative one, institutions cannot simply be factually identified. Specific institutions that democracy demands, therefore, will depend on the theory used to justify that institutional design. While some institutions, such as freely held elections, are universally required for all forms of democracy, others depend more crucially on the specific justifications for democracy being applied. In this part of the book, I proceed by discussing and analyzing the problems that confront the Haitian people in their journey toward democracy. I then describe and analyze the attempts made by the Aristide and Preval governments to stabilize and consolidate the transition to democracy. In addition, I make judgments about those attempts, and I suggest policies and institutional changes that will satisfy the demands of the epistemic democratic theory.

While Aristide's return and the election of his successor, René Preval, clearly represent very positive triumphs, these are, unfortunately, only small steps in the transition to democracy in Haiti. Stability remains frustratingly elusive, and renewed violence is a distinct possibility. While the tenure of the only credible peace-keeping force, the UN peace-keeping force, which was set to leave Haiti on February 6, 1996, upon the expiration of Aristide's term,[1] has been extended several times, until reaching a final date of July 31, 1997,[2] it is almost certain that the Haitian National Police will not be able to function effectively until well after that date. The question, therefore, remains: what will happen now that the Aristide government has been restored to power, the Preval government has assumed power, and the international community appears to be losing interest in helping to create the conditions for democracy to flourish in Haiti?

Haiti has never had a secure democratic government, and it is not clear that there are enough elements of civil society to provide a proper foundation for one within a length of time the U.S. public and the international community would support. Unless significant changes occur before the second democratically elected president in Haitian history, President René Preval, is able to consolidate the preliminary democratic reforms, the successors of Cédras and François will still be there, and the country will still be split between a tiny group of elites and a vast poor majority. What, if any, alternatives exist? The answer begins with a focus on the very complex issues involved in any transition to democracy, especially one that may take place in Haiti.

There is a deeper meaning to the Haitian people's rejection of their military coup leaders than is traditionally suggested. It is a revulsion against a feigned public life, which is in fact little more than a weapon or disguise of private interests. It represents a demand for real democracy and for the protection of human rights. This protest is hampered from within, however, in the sense that it cannot succeed in its larger objectives without fundamental changes in the established structure and in the prevailing ideas of Haitian society— ideas that are, in fact, far removed from the agenda of the traditional politics of Haiti or even international perspectives of the problem.

This problem is not unique to Haiti. Rather, it is reflected in the institutional structures of many developing nations. For example, the dominant political regimes of the less-developed economies, and even their critics, often start with the desire merely to imitate and import the institutional arrangements of the rich industrial democracies. They do this in the hope that, from similar institutional devices, similar economic and political consequences will result. Such imitation, however, has not led to these desired results. The failure of these efforts at emulation may nevertheless be useful to the development of new institutional structures. Such efforts could end up driving these countries into an involuntary institutional experimentalism, which may shed light on the suppressed opportunities for transformation. So if Haiti begins on this path, it is possible that positive results may follow.

Institutional structures must be developed and secured. Economic and political stability must be assured. Corporatist social and political structures must be transformed so that the powerless get their fair share of the basic necessities of life. The rule of law must become paramount in the formal institutions and practices of government, and in the affairs of daily life.

To satisfy the epistemic value of democracy, these issues must become grist for the mill of public debate, and their complexity understood. Although these issues may be theoretically severable, they are also inextricably intertwined. The rule of law, for example, must be consolidated not only to protect human rights, but also to help secure a satisfactory level of economic, political, and social development. Moreover, an independent judiciary is crucial to the process of consolidating the rule of law. This is a good starting point from which to view the specific case of Haiti.

The role of an independent judiciary in the transition process is, of course, extremely complex. One major complication is the very fact that the institutional structures necessary for a viable democracy remain in varying stages of development in Haiti. The transition to democracy is usually represented in one of two distinct stages. In one stage, a country is attempting to adjust norms or institutions toward the strictures of the democratic rule of law. In this preliminary stage of development, it is necessary for the institutional structures associated with a democratic government, such as an independent judiciary or competition between different political parties, to be developed. In the other stage of development, the democratic institutional structures exist in a developed form, but their stability is not completely secured.

Haiti is clearly in the first stage of development. The nation not only needs to develop institutions, it must also train a large number of people to run them. But what is even more ominous for the success of any possible transition to democracy in Haiti is the fact that its institutional structure, particularly its judicial structure, is less developed than that of virtually any nation that has attempted this precarious transformation. The problem is further exacerbated by Haitian history. Social tensions and conflicts sometimes coercively interfere with the creation and development of viable institutional structures, and it is no exaggeration to claim that Haiti has never had a true system of justice. For decades, the FAD'H systematically violated and ignored internationally—and nationally—recognized human rights in its treatment of civilians. Before Aristide's reinstatement to office, even to speak of a "Haitian system of justice" would have dignified the violence and brutal use of force by soldiers and attachés, the corruption of judges and prosecutors, and the anarchy of Haitian courtrooms and prisons. More importantly, the system is still unformed, and corruption continues to be a serious problem. It may be years before a real justice system will be able to function properly. The distance between an ideal democratic model and the institutional structure and reality in Haiti is wide indeed.

THE ABSENCE OF MATERIAL DEPRIVATION: A FIRST STEP TOWARD DEMOCRACY

Because the absence of material deprivation is a prerequisite for free and unconstrained deliberation and individual development and fulfillment, a democratic society that justifies itself on the basis of its epistemic value must provide a basic level of material satisfaction for all members of the political order. Further, to satisfy democratic values, the level of material satisfaction must be determined through a free process of deliberation among the people. Indeed, the expression of self-governing capacities must operate both within the formal institutional structure of government and in the everyday affairs of social life. The democratic order must, in any endeavor, satisfy the conditions of equal freedom and autonomy that help define it. But how can a government even begin to fulfill these requirements in Haiti?

The overriding characteristic of the political life and political discourse of Latin American, Eastern European, and other developing nations today is a frustrated desire to escape the choice between a nationalist-populist project and a neoliberal project. The import-substituting, protectionist style of industrialization and the pseudo-Keynesian public finance that accompanied it seem to have exhausted their capabilities. The neoliberal alternative, however, is unable to service the real conditions of sustained economic growth. If taken seriously, this neoliberal economy remains an anathema to the very elites that pretend to champion it. There does not seem to be any articulated and viable alternative to these rejected and unpromising options.

In political-economy terms, and in line with the justificatory theory of democracy developed above, promising alternatives might develop in a seriously underdeveloped nation such as Haiti in the following direction.

1. The democratically elected government must take macroeconomic stabilization seriously. One way of doing this is through a dramatic rise in, and focusing of, the tax rate, which would impose upon the privileged classes and regions of Haiti the costs of public investment in people and in infrastructure.[3] It would, of course, be utterly unrealistic in Haiti to take another approach and conceive of a sound financial system as one based on a drastic lowering of governmental expenditure rather than on a raising and rationalization of taxes. There needs to be a strong preference for a universal, direct consumption-based tax—taxing, in a steeply progressive way, the difference between income and savings—as the means to finance the state while promoting capital formation and productive investment. Haiti will need large amounts of international aid over a long period of time—perhaps several decades—to augment these taxings, because the nation is in financial ruin. This is in no small part caused by the wealthy and military elites stealing the state's funds and then sending their ill-gotten fortunes out of the country to foreign banks. Even many of those people who earn their money legally do not invest it in the development of Haiti.

2. The government must help create the conditions for an "anti-dualist" political economy. This economy has to aggressively attack and overcome the internal division of Haiti into two (or more) economies that are only tentatively and hierarchically connected. What is needed, therefore, is the consolidation and development of a technological vanguard in both the public and private sectors, and the use of this vanguard to lift up and transform the immense, backward second economy of Haiti. Key to this strategy are untried forms of public-private partnership, and decentralized capital allocation and capital management. These two or more economies cannot be allowed to become the platform for an antiquated fordist-style industry that is unable to compete abroad except through internal wage repression and that is incapable of transforming the second economy. For example, networks of small and medium-sized enterprises represent the most dynamic force in many of the economies of the developing nations, including Haiti, and are even paralleled by internal experiments in the large businesses with the greatest potential for growth and innovation. These intimations of an alternative, less-confining industrial

future—changing the organization of firms, perhaps by making them more democratic, as well as the character of regional economies within the country—need to be developed by a deliberate economic program strongly helped by the international community. Indeed, the international community must play a central role in this experiment through monetary and technical assistance. Haiti simply cannot survive and prosper without large amounts of international assistance.

3. Capitalism has to be imposed upon so-called capitalists through the privatization of the private sector (real competition, real refusal of the capitalization of profits through the socialization of losses, real antitrust, real markets in corporate control, real constraints upon nepotism and inheritance, and real private responsibility for the costs of public investment). The government must also develop a parallel set of institutions to compete in the marketplace. Further, the Haitian government, by working with private entrepreneurs and international organizations and agencies, must create and develop public companies. In addition, the government must impose upon these companies a regime of decisive competition and independent financial responsibility. Total privatization of publicly owned companies would not necessarily be a good idea in Haiti.[4]

4. A massive investment in people and infrastructure should be financed by taxes on the people with the goods. There must be a priority of such claims upon the budget, backed by procedural devices with executory force. In addition, preventative public health, sanitation, and food supplementation need to be given precedence over therapeutic medicine. Even more important, the people must be educated. Schools and universities must be opened to everyone, and literacy programs created and implemented. The Creole language, therefore, must replace French in the schools and in the justice system. Finally, there must be a radical shift of the content of education away from the memorization of facts and toward an emphasis upon the mastery of generic practical and conceptual capabilities.

INSTITUTIONAL ORGANIZATION AND THE TRANSITION PROCESS

In the organization of government, politics, and civil society, the alternative to nationalist-populist or neoliberal projects may take the form of a public-law counterpart to the political economy I have just outlined, animated by the same concerns and moving toward the same goals. The organizational structure should help us decide whether a particular democratic society is moving closer or further away from the ideal model. This proposed transformation of institutional organization raises questions, of course, about the significance and independence of the judiciary. I do not believe, however, the problem is any different in Haiti or in other developing nations than it is in any liberal democracy. When we say "independence" in this context we are usually conjuring up the notion of parties being detached from a particular dispute, politics, and sometimes even ideology.[5] This idea remains problematic in many developing nations, particularly in one as underdeveloped as Haiti.

It is clear that the Haitian people, as well as many people in Eastern European and Latin American nations, have not internalized the significance and legitimacy of a constitutional system based on the rule of law. This, of course, is devastating to the attempt to create a democracy that justifies itself on the basis of its epistemic value. This problem is not simply an individualized one. The Haitian culture appears to be strongly resistant to the internalization of universal standards of achievement and competition necessary to an equitably functioning democracy. Rather, Haitians appear to have internalized a belief in the overpowering importance of status and connections, thus crippling the transition to a constitutional democracy. It is a sobering thought that the problems associated with the transition to democracy in Haiti may be intractable. Is it possible to convince the military and economic elites, and the other corporativist forces in Haiti, that they must adhere to the moral bases of a democracy? Is it possible to make them understand that this is the only way to improve their own lives and the lives of their children, as well as those of all the currently disenfranchised people of Haiti—particularly the masses?

The democratization process needs further elucidation. Setting aside the complex question of when a democracy has been consolidated, which I believe depends implicitly upon justificatory conceptions of democracy, the concept of consolidation presents difficult problems of its own.[6] Each of these problems, in turn, must be confronted and overcome if democracy is to take root. Furthermore, the idea of consolidation is intimately connected with the stability of a given political system, and it is plausible to argue that the latter is itself an arrangement—a dispositional property—which, in turn, depends upon certain predictions.

Predictions about the success of any political process, and particularly the process of change in Haiti, are problematic at best. I therefore do not intend to make such predictions. I do, however, wish to discuss briefly some of the most prominent features of any consolidation of democracy and apply these features to the circumstances in Haiti. These features are useful in formulating those predictions on which the claim that the transition to democracy in Haiti can succeed depends. They are also directly relevant to the question of whether the democratization process is moving toward the ideal conditions that help justify and thus preserve any democracy.

The first significant feature of the consolidation that may occur in Haiti is the fact that the process of democratization must take place during one of the worst economic and social crises in Haiti's history.[7] In general, this crisis manifests itself in enormously high rates of unemployment, unacceptably high increases in the already steep infant mortality rate, epidemics, almost total environmental destruction, a dilapidated infrastructure, physical and emotional exhaustion, and a variety of other social catastrophes.[8] Unfortunately, this is not the whole of the matter. There is a multitude of other serious problems. Haiti's human and material resources are either in such short supply or have been so degraded by poverty, illiteracy, malnutrition, disease, violence, corruption, overpopulation, rapid urbanization, deforestation, and soil erosion as to raise serious questions about Haiti's continued survival as a society and as an independent nation-state. There may be nothing to build on.

Even before the most current crisis erupted, between 1991 and 1994, over the military's refusal to restore President Aristide to power, Haiti was the poorest country in the Western Hemisphere. Its per-capita income was $370 a year. In a country of approximately 7 million people, there are fewer than a thousand doctors. The life expectancy is a mere fifty-six years, one in every eight babies dies before reaching the age of one, and 70 percent of all children are estimated to suffer from some form of malnutrition. At least two-thirds of the population is illiterate, and the state school system is so inefficient and small that fewer than 5 percent of eligible students are enrolled in government high schools.[9] As if these problems are not bad enough in themselves, many of the doctors, engineers, administrators, and others with the necessary skills to change Haiti have been killed or driven into exile. Most of those who are in exile do not wish to risk their lives and fortunes by returning to Haiti until positive changes occur. The irony is that Haiti needs these very same people—these skilled professionals—to make the changes that would attract them to return.

The most difficult obstacle to democracy in Haiti, however, may be psychological and cultural. The tradition of a predatory, oppressive state has left Haitians deeply distrustful of government and of foreigners. In addition, Haiti's political culture has long been characterized as an admiration of force. Political disputes are often settled not by negotiation, but through the exercise of force, and respect for democratic procedures and obligations, including reasoned justifications for actions, is minimal.

Furthermore, there is great controversy in the international community about whether this crisis may lead to a change in the economic and social structures of Haiti necessary to allow for a new oligopolization of the economy.[10] It is possible, if Aristide's return and the subsequent peaceful passage of power to René Preval help create hope and a new infrastructure and international aid is forthcoming, Haiti will be able to change its economic structure to create more efficient schemes of production, thereby benefiting all sectors of society. Such a possibility, however, requires massive changes in the Haitian economic, political, and social structure backed up by the combined strength of the international community.

The problem is even more difficult than it is normally perceived to be. The present situation is the outcome of two hundred years of a war of attrition against the people by a small but ruthless ruling class. Under such circumstances, President Aristide and the newly elected president, René Preval, have clearly been constrained in what they could, and can now, do. Indeed, they have ended up doing things rather differently than expected, particularly because they have been made to feel that their time—apart from the end of their terms—was and is minimal. In important ways, then, the hard decisions may be in the hands of the United States and the international community. If so, it is clear that this community must have the will and patience to help the Haitian people make the changes needed to create a true democracy.

Under the best of circumstances, Haiti cannot be changed structurally without some yielding of power by the haves—the economic elites. It is implausible to expect the rural sector to increase its own productivity without massive, long-term assistance. The nation has become food-importing in recent decades because the elites have systematically plundered their own people. The national infrastructure is in tatters. As discussed above,[11] the origins of these difficulties lie in the past. Not all of them, however, are by any means solely the fault of the Haitian people.

Even the reconstruction of Haitian society on a peasant basis cannot restore the country. Haiti's rulers—the military leaders and the economic elites—have siphoned off surpluses for two centuries without contributing even minimally to the education of the people or to the growth of new sources of income. Rulers who profit from stasis are disinclined to risk change. Moreover, if it is to be the policy of the United States, which it appears to be, to sustain at all costs the present distribution of economic power in Haiti, hardly anything can be done that will necessarily have long-range beneficial political consequences.

A second prominent feature of the consolidation, integrally connected to the first, is the clear fact that the corporatist political and social structure that characterizes Haiti must be transformed. It directly impedes opportunities to make the changes necessary to create the conditions that satisfy the epistemic theory of democracy. This corporatism[12] has been described as bifrontal. On the one hand, it serves the state by allowing it to control different sectors of civil society, and, on the other, it involves the establishment of cleavages of privilege and domination on the part of different social groups within the very structure of the state. The groups that form the constellation of corporative power in Haiti include the armed forces, the Catholic Church, the trade groups, a variety of civic organizations, and the economic elites. During the military dictatorship, the armed forces in Haiti and their civilian front (attachés) assumed total power and influence in, and completely violated and destroyed any semblance of, democratic practices and institutions. Indeed, the military forces consolidated their rule by intentionally and ruthlessly suppressing Haiti's once diverse and vibrant civil society. The military systematically repressed virtually all forms of independent associations in an attempt to deny the Haitian people any organized base for opposition to the brutal dictatorship. Their apparent goal was to push Haiti back into an atomized and fearful society reminiscent of the Duvaliér era. The strategy seemed to be that even if the international community successfully returned Aristide to power, he would have great difficulty both in transforming his popularity into the kind of organized support necessary to exert civilian control over the army and in creating a democratic institutional structure that would aid in that endeavor.[13]

The range of organizations targeted by the army's campaign of repression was all-encompassing. The army viewed any popular association as a potential avenue for organized opposition. Indeed, it swiftly suppressed even the most minor signs of public protest through intimidation, arrests, beatings, and murder. The cost has been astronomical. The very civil society that Haiti needs to confront its desperate economic and social problems has nearly been destroyed. The church has played positive and negative roles in the life of Haiti. The established Catholic Church has for years been siding with the military. Indeed, the Vatican is the only nation to have recognized the political legitimacy of the military coup,[14] and the church hierarchy has consistently opposed Aristide.[15] Local churches, however, have long helped the people of Haiti by nurturing the populist groups in the rural areas.

Until the September 1991 coup,[16] Haiti boasted a huge assortment of peasant associations, grass-roots development projects, trade unions, student organizations, church groups, and independent radio stations. In the rural areas, local groups, generally known as "popular organizations," formed literacy programs, rural-development projects, and farming cooperatives, often with international support. Churches nurtured this movement, and lay involvement in church activities increased dramatically. Some of the associations developed into political groups to deal with questions of land distribution, human rights abuses, and corruption. There was also a vibrant set of organized groups in urban areas. Politically active trade unions, professional, student, and women's organizations, and thousands of block associations and community groups flourished. A lively group of radio journalists provided a forum for organizational activities and denounced attacks on this independent civil society. The trade unions have been enormously affected by unemployment and by the reduction of any state aid. This action has, of course, sometimes adversely affected parties normally allied with democratic governments. These groups have also been decimated by the trade embargo.

Thus, an incredibly diverse civil society existed and waits to be resurrected. Unlike many nations that have made the transition from dictatorship to democracy, Haiti's civil society was extremely advanced. But, unlike most nations that are attempting the transition to democracy, Haiti's political parties remain undeveloped. Indeed, these parties are among the least advanced segments of Haitian civil society. The strength of Haitian civil society was to be found in its diversity and breadth outside of electoral politics. This must be changed. Electoral politics must become the lifeblood of a Haitian democracy.

The great unknown factor, which is related to the controversy

surrounding the assessment of the first feature of consolidation—
the economic and social crisis—is whether the previous dominant
economic groups remain all-powerful or have instead been reduced
to puppets of the military during the dictatorship, and, if so, whether
they will reassert their power or yield some of it to the people. During most of Haiti's history, the military did the bidding of the elite
classes by protecting their economic monopolies and brutally suppressing the vast majority of the poor. In turn, the rich paid off the
dictators. During the coup, things changed. The military took over
the country's ports and landing strips, thus enabling its high-ranking
officials to prosper in the illicit drug trade. Even more significant for
the future of Haiti is the fact that the military increasingly prospered
through its control of state monopolies, such as the telephone company. For example, Colonel François took over from the rich the old
monopolies in flour, sugar, rice, and cement.[17] In fact, it was alarm
over these military incursions into the economy that was behind
some of the economic elites' support of the Governors Island Agreement and the return of Aristide. The question remains, however:
what will the economic elites do now that the military dictatorship
is over and two successive democratic governments have come to
power?[18]

The last feature of democratic consolidation in Haiti that I wish
to discuss here is tightly interwoven with the first two. It is the deficiency in the fulfillment of the requirements of the rule of law.[19]
This deficiency pervades Haiti. It acts as an inhibiting incubus to any
possible positive democratic development. It destroys the quest for
changes in institutional design and completely violates the normative bases of a democracy. Indeed, following the rule of law is a necessary prerequisite to the protection of human rights and to the development of a moral consciousness in the citizenry.

Members of the FAD'H systematically ignored basic human rights
in their treatment of civilians. Internationally recognized human
rights, which are frequently codified in Haitian law, were intentionally and persistently violated. The pattern of abuses included the
following:[20]

> —Haitians [were] routinely taken from their homes or the streets
> and thrown into detention by members of the FADH, with no legal
> basis whatsoever and with no access to judicial protection. Mem-
> bers of Haiti's opposition groups have been particular targets of ha-
> rassment and arrest. The government has arrested and detained
> political activists, union officials, journalists and church leaders.

—Judges have been detained and beaten for ruling against members of the FADH.

—Attorneys have been harassed, threatened, and murdered for challenging the FADH or its allies in the civilian courts.

—No member of the FADH has ever been charged or prosecuted before a civilian court for ordering or executing any human rights abuse in violation of the 1987 Constitution, despite widely available evidence implicating the FADH in the assassination of political opponents and the massacre of civilians.

—The FADH ignore[d] judicial orders, including orders to arrest soldiers or officers accused of human rights abuses.

—The abuses inflicted on those held in Haiti's overcrowded prisons and detention facilities [have been] particularly severe. Detainees [were] beaten regularly. Others [were] deprived of nourishment or medical attention. Prison guards exploit[ed] this poor treatment to extort food or money from the detainees' families, to make an example for other prisoners and to coerce confessions.

—Violent crimes, some clearly politically motivated, . . . proliferated since the departure of Jean Claude Duvaliér. The government [was] unable or unwilling to stop these nightly rampages in the urban areas—the so-called "insecurity"—apprehending only a few suspects and convicting even fewer. This weak response contrasts sharply with the strong steps taken to repress political opponents.

These acts, of course, undermined the credibility of democratic institutions.

It is not the case, however, that Haiti lacks a comprehensive legal structure that would support a democracy. The blueprint for a democracy is set forth in the 1987 Constitution, which the Haitian people overwhelmingly approved in a March 29, 1987, election.[21] The Constitution contains specific guarantees of personal liberty and political and civil rights.[22] It provides citizens with the basic freedoms associated with a democratic state: the right to life (Article 19), freedom of expression (Article 28), freedom of association and assembly (Article 31), freedom of the press (Article 28-1), and freedom of religion and conscience (Article 30). It also provides citizens protection from prosecution, arrest, or detention unless pursuant to law (Article 24-1). For example, no one may be detained without a warrant unless caught in the act of committing a crime, and no arrest may be made between 6 P.M. and 6 A.M. (Articles 24-2 and 24-3d). No one may be kept under arrest for more than forty-eight hours unless he or she has been brought before a judge who rules on the legality of the arrest and detention (Article 26). Article 276-2 is even more important because it expands all of these protections. It provides that all international treaties ratified by Haiti are incorporated into Haitian law and supersede any laws in conflict with them. This provision is very significant because Haiti has ratified several international conventions.[23]

Despite these provisions, the Haitian judicial system is in disarray. The majority of judicial officials fail to apply the law because they are either corrupt, incompetent, or fear for their lives. Deeds of corruption by the highest government officials (the military) occurred daily for years, yet judicial procedures did not prove helpful in investigating them. A UN special expert first concluded in 1988 that "[t]he ordinary system of justice, organized along traditional lines . . . did not play its role. The cases of torture, ill-treatment and arbitrary detentions led to practically no checks on its part, no arrests, no proper investigations."[24] He also concluded that "[t]he independence of the judicial authorities is not safeguarded and their powers are very restricted. . . . [T]hey have been unable to clear up any of the numerous crimes committed during the past few years."[25] These acts of corruption and incompetence generally undermined the credibility of democratic institutions.

Perhaps even more destructive to the creation of a democracy than these acts of corruption and incompetence, however, has been the domination by the authoritarian military dictatorship over all other state powers and branches of government. For example, Article 263 of the Haitian Constitution requires the separation of the police from the military, but during the military dictatorship the police remained under the control of the army. In the rural areas, section chiefs, charged with performing police duties, have been little more than gang leaders who report to military officials rather than to civilian authorities. In the past, they possessed absolute power in the rural regions and were immune from civilian control. They imposed arbitrary taxes, arrested and murdered people, and had private armies. Some of them even maintained their own private prisons. Although President Aristide systematically replaced these section chiefs, they still maintain power in much of the rural countryside.

Haitian prisons have long been controlled by the military. The prison conditions clearly constitute severe and systematic violations of Haitian law and international standards. Even today, there is overcrowding, poor food, and lack of access to water, medical care, and legal counsel. In addition, the military has dominated the civilian justice system to such an extent, that it has failed to investigate or identify those responsible for massive human rights violations. There has never truly been any judicial independence. Judges have routinely been appointed and removed at the will of the military. Finally, the congressional branch of government has possessed no power. It followed the dictates of the military. It is no exaggeration to claim that the law has indeed been used as a weapon to oppress and terrify the people.

Many of these problems continue unabated. Haiti's justice system simply does not function. It lacks everything: resources, competent personnel, independence, stature, and trust. Court facilities are a disgrace; courthouses are often indistinguishable from small shops or run-down residences in Haitian cities and towns. Judges and prosecutors are trained poorly and chosen often because of their "connections" or willingness to comply with their benefactors' demands. They dispense "justice" to the highest bidder or to the most powerful.

In 1993, the OAS/UN International Civilian Mission to Haiti (MICIVIH) did a nationwide study of the justice system.[26] Based on this study, the mission identified the many serious problems that plagued Haiti's administration of justice before President Aristide's reinstatement to office. Among the most serious were the following:

1. The armed forces, including the army, police, rural section chiefs, attachés, and members of the armed paramilitary group FRAPH threatened, beat, and sometimes killed judges, prosecutors, and lawyers. The most egregious example is the execution in broad daylight of Justice Minister Guy Malary on October 14, 1993. Port-au-Prince chief prosecutor Laraque Exantus, who was named to the prosecutor's office by Minister Malary, was abducted from his home in early February 1994 and has never been seen again. Exantus was responsible for several sensitive criminal investigations, including the Malary killing. Wealthy, absentee landowners hired soldiers or local enforcers to intimidate judges and lawyers representing peasants involved in land disputes. Judges and prosecutors admitted that they are too afraid to issue arrest warrants or investigate cases involving the military, paramilitary groups, or certain civilian supporters of the military.

2. Corruption and extortion thrived at every level of the justice system. Salaries were low, and venality high. People paid the police to arrest a rival; prosecutors and judges demanded payment before opening an investigation or issuing an order. Section chiefs arbitrarily imposed taxes that were not found in any law and then threatened those who refused to pay with prison or a

beating. Jailers demanded payment before a family was allowed to bring food to a detainee, and also extorted money from desperate prisoners aiming to avoid beatings or even worse treatment. Sometimes families were able to buy a relative's release from prison.

3. Most judges and prosecutors were poorly trained and lacked motivation. Many judges, especially the lowest-level *juges de paix*, had never been to law school, had received no specialized training to be judges, and showed little interest in receiving such training.

4. Courts lacked even rudimentary materials necessary to function. Most had no electricity or phones. Copy machines, let alone computers or faxes, were unavailable. Most judges and prosecutors did not even own the texts essential to their work: the Civil Code, the Code of Criminal Procedure, and the Penal Code. Record keeping was in complete disarray, with barely legible orders and decisions, some dating back more than ten years, tacked to walls and doors.

5. Most Haitians viewed lawyers and judges—and virtually anyone connected with the justice system—with well-deserved scorn and contempt. People would avoid contact with the system unless it was the last resort. It was expensive, corrupt, and largely mysterious, as all the laws and most of the proceedings were conducted in French, a language most Haitians can barely understand and only a wealthy elite can speak or read. Haitians tried to resolve disputes on their own, sometimes in inventive and acceptable ways appropriate to a country with deep poverty and high illiteracy, and sometimes in deplorable ways best described as "vigilante" justice.

6. The most powerful sectors of Haitian society—the wealthiest families, government officials, and most of all the entire military apparatus—enjoyed virtual impunity. Soldiers were never prosecuted in civilian courts for abuses committed against civilians, despite the constitutional requirement to that effect. This impunity fueled the cycle of violence and the population's cynicism about "justice" in Haiti.

7. Haiti lacked a professional police force.[27] Until very recently, the police had been members of the armed forces, and received no police training. Members were rotated in and out of the police and army; in some cases, an officer literally had two uniforms hanging in a closet and would pick out the appropriate one—po-

lice blue or military khaki—depending on the month or the assignment. Haiti's police did not "walk the beat," investigate crimes, or perform other normal policing functions. Rather, they beat people, rode in trucks with high-caliber weapons, and shot first and asked questions later—and then only to interrogate the poor person who fell into their hands about his or her presumed political opinions or activities. The police not only were for hire to the rich, but would arrest someone on a mere complaint based on flimsy evidence provided by a jealous neighbor, jilted lover, or ambitious farmer who wanted more water from the irrigation canal or a piece of particularly fertile land. Law enforcement was intensively political and personal, not neutral and objective.

8. Although Haitian law creates elaborate procedures governing arrests, detention, and prison inspections and monitoring, all these were systematically breached. Before Aristide's return, most arrests were accomplished without benefit of a warrant. The person arrested often had no idea why he or she had been detained, and family members often did not know where the person was or whether he or she had been detained or simply abducted. In reality, historically, there was no difference between a warrantless arrest and an abduction. Without a "paper trail," the person slipped into the black hole of Haitian detention centers, official and unofficial. These centers uniformly failed to keep registers as they are required to do under both Haitian and international law. Unofficial detention centers, of course, are illegal, so access to family, lawyers, and medical care—in short, the outside world—was impossible. It was precisely during these extensive periods of incommunicado detention that the detainee was most at risk of being tortured, beaten, or killed.

9. Conditions in Haitian prisons and detention centers were inhumane and cruel. Most often decrepit remnants of garrisons built by the U.S. occupying forces seventy years previously, with some even dating back to the French colonial era in the eighteenth century, these prisons lacked all basic services: electricity, potable water, toilets, and medical supplies. Even in a country as desperate as Haiti, where most of the population does not have access to such facilities, the prisons were materially worse. Detainees were kept in close, overcrowded quarters, and prisoners were forced to sleep on the floor. Until recently, men and women prisoners had not been segregated. Sexual abuse was common; tuberculosis, HIV, and other viral diseases were easily transmitted.

Children were kept with adults. Haitian law requires a separate facility for youthful offenders, but this requirement, as many others, existed purely on paper. A Haitian proverb summarizes well the attitude toward the legal system: "law is paper, bayonets are steel."

While the Aristide and Preval governments have vigorously attacked these illegal practices, many of them, in varying degrees, continue to haunt Haiti's justice system. Indeed, it will take years to improve the administration of justice in Haiti so that it reaches an acceptable level. The Haitian government must change this system if the democracy is to have a chance to grow.

The violation of legal norms, however, is not restricted to the newly replaced military leaders or their supporting cast. Unfortunately, such behavior is a distinguishing mark of Haitian political and social life at large, and it has existed throughout the country's history. This failure to follow the rule of law is evident both in social practices and in the actions of governmental bodies. This tendency of unlawfulness, however, does not infect only public officials—it infects the general society. Indeed, this mentality correlates with a general trend toward anomie in society as a whole. It manifests itself in such things as corruption in private economic activities, nonobservance of efficient economic norms, and noncompliance with the most basic rules of society. It normally appears in one of two ways. People in Haiti may adopt a "finalist attitude," where they agree with the goals of a rule, but do not follow the commands of the rule. Conversely, they may adopt a "formalistic attitude," where they blindly comply with the commands of the rule, but ignore its goals. Both of these attitudes are incompatible with, and thus contribute to the continuing difficulty of, securing adherence to the rule of law. They adversely affect the attempt to create a moral consciousness in the citizenry.

The problem may be intractable because it is so pervasive and, therefore, difficult to change. The tendency toward unlawfulness in Haitian public and social life is often the product and the cause of collective-action problems, such as those with structures that game theory labels "prisoner's dilemma," "assurance game," "chicken game," and so forth. Frequently, the combination of expectations, interests, possibilities of actions, and their respective pay-offs is such that the rational course of action for each participant in the process of political or social interaction advises him or her not to comply with a certain norm, despite the fact that general compliance with it would have been for the benefit of everybody, or almost everybody. This kind of anomie may be called "dumb anomie"[28] because it refers to situations in which the compliance with a certain norm would have led the social actors to a more efficient result—in Pareto's terms—than what they obtain in the actual situation of not observing norms.

"Dumb anomie" is intimately connected with the stunting of Haiti's economic and social development. First, there is a direct conceptual connection between that kind of anomie and failures in economic productivity. Indeed, "dumb anomie" is identified by the inefficient results of processes of interaction, including economic ones, that do not observe certain norms. Second, it is clear that anomie affects the process of capital accumulation. For example, when the behavior of people intervening in the process of production—even that of judges and governmental officials—is not sufficiently predictable, productive investments decline or claim disproportionate profits.

Therefore, it is critical for the life of the Haitian nation to consolidate the rule of law. This is important not only to secure respect for fundamental rights and for the observance of the democratic process, but also to achieve satisfactory degrees of economic and social development. It is also obvious that the consolidation of the rule of law, with the consequent overcoming of "dumb anomie," requires strengthening the independence, reliability, and efficiency of the judicial process.

To do this, Haiti must satisfy the guarantees that derive from the idea of due process of law. These guarantees are concerned with the way in which an act of state coercion—which, because of its very nature, infringes upon an individual right and thus must be specially justified—may be exerted on a particular individual. The general principle in a liberal democracy is that when a government act coercively deprives an individual of a vital good, as many independent powers of the state as possible should intervene to ensure that such an act is truly necessary for the good of society. The legislative branch of government necessarily intervenes in regulating constitutional rights. It draws a balance between constitutional rights and determines the conditions under which some of them may be limited for the sake of others. While the necessary generality of this legislation guarantees some degree of impartiality, it is clear that the power may be arbitrarily applied. Thus, the power of the state to perpetrate an act of coercion on an individual must necessarily be mediated by an independent judicial power. Indeed, the ideal of a liberal democracy is that a judge should always intervene between an individual and an act of state coercion.

As many commentators argue,[29] there are two main justifications for interposing a measure of due process between the coercive deprivation of a good and the individual who is the victim of it. The first is an intrinsic value resulting from the fact that the individual in question is not merely an object to be manipulated, but rather a part of a dialogue in which the prosecution tries to convince him or her of the rightness of the coercion as part of a cooperative search for truth. The second justification ascribes to due process an instrumental value; it is viewed as a mechanism for the impartial application of laws. Both justifications, of course, complement each other. To have a dialogue in which the person affected is an active part of the power process is the best way of achieving impartial applications of the law.

The general guarantee of due process of law implies a series of other guarantees; for example, it implies due process requirements associated with access to the jurisdiction of courts. Thus, there must be guarantees related to the conditions for standing, the availability of appropriate remedies, such as *habeas corpus* and injunctions, which protect basic rights, the protection against being tried *in absentia,* the possibility of appeals, the availability of legal assistance, the proximity of courts, and the openness of the judicial procedure, as well as the efficiency and expedience of that procedure.

Other crucial due process guarantees are those related to the characteristics that the judicial process must satisfy, which include the observance of the democratically enacted laws, the unrestricted search for the truth about the facts, and the impartiality of the judge between the parties involved in the process. Additional implied due process guarantees include those associated with the conditions that state coercion must fulfill, such as not imposing cruel or inhumane punishment, being rational in enforcing the purpose of social protection that the law was passed to meet, allowing the individual the possibility of avoiding prosecution and punishment if he complies with the legal requirement (an idea that rejects retroactive and vague legislation), and not punishing an individual for the commission of involuntary acts.

In Haiti, as well as in most nations undergoing the transition to democracy, the ideal of the due process of law has not been actively enforced. Indeed, respect for the guarantees of due process has suffered from considerable oscillations and from a combination of progressive illegal and unconstitutional legislative and executive acts, and judicial decisions that intentionally disregard those guarantees. This has occurred despite the fact that such guarantees are clearly recognized in the Haitian Constitution.

The problem runs deeper. It is clear that the guarantees in the constitutions of nations such as Haiti do not explicitly include all the necessary remedial devices, such as *habeas corpus* and injunctions, that allow access to the administration of justice; and it is obvious that without these remedies the rights become meaningless. The existence of efficacious remedies inheres in the very rights guaranteed in a liberal democracy. In spite of this recognition, Haiti does not have remedies sufficient to protect guaranteed rights, or, if it has the necessary remedies, the authorities have been almost powerless to enforce them.

Legal assistance is another guarantee that is sorely lacking in Haiti. A major reason for this is that it is costly, in part as a result of the length of the judicial proceedings. Further compounding the problem, there appear to be no systematic mechanisms for free legal assistance for poor and incompetent people. It is also true that courts are not generally accessible to large segments of the population, both because of geographical location and because their procedures are too cumbersome, expensive, and slow for dealing with the kinds of controversies common to the large majority of the population.

The judicial process itself raises grave concerns. In Haiti, historically, there has been institutional instability because of the large degree of dependence of the courts, particularly the Supreme Court, on the political process. The Haitian Supreme Court is unstable because it frequently reverses its own opinions and because its justices are often replaced. Indeed, almost every new government has had a judiciary, or at least a Supreme Court, of its own choosing. For example, one of the first acts that the most recent military dictatorship undertook was to assault the legitimacy and power of the judiciary, and the military leaders selected judges who would legitimize their seizure of power. With the return of civilian government, the opportunity to shape the judiciary comes directly after the previous military assault on it.

The due process guarantees that should be granted in the normal course of the judicial process are further impaired in Haiti because of the extreme slowness of the proceedings, the secretiveness and exaggerated ritualism in which they are conducted, the delegation of many judicial functions to clerical employees, the ex-parte communications in which many judges engage, and the endemic corruption of the system. All of these factors destroy the impartiality and expediency of the administration of justice.

However depressing these factors appear to be, and however debilitating to the strengthening of the rule of law and to consolidation of democracy, all is not lost. There are signs of hope. For example, major progress has been made in the procedural conditions for the protection of human rights—by the ratification of several international agreements, such as the American Convention on Human Rights.[30] Moreover, Article 276-2 of the Haitian Constitution provides that all international treaties ratified by Haiti are incorporated into Haitian law and supersede any conflicting laws. Most significantly, the Aristide and Preval governments have realized the importance of following the rule of law to the creation of a democracy in Haiti, and have taken important steps to do so.

Nevertheless, there are problems in complying with the requirement of legality under which coercion may be exerted by the state. The major problems associated with the conditions that acts of coercion must satisfy have to do with the ways in which the government detains people and treats them from arrest through imprisonment. Large numbers of acts of torture and maltreatment on the part of the paramilitary forces are still reported, though they have certainly diminished since the reestablishment of democracy. Prisons are still crowded, unhealthy, and nonrehabilitative places. There have been several inmate uprisings. Perhaps the most grievous situation is that of people held in detention during the entire length of their trial, without any possibility of parole. They are in almost the same conditions as convicts, and often the investigation and trial last so long that they serve the entire sentence for a crime for which they may later be found not guilty. To complicate matters, they are not allowed any compensation for this preventive detention. Further, many judges tend to convict a detainee who has been in prison for such a long time. In their minds, a retroactive conviction legitimates his or her imprisonment.

As this discussion shows, historically, the idea of due process has not been actively enforced in Haiti. Respect for the guarantees of due process has simply been nonexistent. Indeed, there is still a long and perilous road to travel in Haiti before the guarantees of due process and the rule of law are sufficiently consolidated to overcome political and social anomie and to complete the transition to a valuable form of democracy. Despite the recent setbacks, however, progress has been made. Indeed, discussions about the present ailments in the administration of justice and ways of overcoming them are in the forefront of the public debate. Even more importantly, the work of the National Truth and Justice Commission and the prosecutions of those who have committed gross human rights abuses should act as a strong incentive to improve the administration of justice.

PART FOUR

Moving toward a Deliberative Democracy

THE ACTIONS OF PRESIDENTS ARISTIDE AND PREVAL AND THE INTERNATIONAL COMMUNITY

"Yozesi" (they are surprised). Haitians celebrate the return of Jean-Bertrand Aristide at the National Palace, October 15, 1994. Photograph © Chantal Regnault.

CHAPTER SEVEN

The Aristide Government's Proposal

Strategy of Social and Economic Reconstruction

Part 3 analyzed some of the most serious and perplexing problems that Haiti faces in its transition to democracy. It made clear the distance still to be traveled by the Haitian people in order to fulfill the underlying conditions of the epistemic value of democracy. Under the dictatorship, the levels of material satisfaction were so low, the opportunities for informed debate so debased, the institutional structure so dysfunctional to democratic values, human rights violations so ubiquitous, and the problems of the consolidation of democracy so intense, that any hope of creating the conditions for a deliberative democracy appeared to be impossible. Stated otherwise, the distance between the ideal model and the reality of Haitian life seemed to suggest that democracy could never become a reality in Haiti. Indeed, looking at Haiti directly after the coup regime had been forced out and Aristide had been reinstated to office, one had to ask what could possibly be done to change this bleak landscape. Fortunately, President Aristide was not without a plan, and the Haitian people were not without hope.

The 1990 election of Aristide was not only a rejection of Duvaliérism, but a landslide for popular representation. For the first time in the history of the nation, a majority of Haitians entered into politics. This was a very important step toward democracy for the Haitian population. This election, however, was not simply a formal step toward democracy by clearly organized and identifiable political parties. Rather, the people who took part in the democratic explosion at the grass-roots level used the Aristide candidacy to give formal expression to their lives.

The most important popular expectation to emerge from that election is that the repressive role of the state will be terminated. Merely removing the weapons of the army and paramilitary forces is not enough to fulfill that expectation. What is needed is what I would call a new structure of social relationships, which will have to go beyond political pluralism. It will require the use of state power by several successive governments to achieve at least two major goals. First, the government needs to change the Haitian elites' perspective and restrict their historic capacity for social repression. They must begin to realize that the majority of Haitians are human beings, who should be treated with dignity and respect. The elites must realize that their fate is dependent upon improving the lives of all of the Haitian people. Second, the government needs to make sure that the anger and resentment of the poor is contained and channeled in a positive way to improve their living conditions and create hope for their future.

The Aristide government's plan for social and economic reconstruction (which I will refer to here as the Aristide Plan), which the Preval government has fully embraced, attempts to achieve these goals in a variety of ways. The objective of the government is "to substantially transform the nature of the Haitian State as the prerequisite for a sustainable development anchored on social justice and the implementation of an irreversible democratic order." The Aristide Plan calls for shifting the social balance of power away from the executive branch of government to civil society and local government. To do this, the government means to empower several components of civil society, such as political parties, labor unions, grass-roots organizations, cooperatives, and community groups. The government also intends to create a vibrant private sector with an open foreign-investment policy.

It conceives of a sound macroeconomic policy that creates the proper environment for the private sector as one that eschews "foreign exchange controls, price controls, and other policy induced distortions." The Aristide Plan holds that the strategy implemented to realize these goals must:

—meet the basic needs and fully mobilize the human potential of the people of Haiti;
—demilitarize public life and establish the supremacy of legitimate civilian control over the military;
—establish an independent judiciary;
—strengthen the institutional capabilities of Parliament, other autonomous institutions, and local governments to enable them to play a constructive and informed role in policy debates and implementation;
—limit the scope of state activity, and concentrate it on the mission

of defining the enabling milieu for private initiative and productive investments;

—reduce the involvement of the central government in the commercial production of goods and services;

—redefine the relationship and the distribution of political authority between the central government and local authorities;

—improve the quality of public administration.[1]

To create a democracy, the Aristide and Preval governments have taken, and further intend to take, a number of concrete steps. According to the Aristide Plan, one key feature of the new democratic order is the professionalization of the armed forces. Originally, the government planned to, and did in fact, reduce the then current army from approximately seventy-five hundred officers and men to around fifteen hundred. Remarkably, it has gone even further—the army has been totally disbanded, except for the approximately fifty-person marching band. Law enforcement is to be carried out by a newly created National Police Force. This plan is still in its early stages of development, however, and problems have occurred because some of those selected for the police force are former members of the armed forces who have committed human rights abuses.

The second key feature is the establishment of an independent judiciary that is able "to fairly arbitrate conflicts among the members of society, and provide adequate protection for private sector activity, property rights and fundamental human rights."[2] Parliament has a crucial role to play in the modernization of the economy and society, but, of course, it was severely weakened during the military dictatorship, and although most of the economic reforms have to be enacted through laws, the Parliament was still not equipped to deal effectively with these issues right up until the end of Aristide's term. Parliament's power, therefore, has to be strengthened substantially.[3] Furthermore, under the Aristide Plan, the Haitian government also needs to strengthen the Superior Court of Accounts "to improve the level and the quality of public debates in the country, to monitor executive performance and to provide institutional counterweight."[4]

In addition to these two key areas of reform, the Aristide Plan calls for the modernization of the state sector. It requires a reduction in the civil service to approximately half of the civil servants (45,000 during Aristide's term). This is to be achieved through voluntary departure encouraged by generous severance packages. The plan also requires an improvement in the level of professional competence. The scope and content of government activity is to be altered by moving away from "tedious micro-management toward a more strategic approach." The smaller civil service will concentrate on a more limited number of objectives. "It should refrain from excessive regulation and focus on broad policy questions."[5]

In the first year of Aristide's reinstated term, his administration was quite successful in implementing some of these seemingly impossible reforms. Aristide dismissed most of the army's high command and radically reduced the number of troops. Later in his term, he abolished the army.[6] He achieved this by appointing new officers, who then dismissed the troops involved in past human rights abuses. A new civilian police force, operating under the authority of the Ministry of Justice, is in the process of being trained and is partly in operation. Work has also begun on reforming the judicial system. Furthermore, Aristide created the National Truth and Justice Commission to investigate and write a report on human rights violations. The commission has finished its investigations, but, as of November 1996, it has not completed its report. Moreover, parliamentary elections took place in July 1995, and presidential elections took place in December 1995.

Perhaps even more significant, Aristide appointed an international team of prominent lawyers to assist the Ministry of Justice in the investigations and prosecutions of some of the most notorious human rights cases. Preval has continued these investigations and prosecutions. Initially, the team has been focusing on seeking justice for the murders of Antoine Izméry, Guy Malary, Jean-Claude Museau, and Jean-Marie Vincent, all of whom were murdered because of their outspoken opposition to the coup.[7] The attorneys started their work by compiling all of the public information regarding these murders, and they have already turned these files over to the minister of justice. The team members are presently interviewing witnesses, collecting documents, and piecing together information. They have helped create investigative teams of international and national police, and they have worked with prosecutors and judges in the development of cases for prosecution. Several *ordonnances* have been issued, many people have been arrested, and, in the Museau case, several defendants have been convicted *in absentia* and sentenced to long jail terms. In the Izméry case, not only have several defendants been convicted *in absentia* and sentenced to long jail terms, but one defendant, Gérard Gustave (a.k.a. Zimbabwe), a ranking member of FRAPH, has been tried, convicted, and sentenced to life imprisonment at hard labor. This is the first time in the history of the Haitian nation that someone has been fairly tried and convicted for a human rights violation, and the conviction has had a profound impact on the nation's psyche. People now believe, to some degree, that justice can be achieved and that the rule of law is an important aspect of a democracy.[8]

Moreover, five special investigative teams have been organized and have started investigating approximately seventy-six cases. Each team consists of a member of the UN Civilian Police (CIVPOL) and two members of the newly trained and newly created Haitian National Police. The investigative teams first report to the director of CIVPOL and to the director of the National Police. They then report to a minister of justice appointee who directs the investigative teams. The latter is the liaison between the *commissaires* (public prosecutors), judges, and the minister of justice. In addition, victims' committees have been organized in every criminal jurisdiction of the country. These groups are soliciting victims to come forward and detail the atrocities committed against them and to name the perpetrators of these crimes. Lawyers hired by the government are filing lawsuits in these cases. These committees not only gather information, but also exert pressure on the actors in the system to do their jobs—to seek justice.

The international team of legal advisers is overseeing these operations and conducting parallel investigations into some of the major cases. Under President Aristide's rule, the team reported directly to him. Under President Preval's rule, it reports first to the minister of justice. In this way, different kinds of pressures are put on the Haitian officials who are responsible for enforcing the law.

These impressive advances on the political front have not, unfortunately, been accompanied by progress toward a better material life for the vast majority of the Haitian population. For them, grinding poverty and the daily struggle to survive continue uninterrupted. This is an area where the Aristide Plan has serious deficiencies.

The macroeconomic aspects of the plan are clearly intended to attract large amounts of capital from the World Bank, the International Monetary Fund (IMF), and the U.S. Agency for International Development (USAID). So, for example, the plan calls for removing quantitative restrictions on imports and removing the tariffs, except for those on rice, corn, beans, and sorghum. As the plan makes clear, "for a very limited number of sensitive products a transitory adjustment period not exceeding seven (7) years might be provided. For these products, the tariff level will be cut in half immediately." The Aristide Plan claims that this tariff policy will have significant benefits. The plan's authors hold that it will eliminate contraband and its associated corruption, reduce the cost of living, enhance the competitiveness of exports, establish a competitive playing field for all economic agents, and curb the powers of domestic monopolists.[9]

Nevertheless, the plan recognizes that this tariff policy will require adjustment assistance to the productive sectors, such as agriculture (basic grains– and rice-producing areas). It also recognizes that the trade regime distortions are not sufficient to allow for resumption of export performance. Thus, Haiti is "requesting" that its North American trade partners provide "maximum favorable treatment with respect to quantitative restrictions and tariffs (including those on the value added by the assembly sector) for the next ten years." In conjunction with this request, the plan recognizes the need to improve domestic tax collection "for both social equity and medium term economic stability."[10]

Finally, the Aristide Plan calls for the divestiture of publicly owned companies. This is seen as necessary because of mismanagement and because of the associated opportunities for corruption. The plan also suggests that the divestiture should include the implementation of an appropriate regulatory framework and antitrust legislation. To limit the possibility of having the divestiture increase the concentration of wealth within Haiti, the government "will seek out Foreign investors, domestic savers from the professional categories and the members of the Haitian Diaspora." Part of the ownership will be transferred to traditionally excluded members of society, particularly to the families of those murdered, tortured, or otherwise harmed by the military coup. The required reforms of the retirement and social security system "will expand the opportunity to widen the ranks of financial asset owners."[11] Half of the proceeds from the divestiture will be put into infrastructure investments "in the poorest areas and low cost urban and rural housing." The other half "will be invested in a permanent trust fund whose annual proceeds will be used to subsidize education and health for the rural poor."[12]

Clearly, the economic dimension of the Aristide Plan is open to powerful criticism. To begin with, the new structure of social relationships that it requires implies that the state will create a level playing field—a fair chance of access to power—not only in politics, but also in economic and social life. Given Haiti's past and current situation, this equality of opportunity cannot simply mean a noninterventionist economic policy, an extreme version of "laissez-faire" economics. In fact, the Aristide Plan seems to go even beyond the "free-market" expectations of the IMF and the World Bank. For example, as stated above, it calls for the removal of all import tariffs, except on a few cereals, thus clearly favoring the traditional elites who will dominate the trade in imported products. It is surely not conceivable that they will suddenly learn to behave as fair competitors once the state removes itself from regulating economic life. Even more disturbing, the Aristide Plan seems to neglect the capacities and interests of thousands of small urban entrepreneurs and artisans, as well as those of millions of peasants. For example, removing tariffs on hand-crafted products may quickly put out of business a large number of the artisans who have supported Aristide and the transition to democracy. In addition, the unrestricted importation of food may further diminish peasant revenues and encourage both rural and urban unrest.

The divestiture or privatization plans may cause long-term problems.[13] In theory, removing the state from vital enterprises will significantly reduce corporativist influences and help reduce inflation. On the other hand, the political pressures that consumers may have been able to exert on the government to keep down the prices of state-provided services will no longer exist under the divestiture recommended in the Aristide Plan. At the same time, the monopoly status of the new private companies will prevent the activization of free-market forces to keep prices competitive. Absent the unlikely dissolution of these monopolies, the privatization aspect of the plan may prove to be a disaster for Haiti's economy.

On top of these shortcomings in the Aristide Plan, the international community is not helping to alleviate Haiti's economic problems. Instead, it is exacerbating them. In order to foster real stability and stem the flow of refugees to U.S. shores (the real concern of the Clinton administration), the root causes of poverty in Haiti must be addressed. Unfortunately, the Clinton administration is supporting the imposition of a sort of boilerplate World Bank/IMF "structural adjustment" program in Haiti. It restricts wages, favors the export-oriented private sector at the expense of small-scale food producers, and forces resource-stripped local producers to compete with subsidized, highly capitalized foreign companies.[14]

USAID, the World Bank, and other donors claim that one of their primary goals is to alleviate poverty, and early in Aristide's reinstated term of office, they put together an unprecedented $1.2 billion aid-and-loan package for Haiti. Past support of export-led development with anti-poverty programs added on, however, has met with little success. In January 1995, the IDB issued a joint donor report on the proposed economic recovery program in Haiti.[15] It suggested three major shortcomings of past assistance programs: no national owner-

ship, little measurable impact on basic economic and social indica-
tors, and no sustainability. Given this stunning admission of failure
from the agencies that put more than $2 billion into Haiti during the
1980s, it is certainly appropriate to ask why they are not following a
different strategy now.

In point of fact, until quite recently, Haiti's poor majority has
been excluded from any decision-making role regarding the economy. The same is not true for the elites. The Haitian government–
sponsored, USAID–funded Presidential Commission on Modernization and Growth, dominated by Haiti's business elites, has had an
official policy-advisory role. This allows the elites to travel to the
United States to seek increased support from the Clinton administration, Congress, and potential investors. There is, however, a serious
problem with this access. It is one-sided. No parallel programs or
efforts exist to draw expertise, priorities, or advice from the more
than 90 percent of Haiti's population who make their living from
small-scale agriculture, artisan production, and other small enterprises.

The Clinton administration's support of macroeconomic policies,
and the Aristide and Preval governments' agreement with these policies will create as great a threat to democracy as the armed right-
wing paramilitary forces that continue to haunt the Haitian nation.
Without a basic change in economic development policy, as suggested in chapter 6 above, the stranglehold of poverty on the Haitian
people will remain unbroken, and their hard-won progress toward
democracy will quickly erode.

The Haitian government's most difficult challenge in creating a
democracy will not only be that of encouraging political pluralism
in the formal sense, which is certainly a very difficult but indispensable task. Even more important, successive democratically elected
governments must decide whether the economic plans that have
become one of the central fixtures of their democratic program—
and that have brought the Aristide and Preval governments international support—will simply be imposed on the Haitian people, or
will be negotiated out of a truly participatory dialogue with all concerned parties.

It does have to be said that, unlike in the past, there has been a
real attempt by the economists who drafted the economic program,
Leslie Delatorre and Leslie Voltaire, to ask for critical views from
many Haitians who are not part of Aristide's faction. This openness,
of course, signals an extraordinary change in Haitian politics. Those
who have criticized the plan, however, are not necessarily the peas-

ants who will be most adversely affected by it. Thus, the debate must include not only international agencies, Haitian expatriates, political parties, and the elites, but the voices of the very people whose future is most at stake—the vast poor majority. If their voices are not heard, the requirements of the epistemic value of democracy will simply not be observed, and the transition to democracy will surely be set back.

All is not lost, however. There are signs of hope. As the December 1995 presidential election grew near, this debate became central to the campaign. At that time, President Aristide refused to accede to the demands made by the international community for total privatization of the nine major government-owned enterprises. He not only disagreed with total privatization on substantively solid grounds, but also listened to the public uproar against such a policy. As a result, the international community withheld the promised funds, claiming that the Haitian government's refusal to privatize totally these government enterprises violated the terms of their agreement. The debate continued into President Preval's term. Unlike Aristide, Preval seemed to favor the plan of total privatization, at least publicly. Others in his party and many of the masses disagreed. While disruptive, the national debate is a positive step in the transition to democracy; it is a step in the development of public dialogue.[16]

CHAPTER EIGHT

Haiti since Aristide's Return

A Closer Look

It is an extremely positive sign indicating that the rule of law is beginning to take root in the Haitian culture that those who committed massive human rights violations during the coup period (1991–94) are now being investigated and prosecuted. The parliamentary elections of June 1995 and the presidential election of December 1995 also point to the creation of a democratic infrastructure.

WHAT TO DO ABOUT MASSIVE HUMAN RIGHTS ABUSES

One way of encouraging the collective sense of the possible in Haiti and achieving some of the other suggested goals required by a deliberative democracy—making the rule of law an essential part of public and private life, changing the habits of social interaction, guaranteeing economic survival, and creating viable democratic institutions—is to address the question of how to deal with the massive human rights violations committed by the military dictatorship. These cases involve what Kant referred to as "radical evil"—offenses against humanity that are so widespread, persistent, and organized that normal moral assessments are woefully insufficient as an explanation for these actions.

Formulating a policy to deal with this issue depends to a great extent on the purposes of punishment and the prevailing justifications for democracy. Further complicating the problem is the fact that any government attempting to make the transition from dictatorship to democracy must design a dual human rights policy, which deals simultaneously with the future and the past. As to the future, a number of laws may need to be passed to protect and prevent the violations of human rights; as to the past, a strategy must be devised that will punish those responsible for prior atrocities and heal the wounds caused by the commission of those acts. This may require extensive investigations and a series of human rights trials.[1]

Any sensible starting point must focus on moral opprobrium. This is, of course, a required condition of a deliberative democracy. Even if one rejects a retributive theory of punishment, it is difficult to draw any conclusion other than that those who have committed human rights atrocities deserve to be prosecuted and convicted under the law. This is necessary in order to inculcate in the collective conscience of the polity a sense that no sector of society stands above the law and that under no circumstances may a human being be treated as a mere object, or a means to a goal, no matter how important the goal. Some degree of retroactive justice for massive human rights violations may help prevent their future occurrence by creating a positive system of values—a moral consciousness—in that society. Indeed, the basic justification for a democratic government is the promotion of human rights. Such a government is simply illegitimate if its actions are not directed toward reaching this goal.

Moreover, punishing violators of human rights can be viewed as an act of justice that serves the goal of vindicating the dignity of the victims. While this is a unique argument, there is intellectual support for this position. In the literature, Immanuel Kant[2] comes the closest to supporting this position. He defends punishment simply as a just response to a criminal degradation of another human being. He rejects punishment as a means of deterrence or social control, for making an example of offenders degrades them by treating them as a means to an end. He champions the biblical formula of "an eye for an eye, a tooth for a tooth" (Exodus 21:22). In its metaphoric way, this expresses a principle of equality between victim and perpetrator. By insisting on equality as the guiding principle of punishment, Kant makes the victims the center of concern. He defends punishment as the first duty of social organization. The failure to punish renders the rest of society—those charged with a duty to punish—complicitous in the original crime. Indeed, Kant claims that the failure to punish implies a continuity of the criminal's dominance over the victim. In this view, a primary function of punishment is to express solidarity with the victim. Kant rejects the abandonment of the victim to his or her "private" tragedy.

Nevertheless, when one analyzes actual cases of human rights abuses, it is clear that it is extremely difficult to punish people who have committed these acts without threatening the justificatory theory, birth, and development of a democracy.[3] These problems in carrying out justice have moral, political, and legal implications, each of which raises its own set of complicated questions.[4]

The first level of concern is moral. Human rights violations seem to surpass the boundaries of moral discourse. This problem is illustrated by the failure of language to convey accurately the descriptive content of the moral condemnation appropriate to these acts. If we cannot produce an appropriate moral evaluation of these acts, it may be because they are alien to us. It is possible that those who committed these acts believe in concepts that are simply incomprehensible to us and lead to actions that are incommensurable under our conceptual schemes. This poses the problem of whether a state can legitimately carry out moral discourse outside its boundaries and thus subject agents who do not share the assumptions of that discourse to courses of action based on its findings. This problem, of course, destroys any possibility of grounding public moral responsibility in consensus because even moral disagreement is foreclosed by conceptual divergence.

Other moral problems exist, even if the problem of conceptual relativism created by the occurrence of these deeds is overcome. For example, the type of collective behavior necessary for the commission of these acts would not have been successful without strong conviction by the perpetrators of the deeds. Sincere conviction poses problems for moral evaluations, regardless of whether the society agrees with the substantive content of the conviction. In addition, the mistaken character of the conviction has to be demonstrated. This raises questions about the foundations of human rights, and about their scope and balance when several of them are in conflict.[5]

Another moral problem concerns the diffusion of responsibility. These deeds simply could not have been committed without the assent of numerous people in the society. There are those who planned the acts and those who executed them. There are those who in some way supported the illegal actions, by giving information to the perpetrators or by lending material support. Indeed, this may even include victims. There are also many people who cooperated through acts of omission. Are we to punish all of the numerous judges who failed to enforce the rule of law; journalists who failed to report the atrocities; diplomats who concealed or attempted to justify the position of their governments; and everyday citizens who decided to turn a blind eye to what was happening, refrained from telling others of these atrocities, or even justified the deeds? This would lead to a view that, if almost everyone had some complicity in these acts, everyone is guilty, and thus nobody is guilty.

There is also the central moral problem of justifying legal punishments for these acts. A retributivist theory of punishment presents significant problems of justification. This is particularly the case given the diffusion of responsibility argument. Stated otherwise, retribution is concerned with equality, and this means either subjecting everyone who was possibly involved—through acts of omission or commission—to punishment, or subjecting nobody to punishment. Preventionism as a justification raises the question of whether greater evils are risked—such as destroying the stability of an already tenuous democratic system—by punishing the actions. It is also doubtful whether the punishment of these acts is, in fact, effective in preventing the occurrence of similar deeds. In addition, some argue that punishing these acts makes the leaders of authoritarian regimes more reluctant to surrender power. Indeed, General Cédras is a prime example. During the approximately 2½-year negotiation period with Aristide, he refused even to consider stepping down until a complete amnesty was in effect.

Many of the moral problems associated with punishing human rights violators deal with the questions of who is entitled to define the balance and scope of the rights, what the limits of the responsibilities of punishment are, and what the appropriate measures to take may be. There are also questions about who is entitled to intervene in order to prevent or punish these acts. Further complicating matters is the fact that, at some level, these are epistemic moral questions that are concerned with issues of political responsibility. Their resolution is usually reached within the scope of a vision of democracy.

Some of the moral problems associated with the justification of punishment are strongly related to the concerns of political scientists. Indeed, political scientists have argued that the question of how to deal with massive human rights violations is one of the most difficult obstacles to overcome in the transition to democracy. Some warn that excessive concern with the past may alienate entire social groups from supporting the democratic system and may be the cause of resentments that severely harm the success of the transition. Others argue that the energy of the revolutionary moment should be better employed in future-oriented tasks, such as designing a constitutional structure to protect democratic values.[6] Still others believe that some degree of retroactive justice for massive human rights violations helps prevent their future occurrence by creating a positive system of values in that society. For example, punishment may ensure that no groups are above the law, and thus help in consolidating the value of the rule of law. From this perspective, it is necessary to investigate and prosecute the perpetrators of massive human rights violations as an essential part of the technology of consolidating democratic regimes.

The third level of concern raised by the question of how to deal with these evil acts is the subject matter of legal theory. For example, when officials investigate deeds committed during a previous regime, and those responsible for the acts are tried under the rules of a different regime, a problem arises as to which rules apply. The question is whether the rules in force when the deeds occurred or those in force when the deeds are considered for punishment should be binding on the bodies investigating or trying the cases. The deeds may have been lawful when they were committed, or, if not, amnesty laws may have been passed subsequent to their commission. This poses problems for the scope of the principles prohibiting retroactive punishment.

Sometimes these problems deal not with the questions concerning the criminality of the acts at issue, but with other aspects relevant to their punishability. For example, the set of legal justifications and excuses available under the law at the time of the commission of the acts may be different from those available under the law at the time and place of the trial. Furthermore, the procedures or statute of limitations or jurisdiction may have been modified to allow for investigation and trial. All these problems raise questions about the validity of retroactive legislation.

Ascribing legal responsibility to the agents may also be problematic for reasons other than the moral ones mentioned above. For example, if those who executed the deeds are seen to be responsible agents and not mere instruments of those who planned and ordered the acts committed, difficult questions arise about the criteria of agency and causality.

Another legal issue concerns the effect of international law. Some of the legal problems—specifically questions about jurisdiction, retroactivity, and the definition of the crime—are meant to be solved by resorting to international law, but this generates another set of problems. What is the relationship between the international law and a national law that may conflict with it? What is the capacity of international law for legitimating and empowering judicial tribunals? Some of these concerns are related to the question of the right of foreign states or international organizations to intervene in the internal affairs of a state in which human rights violations are allegedly being committed. Sovereignty may be at stake.

Resolution of these moral, political, and legal dilemmas determines the appropriate responses to human rights violations. These responses are wide ranging and may be implemented in isolation or in combination with one another. Some individuals may be released with impunity; private revenge may be allowed; full-fledged trials may be held for all those possibly involved or for the most responsible; civil compensation may be allowed for the victims and their families; people may be dismissed from the relevant organization (e.g., the army); an inquest leading to an official report of the patterns of the human rights violations may be held; symbols of repentance, such as monuments to the victims, may be deployed; or selective or indiscriminate amnesties and pardons may be enacted.

In sum, the moral concerns translate into political and legal considerations that the democratically elected Haitian government—if and when it actually has real power in Haiti—must face in any attempt to take legal action against the military and paramilitary forces.[7] The conditions under which Aristide resumed office and those that allowed Preval to succeed him (and it is not yet clear whether those conditions were a result of simple negotiation or of a decisive routing—with international help—of Cédras, François, and the rest of the coup leaders) will, of course, determine, in part, the limits of the possible. Whether the amnesty law that the Haitian Parliament passed, which apparently grants amnesty for political crimes but not for human rights violations, will become a reality in the transition to democracy is a key unknown factor, as is the extent to which other measures of purge, investigation, or reparations will be possible.[8]

Clearly it will be difficult to sustain prosecutions for the coup itself or for affronts against democracy. Punishing many of the perpetrators of these crimes could destroy the stability of an already fragile democratic system. It could alienate entire social groups from supporting the democratic system and be the cause of resentment that severely harms the chances for a successful transition to democracy. The military and paramilitary forces might stage another coup to protect its leaders and rank-and-file soldiers from prosecution. Thus, a broad amnesty may be an absolute necessity for the very survival of the nascent democracy.[9] But what about the crimes that, under international law, cannot be subject to a blanket amnesty? The incorporation of international human rights treaties directly into Haitian law gives rise to an obligation on the government's part to take action against those who have assassinated, caused to disappear, tortured, and arbitrarily jailed thousands of Haitians. Complying with that obligation will require staunch international and domestic support. Even assuming the best possible scenario, significant impediments remain to prosecutions or even to investigations of the abuses that were committed.

A key problem is defining the chain of responsibility for both criminal and civil purposes. Although the military has a clear-cut command structure, the relationship among the military, the police, the attachés, and other private goon squads is less clear for purposes of attributing both state and command responsibility. The lines of communication between the coup leaders and the attachés and rural section heads have been ambiguous—the attachés and section chiefs were adjuncts who received orders and independent actors. Nonetheless, a plausible argument can be made that these individuals, over time, became agents of the state, so that all their actions may be attributed to the state. In any case, even if their deeds cannot be directly attributed to the state, it is still responsible for not adequately investigating and prosecuting those responsible for them. A similar problem arises with respect to the economic elites who bankrolled and otherwise supported the coup, and who may have been involved in death squad–type activities. Should these individuals be held criminally or civilly liable for the results of their actions?

One other serious problem presents itself. The Haitian justice system may not be equipped to prosecute those accused of massive human rights violations because it is immature and corrupt. Trials that violate due process norms are unacceptable to democratic values. Finally, many prosecutors and judges simply fear for their lives in the event that they prosecute the relevant actors.

It is clear that the question of how to deal with past human rights violations gives rise to a number of complex issues for successive post-coup governments in Haiti. Whatever the difficulties, the Haitian people must face up to them and work toward a resolution. The transformation of Haitian society is fraught with many dangers, and how the Haitians deal with this area is crucial, as it will help determine whether, and to what extent, Haiti will become a viable democracy.

PROSECUTIONS: THE ZIMBABWE TRIAL

Moral, legal, and political problems notwithstanding, the Aristide government decided to pursue retribution for some human rights violations by selecting representative cases. Several prosecutions undertaken upon Aristide's reinstatement to power stand out for review. As stated above,[10] the government prosecuted and convicted several people *in absentia* for the murders of Antoine Izméry and Jean-Claude Museau.[11] Even more significant is the conviction of Gérard Gustave (a.k.a. Zimbabwe), an infamous attaché and a mid-level FRAPH official, for the murder of Antoine Izméry. His trial is an example of both the government's attempt to take positive steps to create a democracy and the distance that remains to reach that goal.

The Factual Background

During the coup years, Antoine Izméry, a wealthy Haitian business-man of Palestinian descent, was well known in Haiti for his outspoken support of then ousted President Jean-Bertrand Aristide. Izméry was one of the largest financial backers of the campaign that brought Aristide to power in the presidential elections of December 1990. Since the coup d'état of September 1991, he had been engaged in the campaign to restore Aristide to his constitutional position. Izméry had joined other Haitian political activists in creating the Joint Committee for the Emergence of the Truth (Komite Mete Men Pov Verite Blayi) (KOMEVEB). KOMEVEB emphasized the need for a just transition of power and opposed any moves to grant impunity to government agents responsible for human rights violations.

Izméry was well aware that opposition activists in Haiti faced serious personal danger. Agents of the de facto regime assassinated his brother Georges Izméry in May 1992, in what is believed to have been a mistaken-identity killing in which Antoine was the intended target. Beginning in May 1993, a number of activists close to Izméry were abducted in Port-au-Prince by armed men and taken to clandestine detention centers, where they were tortured and interrogated about the political activities of Izméry and Father Yvon Massac, one of the co-founders of KOMEVEB. By August 1993, these abductions were becoming more numerous, and the military and police began to target activists from popular organizations close to KOMEVEB.

In early September, KOMEVEB organized a memorial mass at the Church of Sacré Coeur de Turgeau to commemorate the September 11, 1988, massacre at Saint-Jean Bosco Church, Father Aristide's parish church. There was also to be a photography exhibition of the victims of the massacre and the 1991 coup. On leaving the mass, the participants planned to march to Jeremie Square near the Champs de Mars in Port-au-Prince and cover the walls with posters and photographs of President Aristide. The mass was to begin at

7:30 A.M., followed by the march, culminating in the placing of posters. The posters called for the return of Aristide, which was then scheduled for October 30 under the terms of the Governors Island Agreement. On the evening of September 10, UN envoy Dante Caputo telephoned Prime Minister Robert Malval to say he had heard that a massacre would occur if the mass and march took place as planned. Malval called Father Antoine Adrien, a famous religious figure in Haiti, and urged him to use his influence to cancel everything. Adrien was at home sick and had planned not to go, but, following the call, he went to the church early to try and persuade Izméry to cancel.

When he arrived, he found trucks circling the church filled with armed police and attachés. A funeral mass was in progress in the church. While they waited for that mass to end, Adrien, Izméry, and other priests debated what to do. Ultimately, they agreed to cancel the march and postering, but Izméry insisted that the mass go ahead because so many people had turned up and because they should not give way to the same people who had caused the very massacre they were commemorating.

The funeral over, people filed into the church. At this time, a person entered the church and marched down the aisle, shouting words to the effect, "You who are organizing this will have on your hands the blood that is spilled today." Adrien opened the mass by announcing that there was no need for anyone to feel provocation or take offense because the proposed march had been canceled in the interest of preserving peace. Soon after that, the mass in progress, a group of four or five attachés, one with a gun, marched to the front of the church where Izméry was standing to the left facing the altar. Zimbabwe grabbed Izméry by the scruff of the neck, and he and other attachés pulled and pushed Izméry through the rear door on the left side of the church out into the street. When they got him to the street, they forced him down on his knees with his hands behind his head. By this time a dozen men had surrounded him. A man identified as Gros Fanfan, a former Macoute known to be an attaché leader, then approached Izméry and shot him twice in the head at point-blank range. A second victim, Jean-Claude Maturin, was also shot, apparently because he had become an inconvenient witness.[12]

Some people fled as soon as the thugs seized Izméry. Others, including some of the priests, thought Izméry was being arrested, and, as Adrien said at the Zimbabwe trial, felt relieved because at least he would be "safe" (he had been arrested many times before). As soon as the crowd heard shots, everyone ran for cover. Some hid in the pulpit and about thirty took refuge in the sacristy next door. The group charged with carrying out the assassination included at least fifteen people. Witnesses identified both military personnel and attachés. Among the identified attachés were Gérard Gustave (Zimbabwe), Ti Nono, Ti Blan, and Gros Fanfan. The plotters had equipped the group with automatic handguns and hand-held and mobile radio equipment. The attack was well coordinated and aimed solely at Antoine Izméry. Armed men took control of the church grounds and the adjacent street. They violently dispersed passersby. Other armed men, some carrying machine guns, blocked traffic in order to create an outer controlled zone for the executions.

The Trial

The trial of Zimbabwe, which took place on August 25, 1995, raises a number of important issues, and allows one to draw some general conclusions about the newly emerging system of justice in Haiti. The facts of the trial, as given here, are conveyed through the eyes of international observers.

Apparently, there were several major problems in the conduct of the trial that raise serious due process concerns and that violate democratic values. These concern the process of selecting jurors, the provision of adequate legal representation, and the role of the audience, all of which must be addressed because, at Zimbabwe's trial, these issues affected the fairness of the process. In addition, despite the conviction, the prosecution was ill-prepared and failed to exhibit an adequate competency level necessary for the fair administration of justice. Perhaps one of the most serious concerns is that the prosecution failed to bring to justice the masterminds behind Izméry's assassination. They are, of course, the leaders of the repression, who are in "golden" exile and cannot be brought to justice. Nevertheless, for the first time in Haitian history, an individual was convicted for committing a political murder after a trial that can be said to have met at least some minimum due process requirements.

Finding a Quorum of Jurors

Observers met with the *doyen* (chief administrative judge) Roger and the *commissaire* (public prosecutor) Jean-Auguste Brutus in the doyen's chambers at 9:30 A.M. on the day of the trial. They asked what had been done to guarantee a sufficient number of jurors because they had not been able to form a quorum on a previous attempt to start the trial, on August 18, 1995. The doyen said he had put out radio messages announcing the trial and stressing the importance of jurors' attendance so that they could do their civic duty. Commissaire Brutus said he had personally visited a number of the *juges de paix*—who, he said, are responsible for summoning jurors—to get them to stimulate attendance; he had also spoken directly with eighteen jurors to assure them of a ride home if the case went on after dark.

This process seems insufficient to ensure a large enough juror pool and an appropriate jury so that due process requirements can be met. It is not clear how prospective jurors are selected,[13] whether from voter-registration lists or otherwise, but none of the prospective jurors in this case appeared to represent the 90 percent majority of Haitians. This exclusion violates the requirements of the epistemic democratic theory. Furthermore, regardless of the shortcomings of the selection process, those who are chosen should receive better consideration. In this particular case, the trial did not end until after 11 P.M., when the main street outside the Palais de Justice was completely unlit. No doubt the localities through and to which the jurors had to travel were equally dark and, therefore, in their minds, unsafe. Given Haitian jurors' safety concerns, legal officers should perhaps consider using a limousine service to assist them in their travels to and from the courthouse.

DEFENSE COUNSEL

The doyen has the power to appoint defense counsel under Section 198 of the Haitian Criminal Code. Since no defense counsel appeared on August 18, 1995, the date when the trial had to be aborted because of the lack of a jury quorum, the doyen wrote to the *batonnier* (chair of the bar association) Rigaud Duplan, requesting that he provide counsel for the defendant. Unfortunately, the doyen's letter named the defendant as Gérard Antoine instead of Gérard Gustave.

By 11 A.M. on August 25, 1995, no defense counsel had appeared, and the doyen summoned the batonnier, who said he had passed the request to two *étagères* (trainee lawyers), who were to interview the defendant in the National Penitentiary (Pénitentiaire Nationale). They went there but found no one answering to the name on the trial list, and they did nothing further to find the defendant. The batonnier is a former anti-Aristide minister of finance, and the doyen and commissaire believe he was acting in bad faith, hoping the trial would be postponed to a time when its political importance could be limited. Brutus also told the observers that an experienced defense lawyer (Manasse) had agreed to take the case but had been dissuaded by the batonnier, who warned him the case could be dangerous for him.[14]

The doyen told the batonnier to find defense counsel immediately, or Brutus or the doyen himself would act in that capacity, for the trial was not going to be postponed. By 1 p.m., a defense team of seven lawyers assembled, of whom at least three, led by Professor Wilfrid Léger, were clearly very experienced and forceful advocates.

In the future, providing adequate defense counsel should not be left to the batonnier. The international team of lawyers selected by the Aristide government to help in the investigation and prosecution of those who have committed massive human rights violations was particularly concerned with this problem. Indeed, a major part of its role is to promote respect for international human rights under the Haitian justice system. Thus, it has recommended that particular attention be paid to Article 14 of the International Covenant on Civil and Political Rights (ICCPR), notably Paragraph 3.[15] These lawyers proposed as a first step that, in cases of murder and other crimes of maximum severity, counsel should be available as a matter of course. Sufficient time must be given for the defense to prepare its case, review the dossier, and consult with the client. "Counsel," in a country that has a sizeable bar association, should not mean an étagère, but rather a trained lawyer with a minimum of five years' experience or at least considerable criminal trial experience.

This is not to say that Zimbabwe's lawyers did not do a competent job of representing him. They were particularly effective in their exploitation of the code of criminal procedure, and, although they did not seek a postponement or insist on a less exhausting trial schedule (by U.S. standards, at least), in any future case charging major human rights violations, we should expect defense counsel to insist on the government's respecting all their clients' rights under the ICCPR.

PRETRIAL PREPARATION OF WITNESSES

Apparently, pretrial witness preparation does not take place in Haiti. When international observers first talked to Commissaire Brutus about preparing the main witness against Zimbabwe before the first hearing, he said, in effect, "Don't worry, we'll pin him down. We know how to get the truth out of these people." I suspect that this does not reflect a lazy or laissez-faire attitude, but more a sense of the trial process as one in which evidence simply unfolds, and, therefore, a feeling that to prepare witnesses amounts to rehearsing them and tampering with the truth.

The dangers of this approach were most clear from the testimony of witnesses Father Yvon Massac and the ex–prime minister, Robert Malval. Massac arrived somewhat irritable, without having been called by Brutus, and he volunteered to testify. Malval had received a summons but had no idea why because he had not even witnessed the crime. Brutus had not spoken with him and apparently had no plans to do so before putting him on the stand. Several international observers spoke with Malval in the doyen's chambers, and, finding how unenthusiastic and unclear he was about his participation in the proceedings, they then went into the courtroom and suggested to Brutus that it would be most appropriate to speak with him. Brutus ultimately did so, but only briefly.

Father Hugo Trieste was summoned as an afterthought, largely at Father Adrien's suggestion. The doyen's telephone is chronically nonfunctional, however, and the only way of contacting Father Trieste was by radio. Very few people had a radio that could be used for such a purpose, and thus it was difficult to reach him. Trieste was initially very upset at being called in this way and highly skeptical about the integrity of the proceedings, which he expected to be a rerun of the Jean-Claude Museau case, which, by all observations, was not appropriately tried. However, after he arrived and sat with Father Adrien for a long while, he warmed to the importance of the occasion and ultimately gave some of the most telling testimony of all, as will be discussed below. The point here is that his attendance was merely an afterthought and that preparation of witnesses needs to be examined thoroughly. In a democratic society, failure to prepare adequately violates the government's responsibility to the people.

JURY SELECTION

The *greffier* (clerk) solemnly intoned the roll of jurors, repeating each of the 250 names twice. He dropped a small pink card into a large tin box for each juror who announced "present." The roll-call ritual takes up a considerable amount of the day, and more efficient methods could doubtless be found. On the other hand, its ceremonial impact is probably more significant than in Miami, Chicago, or New York, and, because of the importance of respect for the public nature of justice, I would not recommend any major change.

With the quorum of at least thirty names in the box, the greffier shook it, pulled out a card, and read the name. The first juror stepped onto the dais for counsel to look him over and pronounce *"accepté"* or *"rejeté."* The audience soon got the hang of what counsel were looking for and, judging the clothing, age, or other characteristics of each candidate, often chorused the result before counsel spoke. It was all done with good taste and humor. There seemed to be a little colloquy once or twice before a prospective juror was seated or rejected, but otherwise everything was done on appearances. Brutus challenged no jurors, accepting those accepted by the defense, who went for well-dressed, younger people like themselves.

If one desired to get on this jury, the best way was to wear a new suit or cleanly pressed shirt and pants and carry a briefcase. A very yuppie-looking twelve, including two women, took their seats. There were two alternates. No questions were asked of them to elicit bias or any other disqualifications. One of their number got up shortly after the evidence started and asked to be excused because he was not feeling well. One was carrying a copy of the Criminal Code as he walked to his seat. Based on the questions they asked, some of them appeared to be law students. Given the very active role of jurors in the proceedings, this may not have been a bad thing, but it comes as something of a surprise to someone with U.S. or Western European training.

By U.S. standards, of course, this is no way to pick a jury. In countries such as Britain, however, where jury challenges (now effectively abolished) were always arbitrarily based on appearances, and voir dire never existed, the Haitian system would seem quite normal. It was impossible to establish how many challenges were available to each side. No one seemed to know. The Haitian Criminal Code is silent on the issue. The only conclusion that seems accurate, according to observers of Haitian criminal trials, is that the defense gets one more challenge than the prosecution. In theory, every citizen of voting age is eligible to sit as a juror. In practice, it would be interesting to know how jury rolls are compiled and how notice is given, especially to the vast and semi-literate masses who live in the slums. The impression of the international observers was that jury service is overwhelmingly a middle-class business. This could have important consequences in some political contexts and for the creation of a democracy.

OPENING PROCEEDINGS

The clerk asked the accused to rise, state his name, age, place of birth, and occupation. Another clerk handed the accused a microphone, and, standing in a half-slouch like a condemned karaoke singer, he gave his name as Gérard Gustave and said he was known as Zimbabwe. He then tried to launch into a statement of the injustices perpetrated against him—his false arrest, false imprisonment, and general mistreatment. The doyen interrupted him and demanded his occupation, which—ignoring audience cries of "attaché"—Zimbabwe gave as *"malheureux."* The word means "unfortunate," but it also seems to convey "unemployed." He claimed to have been a house painter when he had been employed.

The jury was then sworn, and the greffier's assistant read the six-page indictment, at the end of which the judge told the defendant to rise and said he would inform him of what the indictment amounted to in "plain language." In fact, his language was extremely colorful, but it certainly met the human rights requirement that an accused be informed "in detail in a language which he understands of the nature and cause of the charge against him."[16]

The doyen invited Brutus to open his case, and the defense team rose to assert its right to review the file of *pièces de témoignage,* which seemed to be largely the deposition statements taken in longhand by the *juge d'instruction's* greffier. On being handed the three-inch stack of crumpled papers, the defense team said such a volume would require three hours to examine. Cries of "Oooh," and hoots of derision from the audience drowned out the defense team's voices. Then the doyen ruled that a maximum of thirty minutes should be more than sufficient. The crowd loudly applauded his decision.

Finally, having been in court since 9:30 A.M., opening statements started at about 3:30 P.M. The doyen and Brutus had donned majestically suffocating robes, the former's topped by an eight-inch-high black pill-box hat, resembling an overgrown Oreo cookie, with a white band running round its middle. The defense bar was not robed, apparently because counsel did not have time to get dressed formally before being summoned to court.

Brutus rose to his feet, extended his arms, and demanded a moment's silence as tribute to the cruelly assassinated Antoine Izméry. The audience greeted his dramatic beginning with loud applause. Everyone, including the doyen, jury, and defense bar and its client, rose. The room was, however, far from silent. The audience applauded again as it sat down. Then Brutus delivered his opening salvo, which was emotive, theatrical, and apparently exactly what the crowd wanted. His encomium on Izméry was as soaring as his jeremiad against the *"machine infernale"* that conspired to assassinate him was scathing. The audience again accorded him an ovation.

Testimony

The format for giving testimony is substantially different from that in the U.S. or Western European systems. The judge calls each witness to stand on the dais, where he or she is sworn. The judge then asks each witness his or her name, address, and occupation and whether he or she has any family or employment relationship to the accused. These questions are mandated by law, and in this case the doyen apologized to the priests and ex–prime minister for having to ask them.

The judge then asked each witness to recount what he knew of the events in question. When the witness needed a little prompting to move the narrative forward, the judge provided it, but generally he asked very few questions and allowed each witness full rein. Then he asked the commissaire if he had any further questions (he almost invariably did not). In a process that is clearly foreign to the U.S. legal system, questioning passed next to the jury. The microphone circulated from juror to juror until each person's curiosity was satisfied, without any special regard to what in the United States would be considered hearsay or probative value.

The judge then invited the defense bar to question the witness, permitting any number of members of the defense team to pose questions. These questions all took the form of requests to the judge. Generally, the doyen simply repeated the question, but occasionally he put a gloss of his own on it. When one junior member of the defense team asked a convoluted question, the doyen, affecting not to understand, made him repeat it so many times that the poor man looked utterly ridiculous. This procedure seems unnecessarily artificial, and it is hard to see any justification for it when there is competent defense counsel.

The Prosecution's Case

Prosecutor Brutus presented six witnesses, of whom he needed perhaps only two. Much of the testimony was irrelevant to the proceedings. The important witnesses were Pierre, Deshommes, and Fathers Yvon Massac and Hugo Trieste. Neither Robert Malval nor Father Adrien Antoine was useful to the prosecution.

Father Hugo Trieste

At 4 P.M., the audience loudly applauded Father Hugo's entrance to the courtroom, as an arms-linked phalanx of fresh-minted court security guards in their new blue uniforms escorted him to the podium. He took the microphone and the oath and stood facing Zimbabwe. He pointed a straight arm at him and identified him as the man who had entered the Church of Sacré Coeur de Turgeau accompanied by three or four companions, one of whom was armed. He said he saw Zimbabwe take Izméry by the back of the neck and force him out of the church. He said that, in view of the threats they had received before the church service, he felt somewhat relieved, believing that Izméry was only being arrested, as he had been many times before. He testified that they continued the mass until they heard shots, at which time everyone fled in all directions, many to the presbytery.

Asked by the defense whether he wore glasses because he was short- or longsighted, Father Hugo answered: "Both; one eye long, the other short." When the defense seemed perplexed, the doyen explained to the delight of the audience that his eyes were the same way. When the defense pressed Father Hugo, claiming his vision was defective, he simply took off his glasses and said, "Yes, like this it is, but [putting them back on again], thanks to this marvel, with these I can see perfectly, thank you." The audience members stomped their feet and yelled their approval, and the greffier and guards escorted Father Hugo down the aisle of the courtroom to an ovation.

Father Yvon Massac

The crowd also applauded Father Massac as he approached the dais. He started by saying he would not testify in French because it was an insult to the people, 87 percent of whom speak Creole, not to conduct proceedings in their own language. The foundations of the building rocked to the crowd's loud approval. The remainder of the trial was conducted in Creole, except for closing statements. The rest of Massac's "testimony," however, was a histrionic diatribe against the enemies of liberty and justice, the like of which has probably not been heard since the heyday of the guillotine and tumbrels in the French Revolution. Indeed, he inveighed against the abolition of the death penalty in cases such as the present. With courageous gravity and sound legal reasoning, Léger then took the doyen to task for permitting Massac to use the forum as a political soap-box without adding a word of relevant testimony to the proceedings.

On the one point of critical importance, he said that Zimbabwe's profile closely resembled that of the person who had entered the church threatening that the blood shed on that day would "be on the hands of the organizers of this mass." He claimed, however, that he could not be absolutely 100 percent certain that Zimbabwe was the culprit. The defense seized on this uncertainty for all it was worth.

Deshommes

This nineteen-year-old had gone to the Ministry of Justice and volunteered that he had evidence about the Izméry murder. He appeared on August 18, 1995, when the case was initially scheduled for trial. He was very calm and delivered his testimony extremely well. He identified Zimbabwe clearly and distinctly, confirming the role Hugo Trieste had said Zimbabwe played. The jury said "No questions," to roars of approval from the audience, which were redoubled when the defense had no questions either. This was obviously interpreted as meaning that the testimony was incontrovertible.

Pierre

The one-legged star witness entered on his crutches, ringed by security.[17] He was a little nervous at first, but the guards provided a chair for him, and the power of the microphone took over. He thrust out his arm and pointed directly at Zimbabwe, saying: "I saw him outside the church, and he recognized me. He asked me why I was going in, and I said to go and see Father Nicolas. He said I shouldn't stay around if I didn't want to become a victim."

He then gave a very similar account of events to the one Father Hugo Trieste had delivered earlier. His evidence came in a steady and uninterrupted stream. Once again the jury had no questions, which brought loud cheers from the audience.

One defense lawyer then said he had had difficulty following the testimony and asked the doyen to make Pierre repeat his entire evidence. Howls of derision from the audience were amplified more articulately by the doyen, who informed the defense witheringly of its duty to follow evidence and that, if it could not do its job, it should simply sit down. Defense counsel yelled at the doyen; the doyen yelled back; gesticulations whirled; sweat flew from legal brows. The tension in the courtroom was palpable. Eventually, Léger, the most experienced and articulate of the defense team, rose and delivered a stern lecture to the judge on the duty of the defense bar to represent even the most unpopular defendant in the most arduous trial, and he argued that it was not appropriate for the judge to pick on the younger and more inexperienced members of the team who were working long hours for no pay. A ripple of applause and otherwise respectful silence from the audience followed Léger's peroration. In the end, the doyen did not make Pierre repeat his testimony. The prosecution case ended on the highest possible note as the audience applauded and the doyen announced a thirty-minute recess.

THE DEFENSE'S CASE

The defense's case started with the doyen calling on Zimbabwe to take the stand and the required oath. He told Zimbabwe that he had heard the accusation in the indictment and the evidence of the witnesses, and invited him to explain his conduct on September 11, 1993. It was not clear if Zimbabwe had any option about whether or not he answered these questions, if defense counsel could have objected, or if this questioning is standard procedure in Napoleonic Code jurisdictions. If it is, I am curious to know how the legal officials square this action with the right not to be compelled to testify against oneself under Article 14(3)(g) of the ICCPR.[18] In any event, the only defense witness was the defendant. After the judge had put his questions, the microphone passed first to defense counsel, then to the jury, and finally to the commissaire.

Zimbabwe

Zimbabwe said he had not left the house before 9 A.M. on the day of the murder, and that he had only done so in order to go to the Ministry of Information at Delmas to pick up some money: "I was never there at the church—never, never, never. I know nothing about what happened—nothing, nothing, nothing." His hand went repeatedly up to the heavens to invoke God's judgment in his favor. The audience roared derisively, especially when he complained at having been locked up in jail with murderers and rapists and others with whom he had nothing in common. He denied being an attaché, but admitted that he used to hang around the Champs de Mars (presumably Zimbabwe's connection being Gros Fanfan's attachés in the area near the Belle Equipe du Champs de Mars). Much of his testimony was difficult for foreign observers to follow since Father Massac's coup of turning the entire event into a Creole hearing, with the exception of the legal arguments.[19]

When the jury questioned Zimbabwe, one of them asked him if he recognized the one-legged witness who had identified him. When Zimbabwe admitted recognizing him, the audience went wild. This action convinced many observers of the value of juror cross-examination. Other questions seemed less legally relevant to my mind, but what trial lawyer ever knows what is really relevant to a jury?

Zimbabwe addressed his replies to the audience, the doyen, and the jury. He was by turns spirited and scornful, surly and defiant. His biggest difficulty came when the commissaire asked him to explain why he was going to a government ministry to pick up money on a Saturday morning. As soon as the commissaire asked this question, Zimbabwe claimed it must have been a Friday. This statement did little to provide him with an alibi for a killing that took place on a Saturday.

Zimbabwe twisted and turned in what seemed to the international observers to be a lynch-mob atmosphere. Other observers said the crowd's abuse was largely good-humored, however, and, judging by the laughter and general behavior, this was apparently true. There never seemed to be a real fear of the crowd actually trying to get at the accused to exact the vengeance it clearly felt he deserved. The court security police, with side arms and a couple of shotguns, may have provided some disincentive, but international observers do not seem to have felt the same kind of threat of mob violence that people have reported in racially polarized cases in the recent history of the United States. The most troubling spectacles were when, at various stages when the judge and lawyers were out of court, the audience baited Zimbabwe or else he reacted angrily to press photographers who were getting too close.

It was impossible not to feel some sympathy for him, trapped and chained, the butt of everyone's derision. Having interviewed him in detail and seen his reactions in court, many of the international observers felt he had probably psyched himself into believing his own story. The spectacle may have pleased, entertained, or simply provided a release of tension for some in the crowd, but it did nothing to enhance respect for justice. Audience participation of this kind violates notions of due process.

SUMMATIONS AND CHARGE

Summations started at about 9:45 P.M. and went on until just before 11:00 P.M. Both Commissaire Brutus and his chief assistant prosecutor addressed the jury. Three lengthy defense speeches followed the prosecutor's closing arguments. The audience continued to enliven the proceedings, chorusing "Zimbabwe" every time any of the counsel said "Gérard Gustave, alias . . ." None of the speeches made as much as international observers would have expected of the factually crucial parts of the testimony. The defense understandably played up the number of witnesses who were not able to identify the defendant, praising them for their impartiality and honesty. Surprisingly, they simply ignored the testimony that did identify the accused.

Finally, the judge gave the first juror a printed list of questions for the jury to respond to, but no legal principles to apply to the facts or any other analysis of the case, as far as the observers could perceive.

The questions were:

1. Did Gérard Gustave participate in killing Antoine Izméry?
2. Did Gérard Gustave commit that murder with premeditation?
3. Did Gérard Gustave commit that murder as part of a plan with others?
4. Was Gérard Gustave guilty as a principal in that murder?

VERDICT AND SENTENCE

The jury returned after about forty minutes, and its verdict on each question was "Guilty, by absolute majority" (which everyone I asked interpreted as meaning unanimously). The judge did not poll the jury; neither did defense counsel request it, although I was later told that polling is normal practice. No one I spoke with could explain why it was not done here.

Strangely to any U.S. lawyer, the court issued the verdicts in the absence of the accused. The jury left and Zimbabwe was then brought back in chains through the crowd. He obviously knew the verdict, but this aspect of the system seemed badly handled. I believe it is important to both the accused and the jury that the verdict be delivered to him by them in front of everyone. If this is not done, any defendant, and especially someone like Zimbabwe, will doubt that the jury has actually convicted him. The sentence was that prescribed by law since the 1987 Constitution abolished the death penalty: life imprisonment with hard labor.

Conclusion

This trial was a success by most, if not all, international standards. It was a true success by the standards of what I have been told are traditional Haitian trials. It provides a basis for convincing people in Haiti that justice can be achieved by coming forward to testify against murderers. Indeed, I have been told by members of the victims' committees that more witnesses may want to do so in the future.

Nevertheless, there are serious human rights concerns arising from the conduct of this trial,[20] despite the fact that it is probably one of the most just proceedings Haitian courts have ever seen. In addition to those points already noted, on the question of sentence, the UN Standard Minimum Rules for the Treatment of Prisoners, Article 71(1) provides: "Prison labour must not be of an afflictive nature."[21] The Haitian government should look at states' practices on this in light of Article 8(3) of the ICCPR: "(a) No one shall be required to perform forced or compulsory labour; (b) [This] shall not be held to preclude, in countries where imprisonment with hard labour may be imposed as a punishment for a crime, the performance of hard labour in pursuance of a sentence to such punishment by a competent court."[22]

PROSECUTIONS: THE JEAN-RONIQUE ANTOINE AND ROBERT LECORPS TRIAL

The prosecution of Zimbabwe for the murder of Antoine Izméry laid the groundwork for the prosecution of two men for the murder of the former minister of justice, Guy Malary. On July 23, 1996, former army corporal Jean-Ronique Antoine and civilian Robert Lecorps went to trial, accused of Malary's assassination. This is only the second major trial to be held for a crime committed under the de facto coup regime.[23]

After a nearly sixteen-hour trial, the fifteen-person jury found the defendants not guilty of the murder. Jury composition was a major factor in the result. All the jurors were professionals who showed open disdain for the two beggar eyewitnesses presented by the prosecution; two jurors appeared to be close friends of defense counsel; and one juror was an anchorman for the government-controlled news station during the coup period. The prosecution's case was riddled with errors, the chief of which was simply a deplorable lack of preparation for trial. In particular, the prosecutor failed to prepare the eyewitnesses for cross-examination. The defense lawyers were thus able to trap one of them into making numerous contradictions. In addition, the prosecutor presented the eyewitnesses in the wrong order and failed to use damaging character evidence about the defendant. This trial, therefore, hurt rather than helped the administration of justice in Haiti. This is particularly so given Guy Malary's prominent role in attempting to bring democracy to Haiti by enforcing the rule of law.

The Factual Background

Guy Malary was an outspoken and well-respected human rights attorney in Haiti. He studied law in Port-au-Prince, Haiti, received a master's degree from Howard University in Washington, D.C., and conducted Ph.D. course work at George Washington University in Washington, D.C. Malary served as counsel to USAID in Haiti. He also served as president of the Inter-American Association of Businessmen and as counsel to the Central Bank of Haiti. He was a consultant to the ICM and assisted in the training of the human rights observers who reported on the coup regime's human rights abuses. Malary also represented several victims of military violence in their efforts to seek justice. He lent his assistance in a civil lawsuit seeking damages filed in a U.S. district court by six Haitians who alleged they had been tortured under the orders of former Haitian general Prosper Avril. In July 1994, the six plaintiffs were awarded $41 million in compensatory and punitive damages.[24] Some of the individuals implicated in the case held positions in the Haitian military and security forces during the 1991–94 coup regime period.

Pursuant to the terms of the Governors Island Agreement and the Haitian Constitution, President Aristide appointed Robert Malval as prime minister. In July 1993, Prime Minister Malval appointed Guy Malary as minister of justice of Haiti. The international community, including the UN and international human rights organizations, enthusiastically supported this appointment. Soon afterwards, Malary reportedly began receiving death threats.[25] Despite the risk to himself, Malary became one of the few Aristide appointees to occupy his office in Haiti and to conduct business there regularly.

As minister of justice, Malary was in charge of overseeing efforts to reform the judicial system in Haiti, and in this capacity he was responsible for implementing critical aspects of the Governors Island Agreement. On October 5, 1993, he presented the Haitian Parliament with a plan to form a new police force independent of the military and under the control of the Justice Ministry, in accordance with the terms of the Governors Island Agreement and Articles 263 and 269 of the Haitian Constitution of 1987.

Shortly before he was killed, Malary also called for the resignation of Haitian Supreme Court president Emile Jonassaint, a supporter of the coup regime and an outspoken anti-Aristide figure. Jonassaint had come out of retirement at the request of the coup regime and served as putative president of the military leadership's illegal government until Aristide's return. Malary's refusal to recognize the legality of Jonassaint's appointment as president of the Supreme Court sparked the anger of General Cédras and Colonel François. François controlled many of the "attachés" and is the individual most responsible for political assassinations in Haiti.[26]

It was Malary who coordinated the investigation into the murder of Antoine Izméry. Because of Izméry's prominence and the brazen character of the killing, the case was politically explosive in Haiti. Malary urged prosecutors to investigate the crime, even as other Aristide-appointed ministries were being shut down by paramilitary supporters of the coup leaders. At the time of his death, Malary had identified several suspects in the Izméry murder, including several known attachés and a former Tonton Macoute. Despite strong evidence of their involvement, no case against the suspects was ever brought, and the prosecutor in the case resigned.[27]

On October 14, 1993, at 1:30 P.M., Malary left his office in the Port-au-Prince neighborhood of Turgeau because participants in a meeting there had noticed the presence of armed men around the ministry. Accompanied by two bodyguards and a driver, Malary traveled in a Toyota Land Cruiser for approximately four hundred yards when two or three gunmen dressed in civilian clothes fired on the vehicle. Single gunshots rang out, and people in the streets ran for cover behind trees and in nearby driveways. The single shots were followed by a barrage of automatic gunfire. On a side street between the Sacré Coeur Church (the church from which Antoine Izméry was dragged to be murdered) and a funeral parlor, Malary's driver braked sharply, and the vehicle overturned on the driver's side and slammed into a churchyard wall, creating a six-foot-wide hole.

Approximately fifteen minutes following the gunfire, two *Miami Herald* reporters at the scene noticed several gunmen around the Land Cruiser looking through the windshield at the bodies inside. Five bullet holes were visible on the passenger side of the vehicle. The reporters were chased away by a man in his fifties who yelled at them in English, "Get out of our country."[28] They returned to the scene about fifteen minutes later, saw that an ambulance had arrived, and found three bodies—Malary, his driver, and a bodyguard—laid side by side, face-up on the sidewalk. Bullet wounds were visible on all three bodies. A bullet appeared to have hit Malary in his chest. There were also bullet holes on the vehicle's underbody, indicating that shots had been fired after it overturned. Witnesses at the scene stated that an ambulance had already removed a fourth victim from the vehicle—a second bodyguard who had apparently survived the attack but died later of his wounds.

As the bodies were removed, police armed with machine guns stood guard. The ICM was prevented from approaching the scene of the crime for more than an hour. When finally granted permission to inspect the scene, ICM observers saw Captain Jackson Joanis, commander of the Investigation and Anti-Gang Service of the police (Service d'Investigation et de Recherches Anti-Gang) ordering the roundup of frightened witnesses.[29] They also noted that Malary's vehicle "bore the marks of a large number of small-calibre bullets and several holes of large diameter indicating the use of heavy assault weapons."[30]

The Trial

Many hoped that this trial would mark a new era in which human rights violators would be brought to justice—an era in which the justice system would evolve into a properly functioning institution.[31] They were to be disappointed, however. Whether it was because of corruption or fear, the prosecution was incompetent.

Jean-Auguste Brutus, chief prosecutor of Port-au-Prince, and the man who successfully prosecuted Zimbabwe for the murder of Antoine Izméry, failed miserably in his prosecution of the defendants in the Malary case. Prior to the trial, he refused to interview the two eyewitnesses who were to testify against the defendants. He also refused to read the human rights reports about Malary's assassination. Not only was he unprepared, he did a very poor job at the trial.

In jury selection, he failed to dispute the qualifications of the obviously biased jurors. Several of them were closely connected to the defense team. After the verdict, at least three of them cheered and embraced the defense lawyers. Furthermore, he made no objection when one of the two eyewitnesses was kept standing for over two and a half hours in suffocating heat (over ninety degrees) during cross-examination by the jury. The jury vigorously cross-examined the witness, yelling at him, denouncing his testimony, and telling him that he should be the defendant. In the course of this excruciating examination, the witness became disoriented, contradicted his own testimony, and ran out of the courtroom. Brutus did not attempt to protect him during this onslaught by the jurors.

When the defendants took the stand, Brutus did not cross-examine them. Indeed, he did not ask them a single question, and his assistant asked the defendants only two or three inane questions. In fact, in the nearly sixteen hours of trial, Brutus asked only six questions of witnesses, some of whom were appearing for the prosecution.

President Preval and members of the Parliament, as well as the Haitian people, were incensed at this performance. The Haitian Senate has demanded that the minister of justice and Brutus appear before it and justify what many say was a sham of a trial. The government has appealed the acquittals to the Haitian Supreme Court. The defendants remain incarcerated pending the Supreme Court's decision.[32]

Conclusion

This trial was a failure for democracy. It revealed serious problems in the administration of justice in Haiti. Due process was not observed, the prosecution was incompetent, the jurors were biased, and the people's belief that justice does not exist was validated.

In sum, these two above-described human rights trials suggest that democratic institutions are not yet sufficiently developed in Haiti to provide the necessary conditions for a democracy that meets the demands of the epistemic model. In these cases, the governmental actions in the administration of justice failed in assuring that the autonomy of individuals—the victims of the coup regime's actions—be protected. The government also failed in assuring that the protection of the citizen's autonomy be seen in the actual workings of the institutions of government.

If human rights cases are to be pursued, the legal institutions need to be developed sufficiently to convince people that due process is being meticulously observed and that political criminals will be prosecuted by competent personnel after credible evidence has been developed by capable police officials. One way of doing this is to bypass traditional government organs, such as the regular police, prosecutors, and court system, and to create highly trained, specialized investigative units and prosecutors and special tribunals of highly qualified judges to work on these politically important human rights cases. Assuming that all due process guarantees are protected and that the cases are successfully prosecuted, the Haitian people will begin to believe in the system of justice. Perhaps taking steps to create special tribunals will lead to a much needed overhaul of the regular criminal justice system.

OTHER STEPS TOWARD JUSTICE

As the above discussion shows, justice remains the most important and elusive demand of the Haitian people, and its slow implementation has been causing serious frustrations. In response, strong measures have been taken in an attempt to transform the inherently corrupt legal system. In October 1995, the Aristide government created a new investigative structure, consisting of international legal advisers, CIVPOL, and Haitian officials. This new set of investigative teams has been asked to work on approximately seventy-six of the most notorious murders and, at the same time, to help train Haitian police, prosecutors, and judicial officials. The structure of the teams is as follows:

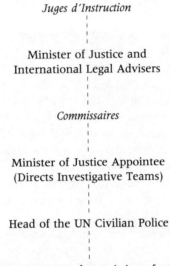

Juges d'Instruction

Minister of Justice and
International Legal Advisers

Commissaires

Minister of Justice Appointee
(Directs Investigative Teams)

Head of the UN Civilian Police

Five teams, each consisting of one
UN Investigator and two members of
the Haitian National Police

The teams have been briefed and trained and are currently investigating those cases. MICIVIH is providing information—its files and other lists of sources. The National Truth and Justice Commission is also providing information. The international legal team is coordinating the efforts.

In addition, victims' committees have been organized all over the country. The committees have been passing out questionnaires and obtaining information about serious crimes committed during the de facto era. President Aristide started this movement by hiring Haitian lawyers to work with the victims. Cases have been filed and are now proceeding. While the pace is slow, the necessary structure is being created. Hope is based on real possibilities for reform. According to Camille LeBlanc,[33] who was originally in charge of these newly hired Haitian lawyers, two hundred fifty cases have already been presented to the *juge d'instruction* by lawyers in Hinche and Mirebala. The *juge d'instruction* has issued approximately fifty *ordonnances*, but no judgments have been passed because there have not been any judges there since July 1995. A doyen and another judge, however, have recently been appointed to try these cases.

The Raboteau Massacre case is also proceeding. This is a case in which military personnel and FRAPH members massacred twenty-seven residents of a poor neighborhood in the city of Gonaives in April 1994. After a public protest, the *juge d'instruction* moved the investigation forward. He spent considerable time interviewing witnesses, approximately forty of whom are prepared to testify at the trial. Five suspects have been arrested, and there are outstanding arrest warrants for two others. The trial started in November 1995, but it has been postponed several times, and as of November 1996 it had not yet been restarted. It was not until February 1997 that the proceedings were reinstituted.

In September 1995, the Ministry of Justice issued warrants for the arrests of several individuals accused of leading or participating in the massacre of July 23, 1987, in the region of Jean Rabel. Unfortunately, the individuals named in the warrants had prior knowledge of their likely arrest and escaped before they could be apprehended. The search for them continues. The bloody attack at Jean Rabel, led by the Tonton Macoutes at the service of a few large landowners, culminated in the murders of approximately two hundred fifty peasants. It is also estimated that the Macoutes wounded over seven hundred other peasants. The attack was seen as the climax in the long persecution of the members of Tet Kole, a peasant association, who were demanding land that had been illegally appropriated by the local wealthy families.

The Jean Rabel Massacre represents one of the most tragic moments in Haiti's long history of land conflicts. Today, as for the past 192 years since independence, Haitian peasants are still seeking the return of lands expropriated from them by wealthy landowners, by the state, and by the security forces that traditionally served both. The 1987 Constitution guarantees a national land reform program. In April 1995 President Aristide inaugurated just such a program, and peasant organizations throughout Haiti, in what they see as a primary component of justice, are continuing to demand the speedy return of lands stolen from them.

Other cases are being filed almost daily. Approximately 804 victims' cases await trial in Port-au-Prince, and the international teams are attempting to determine the stage at which these cases are in the prosecution process. There are lawyers working in each jurisdiction in Haiti on these kinds of cases, but, because the people generally do not have confidence in the lawyers outside of the capital,

Camille LeBlanc and his replacement have often sent a team of law-yers from Port-au-Prince to speak with the victims. There are also victim representatives in each judicial jurisdiction of the country. One of their assigned tasks is to help assure that lawyers, commis-saires, and judges are doing their jobs. The National Truth and Jus-tice Commission should also have information about some of these cases, and the teams of lawyers are also pursuing that information.

Cases are being selected in chronological order. In this way, ev-eryone can see the logic of the prosecutions. There are, of course, some cases—for example, the Izméry, Malary, and Vincent ones—that the international lawyers have pursued as special cases.

In another positive step, all over the country, victims' committees are collecting important data that may be useful for prosecutions. They are also helping to educate people about the importance of following the rule of law. One such organization is the Committee of Justice and Reparation (CJR), founded in late 1995. A former victim, Merlinde Liberus, was originally the head of the CJR in Port-au-Prince. Other former victims are currently serving as members. In addition, ten people were selected to serve on CJR, and five more, for a total of fifteen, will be selected. For each of the other nine parts of the country, there will be representatives from popular organiza-tions and one recent graduate lawyer. There are already two lawyers on the CJR in Port-au-Prince. Camille LeBlanc and the CJR drafted questionnaires in French and Creole to help gather information from the victims. Other government appointees have continued this pro-cess into President Preval's term.

In addition, the CJR has already taken the following steps:

• contacted 274 popular organizations and discussed with them what the CJR's work and obligations are;

• contacted all the new law graduates and asked them to work with the CJR (Ms. Liberus originally received 150 applications from this group and plans were made to hire fifty-four of the ap-plicants);

• made several broadcasts on national radio to announce the creation of the CJR and its purposes;

• helped victims obtain medical care by sending sixty-five vic-tims to the hospital, and helped repair fifty-four of the victims' houses.

This work is certainly a way of beginning to create democracy from the ground up, and it is an example of direct democracy. There can be no real democracy in Haiti without the inclusion of the masses in the deliberative process of discourse and action. While progress remains slow, hope remains high.

ELECTIONS

The vitality of a democratic system of government is generally measured by whether free and fair elections are periodically held as suggested by the standards—the laws and practices—of advanced industrial democratic nations, and as required by the laws of that particular nation.[34] The measurement includes another crucial element: the degree and scope of citizen participation in these electoral activities. If this is a correct formula for the measurement of a democratic polity, then the political system in Haiti is clearly on the correct path toward a properly functioning democracy.[35] While there were undoubtedly some serious problems with the country's recent legislative, municipal, and presidential elections, it is remarkable that they took place at all, given Haiti's history. It is even more remarkable that these elections took place in an essentially nonviolent environment. Increased citizen participation in the election process and in voter turnout is a necessity, however, for the consolidation of democracy in Haiti.

The epistemic justification of democracy adds another variable to the electoral process, however. It questions the value of representative government by suggesting that the use of small groups to make decisions for the larger population causes a distortion in the process of deliberation and that this distortion may have a negative impact on the reliability of the discourse. Nevertheless, some degree of representation is necessary in a large political system because of the impossibility of face-to-face discussion among all the relevant actors and because of the need to respect personal autonomy. Moreover, personal autonomy requires considerable free time for citizens to work on their personal interests. In the epistemic view of democracy, representatives act as the mechanism to continue the discussion begun by the citizens. The discussion has to be continued from the consensus reached by the electoral process so that the concrete conclusions required by general policies can be reached and implemented. Direct democracy, however, should be encouraged whenever possible. This is particularly so in Haiti, where small groups of unelected people have run the nation for almost two hundred years.

There are many standard methods of direct participation by citizens in a large polity. These include plebiscites, referenda, initiatives, and recalls. Thus, while elections are certainly important, institutional structures must also create more opportunities for direct participation by more people through the use of these mechanisms and other, more innovative, ones.

Legislative and Municipal Elections: A Difficult Step toward Democracy

In spite of an extremely complex electoral process, numerous administrative problems, and intense political pressure, the Haitian people went to the polls in large numbers on June 25, 1995, to vote in an election where practically every elective office, except the presidency, was at stake. They freely elected members of Parliament and local representatives. This was only the second time in Haitian history that the government had held democratic elections.

The Provisional Electoral Council (CEP) faced the challenge of carrying out the election process with only four months' notice and within a context totally devoid of electoral infrastructure. Indeed, many of the basic necessities of an election process did not exist. There were no voter-registration polls, local officers, or trained election workers to organize the process. Even with these serious drawbacks, however, the level of citizen participation was quite high. Over eleven thousand candidates, representing twenty-seven political parties or groupings, sought to fill more than two thousand vacant offices, including the seats of 83 deputies, 18 senators, 133 mayors, and 541 municipal representatives. Over 4 million people registered to vote—approximately 90 percent of the eligible electorate—and over 50 percent of those who registered actually voted on election day.[36] This number exceeds the level of voter participation for the parliamentary and municipal elections of 1990, which were universally acclaimed as fair and successfully run. Most important, the elections took place in a climate almost completely free of violence. The Haitian people were demonstrating a firm commitment to the creation of a participatory democracy—a deliberative democracy.

Unfortunately, the election was by no means a perfect model of participatory democracy. In addition to the almost overwhelming administrative problems, many of the candidates and parties were extremely dissatisfied with the way things were run. Expressing concerns about administrative flaws, and, in a number of cases, the fact of having been defeated at the polls, numerous party leaders called for a reformulation of the CEP, an annulment or reevaluation of the June 25 results, and a boycott of the complementary and runoff rounds of the elections. Even with these complaints, however, virtually every candidate from these parties, some of whom had won seats or remained in competition for the runoff elections, remained engaged and did not withdraw from the subsequent electoral rounds. Some mayoral candidates who won clear victories on June 25, among them members of the Front National pour la Convergence Democratique (FNCD), had already been inaugurated and taken office by the time the runoffs occurred. While tensions remained high within the country's traditional elite class as the political landscape shifted, the vast majority of the population, while also appealing for improved administration, appeared calm and satisfied that they were able to express their will through the electoral process.

ELECTION OBSERVER REPORTS

The election was observed at close hand by a truly international audience. The CEP accredited over fourteen hundred international and Haitian observers, and hundreds of journalists were also present. In spite of the many administrative and logistical difficulties, the nearly unanimous consensus of these onlookers was that the elections proved to be a step forward for democracy. All observer missions agreed that people were generally able to express their will freely with no evidence of organized fraud or efforts by electoral officials to favor any single party. There was also a high level of participation in the process by candidates, political parties, and voters. Indeed, Haitian voters participated broadly and, except for rare incidents, peacefully throughout the country—often waiting patiently for long hours in the boiling hot sun to vote.

Access to polling sites and election officials was free and unhindered throughout the country for observers, monitors from the political parties, and journalists. Significantly, for the first time, Haitians participated as accredited observers—approximately one thousand of them. Accredited monitors representing a broad range of political parties and candidates remained at the voting sites throughout the day. While voting began late or with administrative difficulties at many of the sites, in most cases, electoral officials (despite the lack of adequate training in many cases) worked diligently to solve technical problems, and procedures improved throughout the day. Election officials and pollwatchers joined efforts by working into the night, counting, recounting, and certifying ballots, while trying to correct flaws in the process and to assure the integrity of the results. The new Haitian National Police and the Interim Haitian Police (IPSF) worked closely with the 900-strong international civilian police force and the 6,000 UN troops to help establish a climate devoid of violence. With a few exceptions, they succeeded.

All the difficulties notwithstanding, the majority of the observer mission reports, in their overall assessment, accentuated the positive. The OAS Electoral Observation Mission,[37] for example, was of the opinion that "the election has established a foundation which, although shaky, provides the basis for further positive progress toward the continuing evolution of an increasingly peaceful democracy in Haiti."[38] Further, the mission stated that it "hoped that all of those involved in the future elections will profit from the mistakes and problems which arose during the course of the election and will continue to build on the positive aspects in the interests of Haiti and its people."[39] Gay McDougall, executive director of the International Human Rights Law Group, and one of the sixteen members of the Independent Electoral Commission,[40] testifying before the U.S. Senate on July 12, 1995, compared the elections in Haiti with those recently conducted in South Africa. In doing so, she concluded that Haiti's elections had equal, or perhaps less serious, logistical and administrative problems, and equal problems during the counting phase. She also noted that the Haitian elections took place in a climate of peace and cooperation, while South Africa's were marred by serious acts of violence and threats. Even more important, however, she commended the people of both nations for "respond[ing] to the adversities by demonstrating a remarkable spirit of patience, tolerance and commitment to the process."[41]

There were other positive responses from international groups. According to the U.S. Presidential Delegation, the elections represented a step in the building of democracy in Haiti. "A peaceful balloting process occurred in a country where violence has so often marked past elections. This feat is truly impressive when one considers that, but nine months ago, Haiti was under the yoke of a military dictatorship."[42] Nevertheless, this delegation cautioned that "the process was affected by irregularities and administrative flaws that need to be addressed for the second round and the future."[43]

A 62-person delegation fielded jointly by Voices for Haiti, Washington Office on Haiti, Witness for Peace, and Global Exchange also concluded on a positive note: "The elections demonstrated the determination of millions of Haitian citizens to express their political will in the face of confusion, long lines, and fear for personal security. . . . Across the country, we were impressed by the election officials we encountered, who, with few exceptions, worked steadfastly to guarantee the integrity of the process."[44] That is not to say that there were no concerns about the election process: "Our teams did witness a wide array of irregularities, including shortages of materials, administrative difficulties, late openings, lack of secrecy, and incidents of intimidation of voters and election officials. Teams observed isolated instances of manipulation of the process and documented acts of violence by partisans."[45] Despite these problems, the delegation concluded that "the irregularities [it] detected did not seem to be the product of a concerted attempt on the part of any one political party or persuasion to undermine the democratic process at a national level. . . . In [its] opinion, Sunday's vote represents a critical step in Haiti's struggle for democracy."[46]

In contrast to the majority of very positive reports by international observers, only two reports were extremely negative. Unfortunately, it was these two that received the most attention in the international press. One report was by the International Republican Institute (IRI).[47] Initially, the IRI had proposed to provide "leadership training exclusively for non-Lavalas centrist political party representatives," considering Lavalas partisans "undemocratic." Yet, in its June 26, 1995, press release, IRI stated: "It has been the IRI's intent throughout this process to be thorough, independent, objective and constructive."[48] The same press release concluded that irregularities marred the electoral process.[49] On June 27, 1995, the *Washington Post* denounced IRI's conclusion: "Ignoring historical context, [the IRI] applied a test of political-science correctness and, unsurprisingly, found Haiti painfully wanting. This was not constructive, informed criticism. . . ."[50]

Pastor's Report

An individual, Robert A. Pastor, of the Carter Center, wrote the second largely negative report of the election.[51] It stated that the Council of Freely Elected Heads of Government, affiliated with the Carter Center, had sought to play a role of "mediation between the political parties, the Election Council, and the government. . . . But there was not wide enough support in Haiti. . . ."[52] Pastor traveled alone to Haiti to monitor the elections, by his account observing the voting only in selected sections of Port-au-Prince (there were 10,000 voting sites across the country), and issued a report with the following broad conclusion: "There was much good and bad about the June 25th election in Haiti, but overall, of thirteen elections that I have observed, the June 25th Haitian elections were the most disastrous technically, and the counting process was the worst."[53] He also claimed that "the election represents a step out of Haiti's past. Whether it is a step forward or sideways remains to be seen."[54]

Pastor's report was not entirely negative, however. Indeed, he had many positive comments to make about the election. Perhaps most telling was his observation that, in light of Haiti's history of repression and dictatorship, the elections offered hope and a second chance for Haitians to experience freedom through democracy. He concluded that, despite the procedural problems and the lack of experience with local or parliamentary democracy, approximately 50 percent of the Haitian electorate voted. More important, he argued that the election was the most secure and peaceful election in the country's history. The presence of numerous candidates and party pollwatchers at the vast majority of the voting sites represented "the foundation for building a [just] society."[55]

Furthermore, Pastor stressed that the most important difference between the 1995 electoral process and that of both 1987 and 1990 was the level of security.[56] The presence of UN forces and international police monitors, combined with the absence of the Haitian army, provided what in his opinion was a degree of security unprecedented in Haitian history. There was also a considerable increase in the amount of international support, with the UN providing security and an electoral advisory unit to the CEP, and the OAS providing human rights monitors. The election was financed largely by the international community, with the United States providing approximately $12 million.

Major Difficulties of the Electoral Process

Among the major logistical difficulties encountered by the CEP were the lack of adequate buildings for voting and registration sites, and the lack of telecommunications capacity at the polling sites. There were also difficulties in delivering ballots and voting materials to those of the 10,000 voting sites that were in remote rural areas. The only access to these areas was over often impassable roads. Other significant problems included the inadequate census and demographic data, the inexperience of electoral officials, an extremely complex electoral law and process, and a very limited time frame in which to implement the election process.

Other difficulties arose from the lack of coordination and articulation among various international and national players involved in the process.[57] One of the key problems included the limited control of election finances by the CEP. It had reign over only a fraction of the over $15 million donated by the international community. Indeed, the majority of the funds was managed by the UN or went directly to mostly U.S. nongovernmental organizations involved in various facets of the elections—party training, printing of ballots and voting and training materials, civic education, and training of pollworkers.

The funding was restricted further by requirements for it to be spent in the donor countries. For example, ignoring the CEP's requests to have the ballots printed by a Haitian firm, the donor countries decided to have them printed by a firm in California. That firm delivered some of the ballots too late for use in the election. Many materials requested by the CEP were not delivered by international agencies until after delays of between three and six months. These materials included office supplies, vehicles, generators, tape recorders, computers, and copy machines. Furthermore, many of those materials that were delivered were inappropriate: computers equipped with unnecessarily sophisticated software, copy machines without automatic-feed capacity, and the like.

Another crucial flaw in the administration of the election process was the lack of adequate civic education programs for the electorate and sufficient training for electoral officials and political party pollwatchers. International donors decided that, instead of utilizing funds to educate and train pollworkers, the resources would go to contracted international organizations. Unfortunately, the CEP did not have control over the process, and these crucial tasks were never executed adequately. Indeed, perhaps the major problem in the elections was that no one seemed to be in control.[58]

Steps to Improve the Process

Immediately after the first round of elections, the CEP continued to make strenuous efforts to implement the requirements of the electoral law. Complementary elections were held where voting had not taken place or the outcome was deemed questionable because of irregularities.[59] According to specific criteria established by the CEP, elections were rerun where, among other things, voting had not occurred, ballots had been destroyed, and at least 50 percent of the voting sites (BIVs) had not functioned.

Two members of the CEP resigned—President Anselme Remy and Jean-François Merisier—and were replaced by Pierre Michel Sajous and Johnson Bazelais. Other CEP members unanimously elected Sajous as their new president. In addition, on June 27, 1995, Boussuet Aubourg replaced Jaccillon Barthélemy as president of the regional headquarters of the CEP (BED) in the Department of the West.

In order to alleviate the concerns of the parties, the CEP asked all party leaders and candidates to present complaints formally, as required by the electoral law. Moreover, the CEP invited party leaders to engage in dialogue about their concerns in order to achieve specific solutions. In cases in which the CEP received credible information about violence or irregularities related to elections, it forwarded these cases to Haiti's Justice Ministry for investigation and possible prosecution. Examples of the results of such actions are the arrests of Duly Brutus, a candidate for Deputy of the PANPRA Party, and Jacques LaGuerre, justice of the peace in Limbe, who were accused of involvement in the fire that destroyed the commercial headquarters of the CEP in Limbe.[60]

The CEP took other actions. It deployed official delegations of its members to the various departments to evaluate the situation and determine where elections should be rerun. It met with Haitian and UN security forces to design an improved security plan with particular attention to areas of potential conflict. It urged international and nongovernment organizations to accelerate their efforts at civic education and training of election workers. It sought to correct problems with the printing of the ballots that occurred during the first round of the election, by hiring a Haitian firm. Moreover, the CEP worked with representatives from ten parties to implement the Unit for Observation and Control, which allowed party representatives to monitor voting jointly.

In addition to the efforts of the CEP, President Aristide expressed his concern and desire for electoral impartiality by taking immediate action. On June 30, 1995, he promulgated a decree that banned the operation of any television station that received its license during the period of the military regime.[61] This decree affected six prominent television stations, which subsequently went off the air. Furthermore, Robert Pastor offered some recommendations for improving the electoral process.[62] He claimed that the Haitian officials needed both an expanded set of criteria for determining reruns and a certain degree of flexibility for deciding on runoffs. Another of his suggestions was the calling of a "national dialogue" of representatives of the six major political parties and other international representatives to address the major problems of the electoral process, such as the issue of runoffs and the composition of the CEP. Pastor further recommended the appointment of a task force composed of representatives of the major political parties and international mediators skilled in conducting elections. He recommended that the task force be required to produce a report in two weeks, identifying problems and providing suggestions for solving them in time for the next round of elections. According to Pastor, some of these problems included:

1. *Voting sites.* The public was not certain where to vote. In order to alleviate this problem, Pastor suggested that BEC (district or communal level) presidents should visit each BIV site with the president of the BIV, publish the BIV sites and their locations in the newspapers, and list them at the registration sites, the BEC site, and the BIV site at least four days before the election.

2. *Training and practice.* Pastor stressed the inadequate training of the election officials and pollwatchers. As a solution, he suggested a practice run one week before the election.

3. *Completing the vote.* Pastor considered the extension of the voting a mistake that contributed to a compromise of the count. Instead, he suggested that it should not be extended.

4. *The count.* Viewing this as the most crucial stage in the election, Pastor noted the lack of security and the complications surrounding this process. He recommended that these problems could be eliminated by establishing a simpler and more precise procedure.

5. *Institutional memory.* Pastor suggested that, after the runoffs of the parliamentary elections, the president and the new Parliament should concentrate on establishing a permanent elections council that would build from experience of the past.

6. *Changes in electoral law.* Pastor mentioned that most of the worst mistakes made by the CEP in the election stemmed from its disqualifying candidates, leaving no time to respond to legitimate complaints from the parties. He called for revisions in the process.

7. *Mediation.* He called for the OAS, UN, United States, and other foreign governments to help mediate the conflicts between the parties, the Haitian government, and the CEP.

8. *Sample counts.* Pastor suggested that international observers do a quick sample count in order to alleviate fears of fraud or ma-

nipulation. Pastor claimed that a silent sample could assure some security to those who were afraid that the election was a sham and that it was stolen by special interests.

CONCERNS OF POLITICAL PARTY LEADERS, VOTERS, AND CANDIDATES

After the June 25, 1995, election, the leaders of Haiti's political parties called for a variety of actions, including a complete replacement of all or the majority of the CEP, an annulment or reevaluation of the results, and a boycott of the August 13, 1995, complementary elections and subsequent runoffs. In response, both the CEP and President Aristide repeatedly invited the leaders of the parties to dialogue in order to address their concerns. In one attempt, President Aristide hosted a meeting and invited party leaders who were government ministers, originally named as a part of the ongoing efforts toward reconciliation. Unfortunately, this attempt proved to be unsuccessful because the party leaders refused to engage in discourse or discuss specific solutions.[63] Instead, they focused on trying to annul the election. The parties who had won few or no seats seemed intent on attempting to delegitimize the electoral process.

Members of the traditional parties should not have been surprised, however, at the electorate's rejection. Indeed, most international and national observers had predicted it. The National Democratic Institute (NDI) noted that most of Haiti's parties were "largely personality based" with "little base of popular support."[64] NDI remarked that at least nine of these parties supported the coup dictatorship, some of them having sought to use unconstitutional elections on January 18, 1993, in an attempt to legitimize the dictatorship.[65] Nevertheless, according to Pastor, unless the political parties' legitimate concerns were addressed more effectively, the elections currently under way could not be considered a step forward in Haiti's journey to democracy, and his report recommended some ways to reverse their skepticism. For example, he suggested that (1) the criteria for reholding elections should be expanded to permit more elections, and runoffs should be permitted for some mayoral elections; (2) half of the CEP should be replaced by consensus candidates proposed by the parties; (3) a multiparty commission should produce a report on specific ways to improve the electoral process; (4) a new electoral law should be enacted for a more effective CEP; (5) there should be mediation between the parties; and (6) quick counts should be done.[66]

In spite of the calls of the party leaders for a boycott of elections, it appeared that many of the actual candidates—party and independent—remained engaged in the process. The CEP released a list of those running in the complementary election, and only two of the hundreds of original candidates running had sent the required correspondence to the CEP indicating their intent to withdraw.[67]

As far as the vast majority of Haiti's voters was concerned, there appeared to be a general sense of satisfaction that they had been able to express their political will. There were no popular protests supporting the party leaders' calls for annulment of the elections. In contrast, several popular organizations held a protest rally that reportedly drew a thousand people, calling for the election results to be respected. The Haitian people seemed to be more concerned with the need to move ahead with programs that would revitalize the economy, reduce the high cost of living, and establish justice and security.[68]

COMPLEMENTARY ELECTIONS

Complementary elections held on August 13, 1995, covered the areas where voting had not taken place, or had taken place inadequately, on June 25. This applied to approximately 20 percent of the voting sites, and these elections affected races in twenty-one communes and fifteen districts in eight of Haiti's nine geographic departments where administrative snafus had disenfranchised many voters.[69] There were 131 candidates for Senate, 118 candidates for deputy, and 128 mayoral candidates. Although the 32 percent turnout was a bit less than that for the June election, there was considerable improvement in the ability of the election workers to administer the election process.[70] The CEP had taken numerous steps to eliminate the problems that plagued the first round of voting. The IRI attributed the low turnout to voter fatigue, boycotting, and the lack of campaigning.[71]

Prior to the subsequent runoff election held on September 17, 1995, almost all Haitians and international observers seemed certain that parties and candidates linked to Aristide would win overwhelmingly in the races for ten Senate seats and sixty seats in the lower house of Parliament.[72] All parties other than those linked to the Lavalas movement (Aristide's political force) threatened to boycott this election, claiming they would do so because of the administrative chaos and bias by the Aristide-controlled electoral commission in the first round of elections held in June. Defending the election results, Lakhdar Brahimi, UN special envoy for Haiti, claimed that Haitian elections should not be compared to those in the United States. He stated that "[p]olitical parties at this stage of development [were comprised of] small groups of people around one man who has captured the support of the people. And in Haiti there is only one man [Aristide] who has done that."[73]

The September parliamentary and local elections, like the complementary elections held in August, resulted in a low voter turnout. Leaders of the twenty-two opposition parties did, in fact, boycott the vote. They charged that the council overseeing the election was biased in favor of Aristide's party and had failed to redress widespread irregularities in the first round of elections held in June. The effects of the boycott were mixed. Because little campaigning was done, many Haitian voters were not aware of the opposition protest. Furthermore, because the opposition did not withdraw formally, the names of all opposition candidates remained on the ballot. Some thought that the boycott was more symbolic than substantive, with most candidates expected to defy party discipline and take office if elected.[74]

More than a thousand candidates ran for seats in Parliament, on regional councils, and in town halls—all seats where the first round of elections failed to result in a clear majority.[75] Compared with the 50 percent voter turnout in June and the 32 percent turnout in August, an expected low of 20–25 percent voted. Election observers attributed this to fatigue among the voters who, in some cases, had already voted twice in the summer of 1995.

There were, however, positive aspects to this election. Most importantly, no incidents of violence took place at the September election. (In fact, each successive election that year had shown dramatic improvement in organization and a decline in security concerns.) Even though there was a low voter turnout in September, this is by no means an indication that Haitians did not take their civic duty seriously. Indeed, Haitians constantly discussed and debated the elections for months—a healthy sign of participatory democracy. Nevertheless, steps must be taken to increase voter participation or the epistemic requirements of democracy will never be fulfilled.

The Presidential Election

As the December 17, 1995, presidential election approached, pressure mounted from the Haitian civil society for President Aristide to serve out the remaining three years of his term. The president's reconfirmation that elections would take place as scheduled, and that he would turn over power on February 7, 1996, met with widespread disappointment among the population. Popular sentiment held to the position that the coup had stolen three years of administration by the president they had democratically elected, and they wanted him to serve out that time. Enthusiasm for the elections was, therefore, limited. Many analysts believed that this climate of disappointment, combined with the focus on pressing issues such as disarmament and concerns about violence, would affect voter turnout.

According to Haitian and international observers, after initial administrative problems in the first round of parliamentary elections in 1995, each subsequent round had been increasingly well administered. Indeed, at the technical and administrative level, all reports indicated that preparations for the presidential elections proceeded extremely smoothly under the direction of the CEP. Substantive problems that had surfaced earlier, such as inadequate civic education, seemed to have been sufficiently addressed.

In spite of longstanding predictions from all perspectives that the Lavalas candidate was a strong favorite to win, fourteen candidates representing positions across the entire political spectrum registered and were approved. They included representatives of eight political parties and four independents—at least three of whom supported the coup regime.[76] Nevertheless, some parties boycotted the elections.

Though enthusiasm was not intense, all of the candidates were given ample opportunity to present their views on state television and radio stations. Thus, in this election, unlike the case in any of the previous elections in Haitian history, the candidates, including those who supported the coup regime, were able to express their views freely and to reach a wider audience. The government provided police protection at candidate rallies. International agencies provided funding for each of the candidates, allowing all of them combined to place 700 poll observers throughout the country. In order to get their desired observers at the polls, the candidates needed only to submit the names of their designated observers. Hundreds of international observers, including the OAS Electoral Observation Mission and media representatives, traveled to Haiti and had full access to voting sites.

CANDIDATES

The fourteen candidates for the presidency were quite disparate in their political views and backgrounds. They represented a broad range of interests, which illustrates, to a certain extent, the openness of the process. At a minimum, the range of candidates suggests the importance given to including all voices in the debate about what direction the country was to take. The election was clearly a step toward democracy. Simply listing the candidates and describing their backgrounds makes the point.

The overwhelming favorite was the candidate for the Lavalas political platform, René Preval. Preval has a degree in agronomy from the Université des Sciences Agronomiques de Gembloux in Belgium. In 1963, he was forced to leave Haiti because of problems with the Duvaliér dictatorship. When he returned in 1975, he worked at the National Institute of Mining Resources (INAREM). After the fall of the Duvaliér dictatorship, Preval participated actively in various popular and charitable organizations. In 1991, he was President Aristide's prime minister until the military coup of September 30. In exile, Preval served on the private cabinet of President Aristide. After the return of the constitutional government, Preval was named director of the Economic and Social Assistance Fund (FAES).

Victor Benoit, secretary-general of the National Congress of Democratic Movements (CONACOM Party), founded in 1987, was a teacher, a school principal, and a former member of the Senate. After the 1991 coup, CONACOM remained critical of the coup regime; yet, in March of 1994, some CONACOM parliamentarians aligned themselves with the PANPRA Party. They aligned themselves, too, with proposals to resolve Haiti's crisis without the return of the legitimate president. Benoit served as minister of education under the government of Prime Minister Malval from 1993–94. His entrance into the presidential race surprised some observers after his and his party's strong denunciations of the parliamentary elections and the CEP.

Leon Jeune, an independent, worked as secretary of state for the Ministry of Justice on the creation of the new Haitian National Police under the government of Smarck Michel. He was also director of the National Office of Civil Aviation. He was forced into exile in 1991 along with members of the constitutional government and was active in support of the restoration of the democratic government.

Three candidates were members of the then current Senate: Senators Clarck Parent, Firmin Jean-Louis, and Julio Larosilière. Senator Clarck Parent was elected senator for the FNCD Party in 1990 for six years. He ran under the banner of the little-known party PADEMH (Haitian Democratic Party). Senator Firmin Jean-Louis, former president of the Senate, was elected to the Senate for six years to represent the FNCD Party and ran as an independent in the presidential election. Senator Julio Larosilière was elected in 1990 for six years under the banner of the RDNP, and he was also running as an independent in the presidential race. Larosilière led a group of parliamentarians that supported the coup regime and approved its facade Nerette-Honorat government.[77]

Rockefeller Guerre was the deputy representing Cap-Haïtien during the Duvaliér dictatorship. During the presidential election of 1995, he was secretary of state for natural resources and mines. He participated in the race as a representative of the UPD Party (Union of Democratic Patriots). Guerre was a member of the administrative board of the state telecommunications company, TELECO, during the de facto government of Nerette-Honorat.

Gerard Dalvius was a candidate for the little-known PADH Party (Alternative Party for the Development of Haiti). He is a former member of the armed forces and was secretary of state for the Ministry of Justice in 1991 under Prime Minister Preval.

Eddy Volel, who first supported the coup regime and then later the return of President Aristide, ran under the banner of the RDC Party (Reunion of Christian Democrats). Volel originally described the coup d'état as a "patriotic and disinterested gesture" and said that President Aristide should have been condemned "to hard labor for the violation of the Constitution." He quickly changed his position soon after Aristide's reinstatement.

Pastor Vladimir Jeanty ran for the PARADIS Party (Haitian Party of God), the slogan of which is "Jesus." Jeanty fought virulently against the return of the constitutional order, forming part of the ultra-Macoute alliance with Emmanuel Constant of FRAPH, among others.

The rest of the candidates are little known: Jean Dumas Arnold of the PNT (National Workers Party); Marie Alphonse Francis Jean, an ex-official of the army of the FMR (Revolutionary Militant Front); René Julien, attorney of the Amical des Jurists, as an independent candidate; and finally, Dieuveuil Joseph for the Party of the Virgin Mary.

RESULTS OF THE ELECTION

To no one's surprise, the man whom Aristide handpicked to succeed him as president won a landslide victory. On December 23, 1995, René Preval, a distant relative to Aristide, was declared president-elect of Haiti, easily winning an election that many voters shunned. According to the CEP, Preval received approximately 88 percent of the votes—818,000 out of 994,000. This was a substantially higher percentage than Aristide had received in his successful 1990 run for office. Preval replaced President Aristide on February 7, 1996.[78]

Voter turnout was extremely low. Only around 25 percent of the Haitian electorate voted, leading some opposition groups to question the legitimacy of Preval's mandate.[79] Many of those who stayed away said they did so because Aristide was not on the ballot, which serves only to reinforce the most important point about Haitian politics: in or out of the office, Aristide remains the only leader with the power to inspire his countrymen to action.[80] Others stayed away, politically apathetic, because the return to democratic order has brought no tangible economic benefit to most people in the hemisphere's poorest nation.[81] Despite this, the general feeling among Haitians and international observers was that this election was probably the most free and peaceful in the country's history. Marc Bazin, an international economist who finished second to Aristide in the 1990 presidential election, was quoted as saying that the 1995 election was a "huge step forward for democracy."[82]

The presidential election in Haiti thus marked a milestone for democracy there, and a clear success for U.S. policy. On February 7, 1996, for the first time in nearly two hundred years of Haitian independence, one democratically elected president yielded power to another. This incredible feat was one of President Clinton's main goals when he dispatched more than twenty thousand American troops in September 1994.[83]

But the achievement of this milestone must be tempered by the harsh reality of Haitian society. Excessive concentrations of political and economic power and a culture of arbitrary policing remain largely in place. Indeed, Preval faces severe challenges in attempting to create the conditions for democracy. To govern effectively, he will have to demonstrate that he can make hard decisions on his own, without Aristide's input.[84] Moreover, the transition of power has been somewhat awkward. Immediately after the election there were some signs of strain. In January 1996, Preval indicated that, as an economic measure, he would eliminate the Women's Affairs Ministry created by Aristide. In December 1995, Aristide nominated Jean-Marie Fourel Celestin, a former aide who had served as a colonel in the old Haitian army, to a three-year term as head of the new National Police Force. Some felt this decision should have been left to the new president, and the legislature, even though dominated by members of Aristide's Lavalas movement, rejected the nomination on January 16, 1996.[85] Finally, there was a substantial amount of controversy over the number of members of Aristide's government that Preval planned to retain.[86]

Even with these difficulties, and despite their sharp differences in temperament and upbringing, Preval and Aristide have such a close relationship that supporters call them "the twins."[87] While Aristide, a former Roman Catholic priest, grew up in a relatively poor family, Preval grew up in an upper-middle-class rural family and studied agronomy in a prestigious Belgian university. There, he mingled with the Haitian exile community in Europe. When he returned to help Aristide, he was ready to overthrow the Duvaliér dictatorship.[88]

Preval's father was a minister of agriculture before Papa Doc Duvaliér came to power in 1957. The Preval family fled Haiti in 1963, moving to Europe. According to his friends, Preval's experience abroad gave him a much more sophisticated understanding of how the world works than Aristide originally had.[89] "For example, Aristide understands nothing about economics," said a source familiar with both men. He continued: "Preval does. Clearly he is more conscious of the importance of the international community and a good bit more aware of trying to seek some sort of middle ground with the elite. He knows them and they know him."[90]

Preval spent several years in New York, then returned to Haiti in 1982 and opened a bakery. He and Aristide began working together in the mid-1980s when a mutual friend, Antoine Izméry, introduced them. Preval, known affectionately as "Ti René" or "Little René" because of his diminutive stature, was largely instrumental in pushing Aristide to run for president in 1990. Aristide named Preval his prime minister and minister of defense.

As president, Preval has promised to "modernize" the aging state industries and to open them up to private investment. He succeeded in keeping some UN peace-keeping forces in Haiti after the February 7, 1996, cutoff date, for at least six months more—until June 30, 1996. As that date expired, he succeeded in extending the mandate several times, until a final date of July 3, 1997.[91]

SECURITY AND U.S. INVOLVEMENT IN HAITI

As the December 17, 1995, date for the presidential election approached, and less than two months before the peaceful transfer of power from the first democratically elected president in the history of Haiti to the second, Haitians remained extremely concerned about the failure to disarm the military and paramilitary forces still at large in their country and the threat posed to their security and to their fragile democratic process. Simultaneously, on the economic front, the Haitian people continued to pressure the government for policies responsive to their perceived needs. International budgetary support had been at least temporarily cut off because the Haitian government refused to privatize all of its major companies as the World Bank and the IMF claimed it had originally agreed to do. Project funding continued, but the Haitian government and these international financial institutions continued to negotiate over the future of structural adjustment policies.

Disarmament

Many Haitians and international observers, including UN and OAS officials, have long feared that Haiti's antidemocratic forces—the ex-military and paramilitary forces and their supporters—have stored vast quantities of automatic weapons and other heavy weaponry, and could violently attempt to gain power with the departure or downsizing of the UN peace-keeping force, originally scheduled for February 7, 1996, and extended piecemeal thereafter. The Haitian government and many organizations and individuals in Haitian civil society have repeatedly sought assistance with disarmament from the United States and the UN since before the return of President Aristide in October 1994. The UN Secretary-General's Report of July 15, 1994, which details the original mandate of the UNMIH, explicitly states in Point 9 that one of the tasks of the MNF, and now the UN peace-keeping force, is to "assist the legitimate authorities of Haiti in . . . [a]ssuring public order, including the disarmament of paramilitary groups. . . ."[92] As described below,[93] neither the UN nor the United States has adequately fulfilled this mandate. Yet, unless these paramilitary forces are disarmed, Haiti cannot hope to succeed in its attempt to create a meaningful democracy.[94] Unless security is assured, all of the other requirements for the epistemic value of democracy must necessarily remain unfulfilled.

Indeed, the daylight assassination of one parliamentarian and the wounding of another on November 7, 1995, by paramilitary forces, highlighted the growing concerns about the failure of disarmament and the potential to destabilize the fledgling democracy.[95] Unwilling to return to the nightmare of three years of terror and violence under the de facto regime, Haitians increasingly demanded that the government take immediate, effective action to carry out the disarmament campaign and to end impunity.[96] Unfortunately, several reports in the international media described the events of November and December 1995 inaccurately or incompletely, suggesting that the people were taking the law into their own hands and that President Aristide had encouraged their actions.[97] This is simply incorrect.[98]

Violence, Disarmament, and Public Reaction: October and November 1995

The events that occurred in October and November 1995 reflect the hopes and fears that seem perpetually to confront the Haitian people. The issues raised by these events are not, of course, new ones. They have recurred throughout Haitian history. They are, however, particularly important in presenting an example of the difficulties Haitians face as they try to stabilize their democracy.

OCTOBER 26, 1995. U.S. Secretary of State Warren Christopher sent the U.S. ambassador in Haiti, William Swing, a confidential memorandum detailing intelligence reports that the Red Star Organization, under the leadership of former military dictator Prosper Avril (September 1988 to March 1990), " 'is planning [a] harassment and assassination campaign directed at the Lavalas Party [Aristide's political force] and Aristide supporters. The campaign is scheduled to commence in early December 1995.' "[99] Although the information relating to assassination plans has not been corroborated, there is information available that suggests that Avril, a one-time de facto president of Haiti (1988–90), has continued to meet with right-wing supporters to expand his political base.[100]

For reasons that remain unclear, the United States did not share this information with the Haitian government. Even today, the U.S. government is extremely reluctant to discuss with the appropriate Haitian officials the issues raised by these kinds of revelations.

NOVEMBER 7, 1995. After attending the inauguration ceremony for the new prime minister, Claudette Werleigh, at the National Palace, two newly elected members of Haiti's Parliament, Deputy Jean-Hubert Feuillé of Port Salut and Deputy Gabriel Fortuné of Les Cayes, were ambushed and shot by paramilitary forces of the de facto coup regime. (Feuillé was a cousin and former bodyguard of President Aristide. The president was very close to him.) In a well-orchestrated attack, committed in broad daylight, a taxi blocked the path of their vehicle and gunmen opened fire with automatic weapons.

Two media outlets, Radio Metropole and the French Press Agency, incorrectly reported that *both* deputies had been killed,[101] when in fact only Feuillé was dead. On hearing the news, residents of the deputies' districts in Les Cayes and Port Salut, in southern Haiti, reacted with anger. They built street barricades and initiated protests against symbols and associates of the Duvaliérs and ensuing military regimes. Some reports estimated that the Haitian people burned the homes of twenty suspected Duvaliér and de facto coup regime members, and killed a former member of a paramilitary group.[102] The protests spread, and in the days following the shooting of the parliamentarians, thousands of people took to the streets in Port-au-Prince, Gonaives, and Cap-Haïtien, protesting the incident and criticizing the lack of government action for disarmament. The crowds continued to erect barricades, and stopped and searched vehicles and houses of suspected attachés and former military members for illegal weapons.[103] Haiti's Parliament also reacted to the murder and wounding of two of its members. Members of Parliament expressed outrage, demanded that the government carry out disarmament, and questioned and criticized the role of UNMIH. Parliamentary demands continued to increase in the days following the attack.

In response to these outbursts of violence by the people and criticism by members of Parliament, the National Police obtained a judicial order to search the house of ex-dictator Prosper Avril. Apparently tipped off about the search, Avril fled his house just before the police arrived and took refuge in the Colombian embassy.[104] In the course of searching his home, police discovered and confiscated arms and ammunition.

Soon thereafter, the Haitian government discovered that a U.S. embassy political officer had visited Avril's home just hours before the National Police arrived to meet him. A U.S. official claimed that taking this risk—meeting with Avril—was part of a U.S. policy to maintain "contact with a broad spectrum of Haitian society."[105] The *Washington Post* quoted a senior Haitian official as saying: "What are we supposed to think, when they meet with [Avril], maybe warn him, and fail to pass on intelligence that directly affects our safety? What would you think?"[106]

This action is particularly unsettling because Avril is currently a fugitive from U.S. justice. In July 1994, a U.S. district court found that Avril bore "personal responsibility for a systematic pattern of egregious human rights abuses"[107] during his tenure as dictator, as well as for the "interrogation and torture of each of the plaintiffs in [the] case"[108]—six prominent leaders of Haitian civil society. The court ordered him to pay a total of $41 million in damages. What, may we ask, are certain parts of the U.S. government up to in Haiti?

NOVEMBER 8, 1995. The day after the shootings, radio reports corrected the false accounts of Gabriel Fortuné's death. He survived the attack, but had sustained serious wounds. Human rights groups and other members of civil society continued to denounce the climate of violence throughout the country and criticized the Haitian government for failing to disarm paramilitary forces associated with the de facto coup regime. Protests continued across the country.

NOVEMBER 11, 1995. The family of Deputy Feuillé held his funeral at the Port-au-Prince Cathedral. President Aristide, visibly upset by the murder of his cousin, delivered a strong speech mourning the loss of Feuillé and expressed his firm determination to provide security to all Haitians. He also expressed his frustration at the lack of international support for disarmament. The president congratulated the police force for its professionalism in enforcing the law over the past few days, and ordered it to carry out a "legal, total and complete disarmament operation."[109] He also required that the operation conducted by the police be in compliance with Resolution 940 of the UN Security Council.[110] He criticized the international force for searching for weapons only in the poor areas of the country and not in the wealthier areas, where weapons were more likely to be discovered. He appealed to the international community for assistance in the disarmament campaign, and called on the Haitian people to support the police in this entirely legal campaign "with our Constitution and our laws," by accompanying the police and providing information.[111] He continued:

This is what I ask of the Haitian people: don't cross your arms; don't stand there waiting; accompany the police when they are going to enter the houses of those who have heavy weapons. Give them information. Don't be afraid. When you do this, tell the police not to go only to the poor neighborhoods, but to go to the neighborhoods where there are big houses and heavy weapons. . . . Too much blood has flowed in the country. The rich man, the poor man, the big man, and the small man must find peace. And for this to be done, we must take the heavy weapons from the hands of the big men. We must not be cowards. We must not be hypocrites. We must be respectful, but true. And all will benefit from this peace. . . . If we respect ourselves, we must roll up our sleeves, pick up our Constitution, gather the law, support our police to prevent the *zenglendos* from piling up our bodies on the street. . . . Friends of the international community, today, through me, we tell you: we want your help and your cooperation, and we will respect you, march with you so that disarmament is achieved. . . . They assassinated Prime Minister Yitzhak Rabin. The international community expressed its determination to work for peace. It is beautiful. It is grand. Here in Haiti, let us do the same. It is not too late, simply late. It is not too late.[112]

NOVEMBER 11–13, 1995. The police initiated the disarmament campaign. In most instances, the people participated in an orderly manner, providing information and accompanying the police. Citizens also set up roadblocks and searched vehicles. These actions occurred mostly in Port-au-Prince. Numerous reports of people who passed through these roadblocks indicate that people were generally respectful. In some cases, popular protests spilled over into violence that targeted allies of the coup regime. Reports of generalized targeting of wealthy Haitians, however, were completely inaccurate. President Aristide, Prime Minister Claudette Werleigh, Justice Minister René Magloire, and other government officials condemned the violence and reaffirmed that the disarmament campaign must be carried out within a legal context. In Port-au-Prince, the majority of the violence ceased within a few days, and, in general, a state of calm returned to the streets.

NOVEMBER 13–14, 1995. In Gonaives, UN troops intervened to control a crowd of protesters angry at an alleged coup regime collaborator. Some reports indicate that the individual associated with the coup regime fired upon protesters from a house, killing several and wounding eight. Other reports suggest that UN troops fired either into the air or into the crowd, and that they may have been responsible for several deaths. In addition, on November 14, a voodoo priest thought to be associated with the coup regime was killed.[113] The Justice and Peace Commission of Gonaives called on the UN to replace its Nepalese soldiers in the city with other soldiers because of the tremendous animosity that had developed between the people and the soldiers.

In Cap-Haïtien,[114] demonstrators built barricades and searched for weapons. Some witnesses claimed that agitators provoked the demonstrators to violence. On November 13, a group of protesters attacked a radio station; on November 15, another group of protesters attacked the vehicle of a radio journalist who, on the air, had accused individuals of involvement in violence.

Lakhdar Brahimi, the UN special envoy in Haiti, promised that the UN peace-keeping forces would assist the Haitian police in carrying out the mandate of UN Resolution 940 to confiscate arms from people's homes and vehicles. Nevertheless, he criticized the action of demonstrators, stating, "The Constitution and the law say that it is the police [that maintain] order, and not . . . volunteers."[115] Yvon Neptune, palace spokesman and presidential press secretary, emphasized the legitimate right of people to defend themselves when threatened.[116]

NOVEMBER 20, 1995. President Aristide opened a National Dialogue Conference aimed at promoting dialogue on solutions to Haiti's major political, social, and economic problems, which had been planned since the June 25, 1995, parliamentary elections. In recognition of the historical divisions within Haitian society, the intent of the conference was to find common ground upon which all Haitians could advance within the context of a democratic society and the strictures of the Constitution. The conference opened with a tense moment, a broad array of representatives from across Haiti's political spectrum sitting in the same room. In his opening remarks, Aristide stated:

> Tonight, we are opening this dialogue. We have a big, big challenge to overcome. It's the capacity to speak to one another before we even have time to contradict each other. . . . Once we realize that democracy is not made up entirely of people who agree, but of people who have differences among them. At that moment, I will know we are off to a good start.[117]

Over the next several days, the conference increasingly focused on the growing, vehement demands of civic and popular organizations for Aristide to serve out his remaining three years in office. In Aristide's closing speech to the conference, he articulated his sensitivity to the concerns and demands of the people in comments that were misinterpreted internationally as intentions to serve out his remaining three years.[118] President Aristide later reconfirmed the elections would take place as scheduled.

NOVEMBER 23, 1995. An incident in Cité Soleil, one of Port-au-Prince's poorest neighborhoods, highlighted people's demands for security. A dispute broke out between a police officer and a bus driver. Shots rang out and a little girl standing nearby was killed.[119] Some reports stated that a man on a motorcycle fired the shots, and others stated that the policeman did so. The facts remain unclear. Residents reacted angrily and attacked the police station. At some point, units from the IPSF arrived and helped to restore calm. The police withdrew from Cité Soleil. Increasingly, reports have emerged of an armed gang of criminals, the "Red Army," wielding influence in Cité Soleil. The group may have played a role in this incident.

NOVEMBER 25–26, 1995. Although calm had largely been restored to the streets of Haiti, major media in the United States carried numerous articles and reports inaccurately portraying a situation of chaos and mob rule. The *New York Times*, for example, editorialized that, in an "episode of deliberately provoked terror, Mr. Aristide has shaken the fragile tranquility."[120] With the disarmament campaign having achieved only limited success, "tranquility" was not the word one would have used to describe the prevailing public sentiment in Haiti.

As the December 17 election approached, other outbreaks of armed violence made Haitians increasingly uneasy. In addition, revelations in international media reports about the hostility of U.S. agencies and officials toward the Aristide government fueled concerns in Haiti about the lack of international support for disarmament and the consolidation of the rule of law.[121]

U.S. Opposition to Democratic Changes in Haiti

While the U.S. government publicly professes its full support for the creation of a deliberative democracy in Haiti, several actions taken by U.S. government agencies seem to be working against that professed goal. Unless the United States supports the Haitian government in taking the steps needed to establish democracy, any vision of a deliberative democracy in Haiti will remain an illusion.

The CIA used practices in Haiti that are simply unacceptable in the intelligence service of a democratic society. It maintained foreign agents, or assets, on the payroll even after CIA officials had credible information that they were involved in assassination and torture. CIA officials hid information from relevant U.S. government officials and Congress, and directed a misinformation campaign against Aristide.

On a variety of fronts, the U.S. defense establishment, led by the CIA, is clearly continuing to oppose the democratization of Haiti. Indeed, these agencies are protecting the very military coup leaders and their supporting cadre that terrorized Haiti for so many decades. Several well-publicized and verified incidents support this position.

DOCUMENTS

In September of 1994, after the initial international intervention into Haiti, U.S. military forces confiscated a reported 100,000 pages of documents from the Haitian army's headquarters, and another 60,000 pages of documents and photographs, videos, and audiocassettes from the offices of the terrorist group FRAPH.[122] Though the documents were rightfully the property of the Haitian government, the U.S. Army officials who confiscated these records took them to the Defense Intelligence Agency (DIA) in Washington, D.C. Representatives of the Haitian government have repeatedly made oral requests for the documents since shortly after the return of President Aristide to Haiti in October of 1994. Finding itself in the absurd position of requesting its own property from the DIA, the Haitian government made written requests for the documents beginning in August of 1995. In addition to the Haitian government, Haitian human rights organizations and the National Truth and Justice Commission have also sought access to the documents.

The documents are thought to contain significant information both on the whereabouts of arms caches and on human rights violations. They may also contain information about the collaborative relationship between the U.S. government and the Haitian military and paramilitary forces. Ira Kurzban, U.S. counsel for the Republic of Haiti, was quoted by the *Washington Post*[123] as stating:

> The U.S. said, "If you tell us where the weapons are, we will search." But the truth is the reverse. The U.S. has vast amounts of intelligence. ... Why has not the information central to disarmament been shared by the United States? Why have documents central to human rights prosecutions not been turned over?[124]

In addition to the repeated requests for the return of the documents by Haitian government officials and other groups, forty members of the U.S. Congress sent a letter to President Clinton seeking "a complete account of all documents and their immediate return to the Haitian government."[125] The letter stated, "there is absolutely no justification why these materials should be in the hands of our government now that the legitimate government of Haiti has been restored. The fact that these documents have been withheld obviously raises questions about the level of collaboration between elements of the American government and the former military regime."[126] Over fifty representatives of U.S. nongovernmental, human rights, religious, and development organizations sent a similar letter to President Clinton.[127]

During the week of February 26, 1996, the State Department said that Haiti could have some of the documents, but only the "nonsensitive" ones, with the rest to be kept by Washington until the issue is resolved. The State Department has been pursuing Haiti to sign an eight-point "Memorandum of Understanding," which would place detailed restrictions on its right to use the documents.[128] The memo-

randum includes no assurance that the United States will return all
the materials and prohibits Haiti from making public "or otherwise
disseminat[ing]" any it does get if there is "a reasonable likelihood"
that there is a "risk" of causing "unlawful repercussions or abuses."
(This broad language, of course, would include acts of civil disobedi-
ence, such as sit-ins.)[129]

The Haitian government must further refrain from using the documents for its own policy purposes if these go beyond "law enforcement," "legal actions," or human rights investigations. These are,
in turn, to be limited to abuses that took place during the coup regime era. Probes of the U.S. backing of FRAPH or its leader, Emmanuel Constant, would, under the State Department's conditions, be
considered out of bounds. Finally, Haiti would be obliged to keep
and share detailed records on those who see the documents, and
accept the right of the United States to edit the materials as it wishes.
It is, of course, no surprise that neither President Aristide nor President Preval has accepted the documents under those conditions.

FALSE INFORMATION GIVEN TO U.S. TROOPS

A review of classified cables sent by the American embassy in Haiti
to the Defense and State Departments further solidifies strongly held
beliefs about the involvement of the United States with the former
de facto military regime and the U.S. opposition to democratic
change in Haiti.[130] These cables show that, for a year before the U.S.
invasion in September 1994, the Pentagon was well aware of the
abhorrent nature of FRAPH, with American intelligence agencies describing the group as a gang of "gun-carrying crazies."[131] Despite this
knowledge, and even months after the invasion, American officers
told their troops that the country's most dreaded paramilitary group
was a legitimate opposition political party. Radio broadcasts to U.S.
Special Forces units described Lavalas and FRAPH as competing political parties equally dedicated to the country's well-being. Human
rights observers even speculate that the military ordered American
troops to ignore human rights abuses committed before they arrived.
It is uncertain why the Pentagon took a public stance so clearly at
odds with the classified information it had collected in Haiti.

A Pentagon official denied any conflict by stating that there were
efforts in the initial weeks of the intervention to reduce the likelihood of violent confrontations. Emmanuel Constant, the founder of
FRAPH, stated that he was also under pressure from the United
States to help maintain stability.[132] Another accusatory explanation
for the inconsistent stance of the United States is that the Defense

Department and American intelligence agencies were attempting to weaken President Aristide, whom they have long distrusted. They may have also been trying to protect the Haitian informants who might be "useful" in the future.

These cables further indicate that the cooperation between the United States and FRAPH diminished only after U.S. troops intercepted a radio conversation between Constant and other leaders of FRAPH. According to a cable sent on October 3, 1994, FRAPH was "threatening to break out weapons and begin an all-out war against the foreigners" and "named an American official as [its] first target."[133] By January 1995, the State Department was vehemently denying any accusations linking the United States to FRAPH.

60 *Minutes:* FRAPH Leader Affirms Alliance with CIA

On December 3, 1995, Emmanuel Constant, the leader of FRAPH, appeared as a guest on the television program *60 Minutes*,[134] and claimed that he had been a paid employee of the CIA in Haiti from 1991 to 1994.[135] Secretary of State Warren Christopher did not deny this arrangement.

Constant agreed to appear on the program apparently because he was angry with the U.S. government for attempting to deport him to Haiti. Some time after the U.S. occupation of Haiti, Constant was surreptitiously allowed into the United States, but, after repeated demands by the Haitian government for his extradition,[136] the United States began deportation proceedings against him.

Constant's organization was in charge of the terror operation intended to keep Aristide from returning to Haiti. Constant claimed that the CIA encouraged him to provide damaging information about Aristide and that, from this information—certainly fictitious—the CIA created a psychological profile that portrayed Aristide as mentally unstable.[137]

The CIA clearly had a different agenda from President Clinton, for it subverted the president's Haitian policy. The *Harlan County* affair is an incident that serves to prove this assertion beyond doubt. On October 3, 1995, President Clinton sent a troop carrier (the USS *Harlan County*) to Haiti with several hundred American and Canadian soldiers on board. He sent the troops as part of a UN peace-keeping effort to return Aristide to power two weeks later. Although there were only forty protesters on the docks, President Clinton ordered the *Harlan County* to turn back because the CIA and the Pentagon warned the president that these protesters posed a threat to the safety of American soldiers. In point of fact, Constant had organized the demonstration, and he had briefed the CIA station chief in Haiti in advance, assuring him that no American lives would be in danger. Constant claims that he guaranteed the station chief "that the demonstration was simply a media frenzy he wanted to create. That has nothing to do [with hurting American soldiers]—no life was threatened."[138] If Constant is correct, the CIA lied to President Clinton, or Clinton chose to disregard the information. More importantly, if the U.S. and Canadian troops had landed, that action may have averted the U.S. military intervention that took place a year later. Furthermore, Constant claims that the CIA never confronted him about the murders attributed to FRAPH. Instead, he claims that the CIA made him feel that it was grooming him to be the next president of Haiti.[139]

This relationship between Constant and the U.S. government has recently been reinvigorated. According to a December 11, 1995, internal government memorandum, and interviews with informed officials, the United States made a special arrangement with Constant. It was to deport him back to Haiti eventually, and, when that occurred, to do so in a U.S. government plane complete with VIP security and no advance notice for the Haitian government. Regular Haitian airport workers were to be kept away from Constant's plane. Ground services in Haiti were to be provided by Brown & Root, the Pentagon contractor. Haitian Customs would be required to process him at an isolated location. Constant would then be the beneficiary of a program of "crowd control" and a "public affairs strategy" designed to urge Haitians "to remain calm despite the intensity of anti-FRAPH and anti-Constant sentiment."[140]

According to Allan Nairn, a reporter for the *Nation*, these arrangements were finalized on December 7, 1995, four days after Constant called Nairn from an INS prison in Maryland and offered to reveal everything about the relationship between the United States and FRAPH.[141] Nairn tried to follow up the phone call in person because Constant had insisted on a face-to-face meeting, but the INS denied Nairn access to Constant, "explaining that Constant had had a change of heart and no longer wanted to talk."[142]

The change of heart may have had something to do with another arrangement between Constant and the U.S. government. During the week of June 17, 1996, the INS released Constant from prison in Maryland and claimed that he would not be deported back to Haiti because the Haitian government feared that, if returned, Constant would cause serious security risks to the already fragile situation. The INS implied that the Haitian government requested that

Constant not be returned. President Preval has vigorously denied this claim. A variety of serious charges against Constant, including murder, are pending in Haiti. Preval claims that he wants Constant to return and to be tried on those charges. President Aristide has verified Preval's account.[143]

It appears that the claims of Aristide and President Preval are accurate, and that the United States has a different agenda than it has publicly proclaimed. Indeed, when U.S. officials released Constant from INS detention in June 1996, it was part of a secret arrangement that essentially guarantees Constant he will never be deported to Haiti to face the overwhelmingly credible charges of numerous political murders and tortures. Under the agreement, Constant was released into the custody of his mother, who lives in Brooklyn. He is free to live and work in the United States provided that he does not speak publicly about his past association with the CIA. He is also free to emigrate to any country he wants.

The agreement to release him was drawn up by the State Department, INS, Justice Department, and National Security Council. In exchange for his release, Constant dropped a lawsuit against Secretary of State Warren Christopher, in which he claimed to have collaborated with the CIA to make Aristide appear to be a political extremist. In the lawsuit, Constant also claimed that the CIA knew in advance about FRAPH's plan to protest when the first troops arrived in Haiti on the USS *Harlan County*, and that the CIA was intimately connected with FRAPH.

Taking a position that lacks any credibility, the State Department claims that the CIA relationship was not a consideration in the deal to release Constant. The decision to release him, however, clearly contradicts Christopher's stated position. In a March 29, 1995, letter to Attorney General Janet Reno, seeking Constant's arrest, Christopher stated: "Nothing short of Mr. Constant's removal from the United States can protect our foreign policy interests in Haiti."[144]

A recently obtained CIA report issued in 1993 adds considerable weight to the claim that the United States cut a deal with Constant because it feared that he would reveal the unpleasant details of his relationship with the CIA. The CIA withheld much of the report until the week of October 6, 1996, when the document was obtained from the CIA in pretrial proceedings in a lawsuit filed in the United States by Alerte Belance, a Haitian woman who claims she was severely wounded three years ago by four hatchet-wielding FRAPH agents.

The secret CIA report, titled *Haiti's Far Right: Taking the Offensive*, names Emmanuel Constant in connection with the assassination of the justice minister, Guy Malary. It is dated October 28, 1993, two weeks after Malary's murder. It has consecutive sentences mentioning Mr. Constant or FRAPH in connection with the killing. The first sentence says that the Haitian junta's chief of staff, General Philippe Biamby, "and his associates coordinated the murder of Justice Minister Guy Malary, which took place on 14 October, with members of FRAPH."[145] The second sentence says that Mr. Constant and other members of FRAPH met "on the morning of 14 October to discuss plans to kill Malary."[146] At the least, the CIA knew who killed Malary and never informed the democratically elected Haitian government of that fact.

REPORTS OF U.S. SPECIAL FORCES ASSISTING FRAPH AND THE HAITIAN ARMY IN HIDING WEAPONS

Two well-respected newspapers, the *Washington Post*[147] and the *Village Voice*,[148] issued reports about a newsletter called, "The Resister, The Official Publication of the Special Forces Underground," an extreme-right-wing publication whose publishers say they are active and recently retired U.S. Special Forces troops. These reports raise other serious concerns about what the United States is actually doing, and which groups it is actively supporting, in Haiti. The *Village Voice* describes an article on Haiti in "The Resister" published in January 1994 in the following terms:

> Under an editor's note that reads, "The following is a synthesis of several reports forwarded by our members currently deployed to Haiti," the report outlines how "[i]mmediately upon arrival in an operational area [they] met with senior non-commissioned officers of the Fad'H and arranged a meeting with senior representatives of Fad'H, attaches and FRAPH. . . . This was not as easy as it sounds given the treatment these groups had received in Port-au-Prince and Cap Haitian in late September. It called for a very blunt cold-pitch describing [their] hatred of communism and [their] official mission."
>   The unsigned article goes on to describe how attaches and FRAPH members were advised to go underground or take "long vacations"; how "[they] informed them about the plans and timetables for weapons confiscation and told them how to disappear their functional firearms while keeping . . . otherwise useless weapons available to sell during the weapons buy-back program."
>   The piece also describes how Special Forces waged "a clandestine offensive against the Lavalas . . . which in [their] operational areas

managed to drive at least the leadership underground." Finally, it said, "[they] have established an escape line to help Fad'H, ex-attaches and ex-FRAPH members under threat of arrest from the communists reach relative safety in the Dominican Republic."[149]

Leslie Voltaire, President Aristide's chief of staff, speaking about this report, stated: "We cannot comment on the authenticity of the Resister. However, the ramifications of its claims, if true, are so serious for the future security of the Haitian people that we feel it merits further investigation. Unfortunately, there is a correlation between details cited in this document and events that have taken place in Haiti during the past year."[150] Moreover, "[a]lmost from the beginning of the occupation, it was clear that Special Forces troops, mostly deployed outside the capital, viewed FRAPH as friends, not as the thugs and rights abusers described by the State Department and human rights organizations. They talked to reporters about dealing with FRAPH as a legitimate political party and the need for remnants of the Haitian army and police to impose order."[151]

Sources Assert that the United States Blocks Investigation of Coup Crimes

Despite the U.S. government assistance in reforming the Haitian judicial system, certain agencies of the U.S. government have sometimes interfered in the prosecutions of those who are responsible for the approximately five thousand assassinations and other massive human rights abuses that took place in Haiti during the coup regime. The most infamous and well publicized example of this interference is the Marcel Morissaint case.[152]

In the course of extensive interviews, Morissaint gave up a great deal of information on a variety of issues. According to him, he was a member of the Anti-Gang Unit of the police department headed by Michel François. The Anti-Gang Unit's sole functions were to smuggle narcotics and commit political assassinations. Morissaint was not only a member of the Anti-Gang Unit, but also an informant for the Drug Enforcement Administration (DEA) of the United States and for the CIA. He said that people in the U.S. embassy recruited him. He reported to two men at the U.S. embassy in Port-au-Prince, both of whom were African-Americans, who spoke fluent Creole. One apparently worked for the DEA, and the other worked for the CIA. Morissaint claimed that Jackson Joanis, then head of the Anti-Gang Unit, and others, were heavily involved in drug smuggling. These men reported to François, who headed the drug-smuggling operations. This unit imported the drugs—almost exclusively co-caine—from Colombia and exported them to the United States. He implied that the DEA was directly involved in this activity.

Furthermore, Morissaint claimed that he was a member of Zel Sekey, a special Anti-Gang team. Major Renault was the commander of this group. Renault worked under Joanis and François. The team reported directly to Joanis. The other members of Zel Sekey were Eric Avril, Lionel Cadet, Lieutenant Cesar Abellard, and Salem. Every one of these men and other members of the Anti-Gang Unit were heavily involved in the illegal drug activity. Morissaint claimed that Eric Avril actually shot Guy Malary, and that Lionel Cadet, Lieutenant Cesar Abellard, and Salem all took part in the assassination. He claimed that he participated in a discussion of Malary's murder at the Anti-Gang headquarters when he heard the above-mentioned people talking about it. According to Morissaint, Eric Avril said: "The only regret I have is that one of us was wounded." Marcel Morissaint further claimed, of course, that he was not involved in Guy Malary's assassination. He did not wish to testify against anyone regarding drug activity because, he said, "if you testify in a drug case, you and your family are dead." He was also reluctant to testify against anyone involved in Guy Malary's assassination because he feared for his life.

U.S. embassy officials visited Morissaint several times while he was incarcerated. They promised to get him out of prison. They allegedly wanted to bring him to the United States to testify against a Haitian drug czar.

On September 13, 1995, I learned from the Haitian minister of justice, Jean-Joseph Exumé, that, during the week of either August 31 or September 7, Marcel Morissaint had been taken by U.S. troops (or officials) from the Petionville Prison, allegedly to be tried for a robbery. They had taken Morissaint to a hotel, and, the next day, they released him. U.S. officials told Exumé that Morissaint had escaped. According to Exumé, Marcel Morissaint is now in the United States. Exumé would not tell me how he obtained this information. He did not know who took Marcel Morissaint from prison, who in the Haitian government authorized his release, who released him, or any other details.[153]

According to Allan Nairn,[154] U.S. embassy officials have confirmed that Morissaint collaborated with the CIA while working as an attaché for the police. Morissaint was a suspect in the Malary assassination and was receiving money from the U.S. embassy at the time of the assassination.

On March 7, 1997, some of Morissaint's allegations were directly verified when Joseph Michel François was indicted in Miami on charges that he helped smuggle 66,000 pounds of cocaine and heroin into the United States. As one of the de facto leaders, François placed the political and military structure of Haiti under his control to ship the drugs from Columbia through Haiti into the United States.[155]

A former lieutenant colonel and son of a member of the presidential guard that served ex-dictator François Duvaliér, François was trained by the U.S. army at its infamous School of the Americas. As the chief of police in Port-au-Prince, he controlled death squads, vigilante gangs, and vicious plainclothes police (attachés) during the junta's three-year rule. Under his direction, those forces killed thousands of people in an effort to keep the junta in power by repressing Aristide's supporters—the vast majority of Haitians. François was convicted *in absentia* by a Haitian court for his part in the 1993 assassination of Antoine Izméry.

As police chief with a monthly salary of $500, François managed to build a grand villa in Petionville, Port-au-Prince's wealthiest neighborhood. U.S. officials said that he took payoffs for everything of value that entered Haiti's ports, from cement to narcotics.[156] The 41-page indictment charges that François' wealth came in part from his role in plotting to ship 33 tons of cocaine and heroin into the United States. The indictment made the scheme appear easy.

According to the indictment, François's career in drugs began in 1987 when, as a representative of the Haitian military, he received a payoff of between $1 million and $4 million to protect Columbian cocaine shipments. François and his Columbian cocaine connection, Fernando Burgos-Martinez, built an airstrip on the property of a Haitian colonel, Jean Claude Paul, as a landing pad for airplanes loaded with Columbian cocaine. The indictment alleges that François was trusted to courier millions of dollars in illicit profits from the Medellin, Baranquilla, and Cali cartels to pay off the military for use of the private airstrip, supervised off-loading operations, and arranged for storage facilities and the transfer of narcotics to maritime vessels and aircraft in Haiti for importation into the United States. Indeed, after the 1991 coup put François in power, cocaine seizures in Haiti plummeted to near zero.

François installed his friend Marc Valme as chief of security at Port-au-Prince International Airport. According to the indictment, nine people were allowed to smuggle drugs to Miami on commercial flights with the complicity of Valme and his officers. When they arrived in Miami, they received a similar welcome from Evans Gourge, a security officer at Miami International Airport, who made sure they bypassed Customs officials. The thirty-three tons of drugs were distributed in Miami, New York, and Chicago.

Burgos-Martinez, Valme, and Gourge were indicted along with François. Also named in the indictment were Menard Saul, Pierrot Bauvais, Guy Plantin, Derrick Vaughn Maddox, Jean Toussaint, Reginald Molin, Fritz LaFonte, Beaudouin Ketant, and Frantz Cadet. The defendants are charged with conspiracy to possess with intent to distribute cocaine, conspiracy to import narcotics, conspiracy to launder monetary instruments, money laundering, and operating a continuing criminal enterprise. If convicted, each defendant faces a maximum penalty of life imprisonment and a $4 million fine.

With the return of the democratically elected government in October 1994, François fled to the Dominican Republic. He was arrested there in April 1996 by the Dominican Republic authorities and accused of plotting another coup in Haiti. He then left for Honduras, where he was given asylum, but the Honduran authorities helped take part in his arrest. Nevertheless, as of June 1997, François remained in Honduras, successfully fighting the U.S. government's request for his extradition.

A 1994 Justice Department memorandum named François as a target in the cocaine-smuggling case, along with senior members of the Service Intelligence National, a Haitian intelligence organization. The group, founded in 1986 with help from the CIA, was supposedly dedicated to anti-drug efforts.[157] None of the CIA-connected officers was arrested for the drug smuggling, nor was Raul Cédras, the leader of the junta. Information provided to the United States in relation to this case, however, strongly links Cédras to the drug-smuggling operations. Two jailed members of a Columbian cartel have told Justice Department investigators that François and Cédras attended a 1987 party at a ranch in Columbia, thrown to celebrate the Haitian drug connection.[158] The jailed cartel members, Enrique Arroyave and Carlos Marcantoni, who have been federal witnesses in several cocaine cases, told the investigators that the celebration marked the shipment of 66,000 pounds of cocaine into Haiti—the same amount alleged in the indictment. They said Cédras and François, among other senior Haitian military officials at the party, were paid $10 million for their help with the shipments.

Public Security

After the ouster of the de facto regime and the return of democratically elected governance to Haiti, the international community, the

MNF (particularly the United States), and the Aristide government took several steps to reform the institution of public security. The Preval government must continue these efforts. Indeed, the effectiveness of these reforms for the demilitarization of public order is crucial to the creation of a democracy in Haiti. Success will depend upon reforming the police, purging the army and continuing to keep it disbanded, and preventing the paramilitary forces from attempting to regain power through violence. Without security, a deliberative democracy remains a distant dream.

THE POLICE

From the first day of Aristide's reinstatement, Haitians have strongly voiced their objection to the continued involvement of former members of FAD'H in the IPSF and the National Police Force. Nevertheless, recycled FAD'H personnel made up three-quarters of IPSF. The unstated reason for this continued involvement was the concern of the United States and the international community about the need to maintain established institutions and ensure political and ideological counterbalance. The stated reasons, voiced by officials—some Haitian—and by the international community, were that these individuals would bring a degree of experience to the job and that their involvement would discourage violent activities of a major group of disaffected and potentially destabilizing individuals in the society at large. Both of these latter reasons are seriously flawed.

In Haiti, police trainers employ two key criteria for judging the suitability of recruits: competence and training receptivity. A comparison in these two key areas of the two groups that made up the IPSF—recycled FAD'H members and the Guantanamo recruits—illustrates this point. Employing almost any scale to judge these groups and factors—for example, on a scale of flawed to perfect—the recycled FAD'H members measured flawed in competence and flawed in receptivity. The Guantanamo recruits also measured flawed in competence, but they measured perfect in receptivity. The emphasis on IPSF recruitment, however, was almost exclusively placed on former members of FAD'H. Moreover, they were assigned to the most visible duties.[159] The Guantanamo recruits, initially included only because of the strong insistence of the Aristide government, were assigned to low-profile work. Thus, from a technical police-training perspective, the emphasis on using recycled FAD'H members was simply not a rational policy.

In response to the stated reasons for employing FAD'H members—recognition of their experience and the need to discourage them from destabilizing the government—USAID created a program for the training and reinsertion into society of FAD'H members who were not selected for public security programs. In mid-1994, USAID projected a budget for 4,000 former FAD'H members to enroll in this program.[160] Thus, the program was budgeted to absorb many, but not all, of the former FAD'H members who were not integrated into IPSF.

This was, however, only a short-term solution to a longer-term problem. President Aristide, of course, took decisive action in this area, and on November 30, 1994, he named Dr. Jean-Marie Fourel Celestin, a former armed forces colonel and physician at the Military Hospital, as director of the National Police Force.[161] The move was part of the broader efforts to improve the discipline and performance of the police force. Celestin was a member of President Aristide's personal security force in 1991, was forced into exile during the coup regime years, and served as the director of security for the National Palace after the restoration of constitutional order.

Aristide took other steps. On December 5, he issued a presidential decree formally dissolving the IPSF. Over the years, as classes of the newly trained National Police Force have graduated, members of the IPSF have been demobilized. Each month, the government first demobilized the members of the IPSF about whom complaints had been received or whose performances were poor, while retaining the best-performing members with the greatest demonstrated respect for human rights. Of the original number of around 3,000 persons in the IPSF, the government demobilized 750 of them during the first week of December 1994. It transferred the 100 remaining most effective members into the permanent police force. Another approximately 225 persons were designated to duty as unarmed palace guards, separate from the police force and with no other policing functions. Another 900–1,000 police originally recruited from the Guantanamo refugee camp were transferred into the police force. Approximately 400 members of this group will be traffic police in Port-au-Prince, and approximately 500 of them will be trained as rural police. The rural police will eventually be placed under the authority of local elected officials, and will replace the hated section-chief system.

All police will continue to be subject to review if they do not perform up to standards and if complaints are filed against them. Promotions will be made according to performance and respect for human rights and the Haitian Constitution.

Many Haitians continue to argue that the police force is in dire need of more training and experience if it is to eradicate a nearly 200-year tradition of arbitrary behavior and brutality.[162] Furthermore, the United States, while privately encouraging the reintegration of FAD'H into the police force, publicly took action to voice its opposition to Aristide's decision to integrate 1,400 ex-soldiers and other political loyalists into the police force. On December 23, 1995, five congressmen stated that they were freezing $5 million in United States aid for training the National Police Force. In January, however, Congress decided to release the funds, conditioning the release on the expectation that rights violators and others with criminal backgrounds would be screened out.[163]

As a solution to this much-debated issue of security, Canada offered to send in military peace-keepers for another six months after the scheduled departure of UN peace-keeping troops, in order to help maintain stability in Haiti.[164] There was a hope that the handover to Canada might even placate the Haitian elites who have criticized the American-led UN mission as a U.S. occupation in disguise.[165] This speculation was, however, unfounded, especially considering the fact that the United States plans to continue its support for the Haitian police academy by rotating in engineers, road-builders, and the like on training missions.[166] USAID will also continue to operate in Haiti, along with the Department of Justice police-training program.[167]

All of these plans and programs notwithstanding, the fact remains that when the UN peace-keeping force leaves Haiti, these former FAD'H members will once again represent a potentially disaffected, destabilizing group. Yet possible solutions to this problem do exist. One of the most promising comes from a group of Haitian peasants. Upon learning that USAID had set aside approximately $12 million for these reintegration efforts, this group spontaneously suggested that the money be used to sponsor such programs as soil conservation and reforestation, which will help rebuild the country. The peasants have stated that they would work in these programs with former FAD'H members. Their idea is that unnamed FAD'H members must help to rebuild the country they have destroyed and, at the same time, become reintegrated into the society.[168] This is a wonderful example of direct democracy in action.

The Army

The 1987 Haitian Constitution mandates that the country maintain an army, and as President Aristide has pointed out repeatedly, some form of army must exist until the Constitution is legally amended.[169] Since the return of President Aristide in October 1994, public opinion in Haiti urging an abolition of the army has been almost universal. Consistent with this strong sentiment, and notwithstanding its previous plan for a reformed 1,500-member force, the Aristide government enacted a series of reforms that virtually dissolved the Haitian army by February 1995.[170] By June, the army had been effectively reduced to a fifty-man presidential band.[171] The problem remains, however, as to what to do with the purged members of FAD'H. Indeed, during President Preval's term, these disaffected former army members have waged a campaign of violence.

PARAMILITARY FORCES

In order for Haiti to achieve significant and sustainable demilitarization of public order, decisive steps must be taken to confront the paramilitary forces—rural affiliates of section chiefs or urban attachés—that remain underground. Disarmament has not occurred because the United States, the MNF, and UN peace-keeping force refused to alter their position against disarmament. Haitian authorities, of course, simply do not have the power to disarm these forces by themselves. Moreover, complete disarmament may be impractical, if not almost impossible, because Haiti shares a porous border with the Dominican Republic and because huge weapons caches are hidden across Haiti.

Given this reality, the most effective strategy may be to pursue individuals rather than weapons. The theory is that, once their impunity to sponsor or undertake terrorist and criminal acts is challenged by the aggressive and systematic application of legal prosecutions, Haiti's paramilitary forces will recede into the background. Indeed, there have been some positive developments along those lines. For example, for the first time in Haitian history, an attaché ("Zimbabwe") has been convicted of murder for a political assassination committed during the coup period.[172] Emmanuel Constant, a former FRAPH leader, has been arrested in the United States and found to be deportable. (Although it is highly unlikely that he will be deported, if he is, he will stand trial for committing human rights violations, including murder.[173]) Finally, the Special Investigative Units, created during Aristide's term, continue into Preval's administration to concentrate on investigations of serious human rights violations.[174]

This strategy of prosecuting individuals depends, of course, on the existence of a functioning police force and justice system, as well as secure prisons. It also requires a strong linkage among police, judicial officials, and community-based civic-society organizations. The latter groups, which are among the most developed elements of Haitian society, could be called on to help create accountability, partnership, and oversight.

Because the National Police, judiciary, and prison system remain insufficiently developed to perform these tasks, the international community's help is crucial. For example, following the transition from the MNF to the UN peace-keepers, the latter took responsibility for the security of Haitian prisons, and they now share the responsibility of running the prisons with Haitian officials. Current improvements in prison security will have to be maintained when the UN peace-keepers leave Haiti. Moreover, international assistance must not give mixed signals to the paramilitary forces.

The international community needs to help Haitian officials find, obtain evidence against, and prosecute the most notorious human rights violators. The United States must play a central role in this crucial task because the Haitian government is simply not yet able to prosecute effectively those who have committed serious human rights abuses without help. The United States should begin this process by arresting Emmanuel Constant and deporting him to Haiti. There is no lack of precedent for doing so. Between October 1995 and July 1996, the United States deported more than 130 Haitians, ninety-four of whom had criminal records. Moreover, according to the UN Convention against Torture, which both the United States and Haiti have signed, if the United States does not return Constant, then it has to try him in the States, "as if [the offences] had been committed not only in the place in which they occurred" but also in the United States.[175] In addition, the United States should demand that other countries do the same with the Haitian killers whom they are harboring. Cédras is in "golden" exile in Panama. Michel François, who was arrested in Honduras in April 1997 after being indicted in the United States on drug smuggling charges, and the loathed former mayor of Port-au-Prince, Franck Romain, both received asylum in Honduras. Ex-dictator Prosper Avril was rumored to have an offer of asylum from Israel, one of Haiti's key arms suppliers. Finally, the United States should take steps to support Haiti's U.S.-trained police in disarming and prosecuting the thugs still living in Haiti.

THE ECONOMY

As described above, the basic necessities for a life of dignity do not exist for the overwhelming majority of Haitians. Haiti remains a land of widespread abject poverty, where the people face devastating levels of disease (including epidemics), malnutrition, unemployment, and environmental destruction. The epistemic theory of democracy, however, demands an economic structure that can alleviate these disastrous circumstances. Without an economy that attacks these serious maladies, Haiti has very little chance of surviving as a nation, and almost no chance of becoming a functioning democracy. This section thus focuses on Haiti's opportunities for economic development.

The Inter-American Development Bank Loan for Emergency Programs

In December 1995, the IDB announced its approval of a loan for $50 million to support the second phase of an emergency program to "revive the economy and rehabilitate the basic physical and social infrastructure" of Haiti.[176] Funds have been earmarked for repairing ports and roads, drainage, irrigation facilities, markets, hospitals, government buildings, electricity, and drinking water. The funds will also support reforestation as well as coffee- and fruit-production projects. The loan will be administered by the Central Implementation Unit in the prime minister's office. This is a very important loan for Haiti. Without it, the economic prospects would clearly be disastrous. The loan also acts as an incentive for Haiti and the international community to come to agreement on other development issues.

Negotiations with the International Financial Institutions and Privatization

Since Aristide's reinstatement to office, the government of Haiti has been seeking to negotiate a new letter of intent with the World Bank, which would outline the policy framework to be adopted during the period 1995–98 under the Structural Adjustment Program. Approximately $100 million in balance-of-payments support from the international community hinges on this agreement. Simultaneously, Haitian civil society continues to pressure for economic policies responsive to the needs and realities of Haiti's overwhelmingly poor majority.

In spite of the tremendous progress made by the Haitian government in implementing economic reforms and complying with benchmarks of the international financial institutions, the U.S. government continued, as late as December 1996, to withhold some $4,600,000 in balance-of-payments support committed for the 1994 fiscal year.[177] The United States seeks rapid privatization of state-owned enterprises, but the Haitian Parliament has shown some reluctance to pass all of the necessary supporting legislation, including antitrust legislation. The population continues to express concerns that privatization be carried out in a manner that does not undermine the prospects for national development and democracy. Additionally, many Haitians believe that it is unfair for the international community to expect a nation emerging from decades of dictatorship and military rule to move too quickly to privatize, given the social cost of the measures.[178]

Most of the economic aid package has been on hold since 1994, specifically because (first) Aristide and (then) Preval refused to sign the economic reform pact of the IMF, which called for the Haitian government to privatize nine state industries.[179] Over time, however, President Preval seemingly changed his mind and put his support behind the plan to privatize these industries. In May 1996, he apparently reached a preliminary agreement on economic reforms with the IMF and the World Bank, which could lead to the injection of more than $1 billion in badly needed foreign assistance over the following three years.

On October 18, 1996, the IMF board approved the agreement with the Haitian government. This will allow a three-year, $131 million loan to support economic reform. On November 5, 1996, Haiti received the first installment of $22 million. The new aid funds are expected to inject more money into the economy and enable the government to pay long-overdue salaries of public employees, who have become increasingly militant in demanding back pay. In addition, they were unhappy because the Haitian government has maintained a tight money policy, reducing liquidity and refusing to print any new currency in order to keep inflation under control.

As of June 1996, the Haitian Parliament had not yet voted to ratify the agreement.[180] On September 25, 1996, the Senate passed a bill designed to streamline the bureaucracy, which is a crucial step toward receiving $226 million in foreign aid.[181] In the midst of domestic and international pressures, the Haitian Parliament finally passed legislation privatizing the nine state-run enterprises: the Senate passed a bill on August 9, 1996, by a majority of eleven to one (two abstentions), and, after some debate,[182] the 83-seat lower house passed a similar measure on September 5, by a majority of thirty-five to ten.[183]

Parliament's passage of all of this reform legislation is critically important because it complies with the requirements of the agreements made with the IMF and because it sets the stage for privatization. Total privatization, however, is not allowed. The three options now available to the private sector are management contracts, concessions, and capitalization or joint ventures, similar to those undertaken by Bolivia. Concession contracts, however, require parliamentary approval.

The privatization legislation calls for the naming of a five-member commission to oversee the privatization process. Three of the five members will come from the government, one will represent the private sector, and another will represent labor. An existing privatization unit within the prime minister's office will function as the commission's technical arm. The commission's responsibility will be to identify the enterprises to be privatized, the formula to be used in that process, and to accept and award bids.[184]

It is clear that Haiti will soon begin to privatize many of its state industries. Erns Exeus, chief of privatization in the Haitian prime minister's office, has consistently recognized that privatization is essential if Haiti is to modernize its economy.[185] In particular, Exeus has recognized the need to privatize the electric industry. Presently, Haiti's electric company, EDH, a state monopoly, has a production capacity of 217 megawatts, of which only 101 have been functioning. The projected demand by the year 2004 is 1,250 megawatts. It is estimated that by 2000, $970 million will be needed for electricity alone.[186]

Another possible investment opportunity is the telephone company. At present, TELECO has only 55,000 lines serving the entire country of 7 million people, and there is a waiting list of 130,000 persons, who must wait for an average six and a half years. Projected demand by the year 2004 is 288,000 lines. Exeus estimates that a $500 million investment is needed in telecommunications over the next five years.[187]

The transportation industry also needs an infusion of capital. The port of Port-au-Prince, which is the most expensive port at which to dock and unload in the Americas, costs a ship at least $50,000 before it even begins to unload, compared with $1,275 in the Dominican Republic. This, of course, causes ships to unload their goods in the Dominican Republic, and, further, leads to the smuggling of most of the goods destined for Haiti. A $120 million investment is necessary to make the port competitive. Finally, the airport is reported to require $40 million in renovations simply to accommodate international travelers.[188]

Compounding these financial difficulties is the problem of refugees. An increased tide of boat people will certainly be triggered by cuts in international loans. Indeed, the apprehension of 1,000 Haitian boat people in the last week of November 1995 was considered to be a "warning sign" by most Haitians that the withholding of $4,600,000 in economic aid by the United States, and the $45 million in loans by the World Bank and IMF, is taking a toll on the Haitian people.[189] Thus, this issue leaves President Preval the arduous task of balancing two constituencies—one of them being his domestic political followers who oppose free-market reforms, and the other being the international donor nations seeking market reforms.

While money for particular projects continues to flow (such as the IDB loan mentioned above), the government has received no balance-of-payments support from the international community since the beginning of the fiscal year in October 1995. This support is used to maintain basic governmental functions and to import vital goods, such as petroleum.

These economic concerns have combined to affect the currency. After a dangerous devaluation of the gourde (Haiti's currency) against the U.S. dollar, it has rebounded, at least in part, because of intervention by the Haitian Central Bank. In the last several months of 1995, for example, the gourde had devalued from 15 gourdes to the dollar, to 20 gourdes to the dollar;[190] yet, in December 1995, it stood at about 16 gourdes to the dollar. A devaluation of the gourde undermines the purchasing power of average Haitians for food and other basic goods, particularly those that have some import component. This, of course, covers nearly all goods in Haiti. Changes must be made, and soon, or the economic problems will accelerate.

Privatization: What Does it Mean?

The hope for economic reform that will benefit the Haitian people seems to hinge on the privatization plan. Haitians, however, are not clear on what that plan is, how it is to operate, or even if it will improve their living conditions.

In fact, the plan that the Preval administration is sponsoring does not allow for privatization in the real sense of the term. Rather, Preval's economic planners worked out an arrangement with the international lending community, including the World Bank, that involves a scheme of joint ventures. The existing state businesses merge with foreign investors, who must commit themselves to putting up money, technological know-how, and management.[191] The theory is that this scheme will leave the actual Haitian assets in the hands of the state. At the same time, however, critics of the plan are correct in claiming that any future development of these assets will be controlled largely by the desires of foreign management.

The joint venture system is being overseen by a new organization—the Sociétés d'Économie Mixte—made up of cabinet ministers and public representatives, and headed by Rosny Smarth, the Haitian prime minister. According to one Preval adviser,[192] foreign companies that have indicated their interest in participating in joint ventures include the large American telephone companies—AT&T, MCI, Sprint, and Southern Bell—France's Telecom, and the United Kingdom's telecommunications giant, BT. In the electricity industry, Smith Co-generation, EDF, and Hydro-Quebec have all shown interest in Haiti and have been negotiating with the Haitian government. There are also plans to reestablish Port-au-Prince Airport as a major Caribbean concern. France's Bordeaux Airport Authority has shown the greatest interest in running its operations. Cemex, an American-Mexican concern, Holder Bank, and La Farge all want to become involved in reviving the cement business. Jamaican Flour, Maple Leaf, and Continental are interested in the flour mills. An unnamed U.S. firm has shown an interest in managing the ports. Moreover, at some point in the near future, the Haitian government intends to rebuild its tourist industry, which flourished after World War II, its assembly plants, and its small artisan enterprises. Haiti hopes to obtain $800 million in overall support from the international community, with up to $130 million of that amount to be used to reduce its current balance of payments.

While opposition to the joint venture scheme does exist, many analysts claim that it is not intense or widespread. In support of this claim, they cite a highly promoted demonstration against privatization during the week of May 6, 1996, that attracted fewer than five hundred people. Many Haitians, however, claim that the opposition to privatization is quite strong. There have been strikes and demonstrations against the plan in Port-au-Prince. In addition, in the countryside there appears to be little support for the plan. Indeed, many of the rural people believe that it allows for foreign domination of their only resources.

Whatever the extent of the opposition, it did not stop the government from implementing privatization plans. Politicians representing urban areas spoke often of their fears of mass unemployment unless something was done soon. If this was to be avoided, they argued, the Parliament had to approve the plan to privatize, at the latest before the end of fall of 1996. In fact, Parliament did finally respond to these concerns by passing the necessary legislation on September 5.

One crucial element to the success or failure of the plan will be the role played by the elite families, who, for generations, have provided the economic and social link between Haiti's rulers and the international community. They have acted as brokers between Haiti's declining commodity base and the international business interests in Europe and America. In the original World Bank plan, these families were to be denied any real participation in the new economy. Presently, however, the Haitian government and the World Bank are studying the possibility of letting them invest in the joint ventures. The reason for this is clear: these families are the only people in Haiti with the capital and know-how to make privatization work.

Although the Preval government needs help from the elite families, it does not want to give them any real economic power over the plan. A top government official, who is participating in the World Bank negotiations, claims that Preval's plan is to allow them to make their money in banking, industrial parks, and perhaps as agents for automobile insurance, but at the same time isolate them from involvement in the other major industries.[193]

Nobody is quite sure how all of this will work out. Despite the fact that they can no longer count upon the military to secure their operations, the elite families still control disproportionate amounts of Haiti's wealth. One reason for this, of course, is that they do not pay taxes. Things may be about to change, however. For example, around a hundred young and upcoming Haitian businesspeople, educated in the United States and France, and calling themselves "Le Group," have recently organized in an attempt to compete with the old elite families. Richard Coles, who himself is the son of a family that dominates several major businesses, particularly the soft drinks business, leads "Le Group" and openly attacks the older patriarchs. "On a project worth three million dollars," Coles says in disgust, "these guys would rather spend three hundred thousand dollars in bribing public officials than in paying their taxes."[194] In the new Haiti, paying taxes, it seems, is one of the foundation stones (even though it means a lower profit margin) for establishing credibility for these young but highly motivated businesspeople. Whether this organization, if and when it gains economic clout, will help redistribute resources is, of course, unclear.

Nevertheless, there have been attempts by the Haitian government and the international financial organizations to increase investments in Haiti and, at the same time, to collect taxes. During the first two weeks of May 1996, for example, the World Bank officiated at meetings between local businesspeople and the government. These officials strongly encouraged the businesspeople to invest in a free-market system. At the same time, President Preval, for the first time, began to collect taxes. He began this unenviable task by threatening to shut down the businesses of those people who were not paying the required taxes. He actually wound up seizing business properties. In May and June 1996, the government's tax collectors directly confronted former Duvaliérist Gerald Khawly, a businessman who had reputedly made a small fortune during the 1991–94 embargo by selling pirated gasoline. The government claimed that Khawly owed millions of gourdes in back taxes and therefore seized several of his high-priced vehicles—two of his Mercedes and two of his Volvos—along with several of his trucks. Government officials are now planning to shut down his entire operation if he fails to pay his back taxes.

This is an unprecedented step in Haiti. Preval is treading on dangerous ground. Initially, however, this action seems to have had a positive effect. When Preval announced his new get-tough tax collection policy and took this action, delinquent taxpayers came forward and paid $500,000 during the first day of the policy. Only several days later, the government collected the sum of $800,000. By the end of the first week, the government had collected $1,300,000. This unprecedented action is certainly a positive sign that business is going to cooperate with Preval's policy.

While this collection policy seems to be working, not all of the elite families are going along with Preval's plans. Instead, they are working hard to maintain their absolute control over the Haitian economy. Some of the most prominent families have been proposing ambitious plans to build an electrical production plant with Florida Power & Light.[195] They have also spoken of setting up a propane factory with a marine terminal that will act as a transit hub for shipping that flows to and from the Panama Canal through the Windward Passage, one of the world's busiest shipping channels. These families have the advantage of years of experience in maintaining power in Haiti. Recently they have taken on a new role of influence by becoming counsels to foreign governments, such as Panama, Denmark, and Israel.[196]

These problems are compounded by another, perhaps more serious, phenomenon. The real economy of Haiti—the cash-driven black market—threatens to turn Haiti into a department store for smuggled cars, bikes, guns, and, worst of all, illegal drugs. Indeed, it is no exaggeration to claim that Port-au-Prince traffic jams have become a metaphor for the new economy of Haiti. This can be traced to an influx of cars from the United States, nearly all from Florida and New Jersey. Almost unbelievably, in 1995, approximately seventeen thousand cars were imported into the poorest country in the hemisphere. This is a country with very few paved roads, even in Port-au-Prince. Moreover, the roads that are paved are riddled with potholes. The population of Port-au-Prince has overrun the streets. Driving is hazardous and huge traffic jams are the order of the day. In addition, according to a U.S. federal investigator who spends his time checking Haiti's piers for smuggled cargo, one out of every four cars imported into Haiti is stolen.[197] The cars are shipped in at night and unloaded at numerous piers belonging to the elite families. Some of the cars remain in Haiti; others are driven across the almost open border into the Dominican Republic.

Who can afford these cars? Despite its poverty, Haiti has a small upper-middle class numbering approximately one hundred thousand people. Many of these people have grown rich either from the sale of drugs or from smuggling gasoline during the recent 1991–94 UN embargo. This has created a thriving market for new cars. There are also approximately one million Haitian expatriates living in the United States, who buy cars and send them to relatives in Haiti. An entrepreneurial group of brokers has evolved around this trade. They essentially bundle up new cars and stolen vehicles into bulk shipments.

The car-smuggling problem is, however, only a small part of the overall smuggling trade that is undermining Haiti's struggle to rebuild its shattered economy. Fueled by corruption, inefficiency, a lack of resources, and a controversial new tax passed by Parliament in August 1996, smugglers are causing economic devastation and threatening the survival of legitimate businesses.[198]

Although there are no reliable statistics, one widely quoted estimate is that 70 percent of all the sea cargo manifested for Port-au-Prince from the United States is diverted to provincial Haitian ports as contraband. Of that amount, an estimated 95 percent winds up in Port-au-Prince. At the approximately half-dozen provincial ports scattered around Haiti, port infrastructure is non-existent or inefficient, and local authorities are often part of the smuggling operations.

A large proportion of the contraband is made up of such basic commodities as rice, flour, cooking oil, sugar, and condensed or powdered milk. The problem became overwhelming in August 1996, when a 10 percent tax imposed by Parliament on such products took effect. This has, of course, made smuggling much more profitable. Business people argue convincingly that the tax has severely injured legitimate tax-paying businesses while increasing prices for consumers. For example, the retail price for imported rice—about 80 percent of Haiti's consumption—has reached an all-time high of about $30 for a 110-pound bag. Indeed, several major problems arise from the deluge of contraband: the state is losing substantial revenues from the loss of port fees, sales taxes, and other levies; Haitians are being put out of business by dishonest competition; illegal weapons and drugs are being smuggled without any government control; and the restoration of state authority is being undermined.

There is no easy solution to these problems. The Haitian government simply does not have the resources to carry out the battle against contraband. If it did, there would certainly be serious repercussions. For example, the boats that carry the contraband are mooring at provincial ports that are poorly equipped and where most of the unloading is done by hand. This can take 600 to 700 people in a small town where there are no other jobs. A smuggling crackdown, therefore, would leave many people without any job.

Haiti's drug, weapon, and car-smuggling problems pale in comparison to the devastation of the country's historic subsistence base—agriculture. Haiti's bread basket, and the center of what ought to be a thriving rice-growing industry, is the Artibonite Valley. It is almost completely desolate, and if Haiti is to become economically self-sufficient or even move toward that goal, the Artibonite Valley must be restored.

Just off the main road to St. Marc lies the headquarters of the Organization for the Development of the Artibonite Valley (ODVA), a once bold imitation of the Tennessee Valley Authority–type organization, that managed state-owned lands and provided the local peasantry with cheap loans for seed and production. Ironically, it was with the demise of Baby Doc Duvaliér's dictatorship in 1986 that this agricultural experiment became an unmitigated failure. As power was transferred from one repressive military regime to another, the ODVA was turned to a ruin. The state lands were taken over by rich landowners, and the once poor but independent peasants were relegated to sharecropping. Where the state had once lent money at bargain rates, the landowners now set their own new higher rates and demanded 50 percent of any profit made by the peasant farmers. Because the peasants could not meet these terms, production in the valley steadily declined.

Today, the ODVA headquarters is all but deserted. It is impossible to communicate with the managers of ODVA. There is no phone, and the director of the project is seldom there because he lives 200 kilometers away at Les Cayes in the south. Millions of dollars worth of tractors, bulldozers, and trucks sit in ruin in a lot nearby, overgrown by weeds. Some of these machines look as if they never have been used.

Haiti ought to be able to grow enough rice to feed its people and provide an economic base for its peasantry. Under the ardent nationalism of the Duvaliérs, rice production was expanded, and it became a widely consumed food. Today, however, its rice-growing region is in disrepair, and, with the flood of cheap U.S. rice, it seems unlikely that the domestic economy will rebound any time soon. Haiti's agricultural decline has presented easy profit opportunities for American businesses, and has harmed Haiti substantially.[199]

U.S. POLITICS: THE PRESIDENTIAL ELECTION AND POLITICAL MURDERS

Like Aristide before him, President Preval understands that certain elements in the U.S. government, which have long supported successive Haitian military dictatorships, wish to have him fail in office and be removed. Thus, Haiti not only faces grave internal problems, but also has become a pawn in U.S. politics.[200] Indeed, Republican leaders seemed intent on making Haiti's quest for democracy appear to be a provocative sound bite in the 1996 U.S. presidential campaign, demonstrating Clinton's ineffectiveness in foreign policy matters.

Ironically, despite the atrocities committed throughout successive U.S.-supported military regimes—including at least five thousand murders during the de facto regime's rule—it was the murder of a staunch supporter of the de facto regime, the lawyer Mireille Durocher de Bertin, that allowed Republican legislators, and then Senate majority leader Robert Dole in particular, to invoke "moral outrage," and thereby to attack the Clinton administration's self-publicized foreign policy success in Haiti. As a result of this politically motivated action, the Haitian economy has necessarily suffered. Under Dole's sponsorship, Congress passed legislation (known as the Dole Amendment) that suspended approximately $50 million in aid to Haiti.

The decision in September 1995 to hold back American aid came at a time when President René Preval was especially vulnerable. More than $100 million in sorely needed foreign assistance had already been on hold for over six months because of President Aristide's refusal to sell nine state-owned enterprises to private investors. Largely as a result of this reduced flow of aid, which, combined, accounts for approximately two-thirds of the Haitian government's budget, the Preval administration has been unable to get the economy working again. Unemployment remains extremely high (over 50 percent), currency reserves are dropping, and many health, education, and agricultural projects are stalled. The government lacks the funds even to pay its own employees. Yet some U.S. Republicans continue to denounce and derail Haiti's attempt to make the difficult transition to democracy.

The Dole Amendment prohibits the United States from dispensing all but humanitarian aid to Haiti unless President Clinton certifies to Congress that the Haitian government is conducting a thorough and professional investigation of a series of killings that occurred during President Aristide's term of reinstatement to office and during part of President Preval's term—approximately eighteen months, from October 1994 to June 1996—which Dole claims are political or extrajudicial murders.[201] In the original version of the amendment,[202] Dole included in this list "the 20 cases of 'commando-style executions' cited by the United Nations/Organization of American States International Civilian Mission in Haiti on September 12, 1995,"[203] and the murder of Mireille Durocher de Bertin.

De Bertin was an English-speaking attorney who passionately defended the interests of the de facto military regime that ousted Aristide in 1991. She and a client, Eugene Baillergeau, were shot dead on March 28, 1995, by gunmen who trailed them in taxis as they drove on one of the busiest streets in Port-au-Prince. She was one of the Aristide government's harshest critics. Suspicion by U.S. officials fell on everyone from Aristide and his then interior minister, Mondesir Beaubrun, to de Bertin's right-wing political cronies and even her husband. Others suggested it was not in fact de Bertin, but her client, Baillergeau, who was the target, claiming that he was involved in illegal drug activities and killed by other people involved in that illegal trade. None of these suspicions, of course, was necessarily based on solid investigative information.

With the agreement of the Haitian government, the United States sent an FBI team to Haiti within eighteen hours of the de Bertin and Baillergeau slayings.[204] After seven months of investigation in Haiti, however, the FBI called a halt to its efforts because, it claimed, the Haitian government imposed "unreasonable conditions" on questioning government officials. The reality is far different from what the FBI will publicly admit. At a private briefing in Haiti with high-ranking Haitian officials, held directly after the FBI decided to call off the investigation, the FBI stated that it had no real leads into the murder. Indeed, the entire investigation was a total failure—but not because of "unreasonable conditions" imposed by the Haitian government on the questioning of its government officials.[205] Haitians simply refused to speak to FBI officials because the FBI does not understand Haitian culture and mores, and because Haitians continue to distrust U.S. officials. Thus, the FBI's account of the incident is questionable, and it seems likely that the Bureau was simply embarrassed by its failure to solve the crime.

It is interesting to note that the FBI targeted *only* Aristide government officials in this investigation, and attempted to question them without allowing them to claim their Haitian constitutional rights. Some of these officials wound up hiring American lawyers to represent them during the interviews. This is hardly an "unreasonable condition." Furthermore, the FBI never actively pursued the questions of whether de Bertin may have been killed because of Baillergeau's drug connection or whether her right-wing comrades or her husband may have been involved in her murder.

This is not, however, the end of the story. The UN/OAS Report relied upon by Dole in his assessment of the Haitian situation, which in turn prompted his amendment, simply does not state that the twenty killings he highlighted in addition to de Bertin's were necessarily "political." Indeed, Colin Granderson, a Trinidadian diplomat who heads the UN/OAS Civil Mission, claims that the cases comprise a "mixed bag" that includes both pro- and anti-Aristide victims, as well as some who have no apparent political affiliation.[206] "We've never said they were political," Granderson said. "We have said that perhaps some were political, but we are not willing to go further than that. It's very difficult to tell."[207]

Clearly, any strong investigative or factual support for Dole's amendment was lacking. Nevertheless, on January 26, 1996, the Dole Amendment, in the form of Section 583 of Public Law 104–107, became law. The final version of the act reads as follows:

> Sec. 583. (a) Limitation.—None of the funds appropriated or otherwise made available by this Act, may be provided to the Government of Haiti until the President reports to Congress that—
>
> (1) the Government is conducting thorough investigations of extrajudicial and political killings; and
>
> (2) the Government is cooperating with United States authorities in the investigations of political and extrajudicial killings.
>
> (b) Nothing in this section shall be construed to restrict the provision of humanitarian or electoral assistance.
>
> (c) The President may waive the requirements of this section if he determines and certifies to the appropriate committees of Congress that it is in the national interest of the United States or necessary to assure the safe and timely withdrawal of American forces from Haiti.[208]

Even before this act became law, the Clinton administration had made clear on numerous occasions to the Haitian government, at all levels, that a thorough investigation of these offenses is crucial both to establishing the rule of law and to maintaining international support. Nevertheless, when the amendment became law, the Clinton administration again examined the progress of the Haitian authorities' investigation into these so-called execution-style murders. It concluded that, while progress had been made by the Haitian government—it had established a Special Investigative Unit,[209] appointed an investigative magistrate and prosecutor, and sought and received international assistance—the administration could not document sufficient progress to permit it to make the report to Congress required by the Dole Amendment.

At the same time, however, there was another factor at work in determining U.S. policy regarding financial assistance to Haiti: any delay in completing the basic training and deployment of the National Police Force in Haiti would have called into question the timely withdrawal of U.S. forces. Thus, on February 6, 1996, to avoid this serious problem, and after consulting with congressional staff, the acting secretary of state signed a waiver determination, pursuant to Section 583(c) of the act, that continuing assistance was "necessary to assure the safe and timely withdrawal of U.S. forces from Haiti."[210] In April 1996, however, the State Department determined that the Haitian government had made insufficient progress and therefore would soon consult with Congress on how to proceed. The Clinton administration's response was made for political purposes—

to deflect Republican criticism of Clinton's self-proclaimed policy success in Haiti. Dole's claims appear to have no factual basis.

In addition to the Dole Amendment, a Republican congressional staff report,[211] issued on April 19, 1996, made after a brief trip to Haiti, harshly criticized the Haitian government and the American embassy in Haiti for its handling of the de Bertin case and the other allegedly political murder cases. The delegation concluded that the killings were politically motivated, that the Aristide government had masterminded them, and that, in essence, the American embassy had joined in the coverup of the slayings.[212] The State Department responded by strongly denying these allegations.

In an attempt to respond to some of these criticisms, President Preval removed those members of the security forces who may have appeared to be implicated in any of these offenses, appointed a new police chief, and took steps to reinvigorate the Special Investigative Unit formed in October 1995 to investigate a number of high-profile murders committed both during the coup and following President Aristide's return.[213] The investigative police trained by the U.S. Justice Department's International Criminal Investigative Training Assistance Program (ICITAP) were returned to their duties after the previous government had drawn them off to other cases, and the Preval government provided them with office space that is conducive to the special conduct of their investigations. CIVPOL provided advisers, and the Department of State contracted two experienced investigators to work with them. Since then, these people have been working with the Special Investigative Unit and, with the assistance of American lawyers and others, have helped it develop an investigative strategy for certain of the high-profile cases. The FBI has briefed these investigators on its own investigation of the de Bertin case, and has answered follow-up questions and offered assistance in forensic laboratory work. The two experienced investigators hired by the Department of State, however, have been highly critical of the FBI's investigations in Haiti, and believe that the FBI continues to withhold relevant information.[214]

It seems that the more the Clinton administration claimed Haiti as a foreign policy success, the more the Republicans attacked the Haitian government's attempt to make the hazardous journey to democracy. It is important to be clear, here, about the motives of those who were questioning, and continue to question, the Haitian government's role in these crimes. The delegation that drafted the report consisted of staff members of senators and congresspersons who were openly hostile to the Aristide government's attempt to bring democracy to Haiti. Some of them even supported the de facto military regimes that murdered thousands of people.[215] In addition, at the time of the report's issue, Dole would have liked nothing more than to embarrass Clinton, his opponent in the upcoming presidential election. Haiti was a prime medium for this activity.

A second report by the same Republican congressional staff, issued on October 22, 1996, just two weeks before the U.S. election, continued this harsh criticism.[216] The report claims that Clinton administration officials concealed the fact that Aristide stonewalled the FBI probe into de Bertin's murder. Moreover, it claims that the FBI asked to halt its inquiry in mid-1995, but the Clinton administration kept its investigators in Haiti at least three months after the probe stalled. The report cites congressional testimony, declassified embassy cables, and State Department memoranda to support its position. The obvious purpose of the report was, once again, to refute President Clinton's claim to a foreign policy triumph in his handling of Haiti.

The report details a series of mistakes and accuses Clinton administration officials—including Deputy Secretary of State Strobe Talbot and James Dobbins, then State Department coordinator of Haiti—of withholding for months information about suspected criminals on the Haitian government payroll. In response, the Clinton administration harshly criticized the report as being a partisan witch hunt. Indeed, James P. Rubin, foreign policy spokesman for the Clinton administration, responded to the report by denouncing it. He claimed that the report was an attempt by some Republicans to besmirch what virtually everyone in the region recognizes as a victory for democracy.[217] Representative Lee H. Hamilton, ranking Democratic member of the Committee on International Relations, was furious at the process by which the report was researched, written, and issued. He stated:

> I am concerned with how the report was released. In a break with Committee practice, neither I nor any other member was allowed to attach a dissenting view. Despite the fact that the report directly quotes me, I was not even allowed to *review* the report before it was released to the press. Since I just received the report yesterday, I am as yet completing my dissenting opinion.[218]

Hamilton also claims that Republican staffers denied his request to let their Democratic counterparts go along on a key fact-finding trip to Haiti.[219]

There are other, internal, reasons why the investigations into the murders highlighted in Dole's amendment have not been going forward in Haiti. The National Police Force is not yet competent. Even with UN assistance, the fledgling force is hampered by a lack of skills, and criminal investigation is the most sophisticated enterprise of any police force. In addition, the judiciary lacks everything, including the ability to investigate and prosecute crime. The elite families and paramilitary forces still remain powerful, and they simply refuse to allow justice to prevail. Stated otherwise, the country continues to face a security threat from these groups; people are terrified and refuse to cooperate with the police; corruption is ubiquitous.

Many of the problems in the investigations also stem from the lack of cooperation from the United States. For example, the American intelligence agencies and the FBI have refused to make available copies of tapes of two-way radio (walkie-talkie) conversations that de Bertin had the day she was killed. Moreover, the Special Investigative Unit, which is investigating the killings, is being allowed access only to selective materials—those related to some crimes that occurred before Aristide's reinstatement. These actions, of course, act as a strong barrier to effective investigation and prosecution. They block any attempt to move toward the rule of law and the creation of a moral consciousness in the citizenry. A deliberative democracy cannot be created in Haiti until the United States stops working against the democratic forces in that country, whether this is being done on genuine ideological grounds (as is the case for some factions in the United States who still support the de facto regime), or for reasons of internal partisan political point scoring.

CONTINUING SECURITY CONCERNS

As this book goes to press, the fragility of the transition to democracy in Haiti remains a pervasive problem. Security concerns continue to be the focal point of Haitian life, and stability remains frustratingly elusive.

The major source of insecurity is the attempt by the military and paramilitary forces to destabilize the democratically elected government, with the hope of eventually regaining power. In particular, there appears to be a systematic attempt to murder police officers and thus show the Haitian people that they and their families will never be secure under democratic rule. From April 27 to August 31, 1996, nine police officers were assassinated. The ninth murdered officer, Haitian-American Yves Phanor, was a U.S. citizen and a former police officer for the Miami Police Department. He resigned from that department to work for the U.S. Justice Department to help train Haiti's new 5,300-member police force. At the time of his death, he was a supervising instructor for Haiti's police academy.[220] Strong evidence suggests that former coup regime soldiers and their paramilitary allies committed his and these other murders.[221]

Other political acts of violence continue to occur. The grandson of a wealthy industrialist, whose family once employed Preval, was abducted on May 28, 1996. Police have arrested nine suspects in the incident, including two former police officers.[222] On May 29, 1996, highwaymen held up five buses and shot and injured several passengers. Erla François, a member of Preval's governing coalition and mayor of Chansolme, a town 160 miles north of Port-au-Prince, was shot and killed on May 30, 1996, as she waited at a bus stop. In retaliation for these latter two incidents, an angry mob stormed the police station where seven men were being questioned about the bus attacks, and stoned the men and hacked them to death with machetes.[223] On July 23, 1996, Dany Toussaint, the former chief of police, who had been appointed by President Aristide shortly after his reinstatement, narrowly escaped an assassination attempt. Toussaint was driving in Petionville, an exclusive suburb of Port-au-Prince, when two men in separate cars tried to trap his vehicle between theirs. When Toussaint saw a man in one of these cars take aim at him with an automatic rifle, he quickly accelerated and fled.[224] The attempt on Toussaint's life was a clear warning to President Preval and to Aristide.

Unfortunately, in addition to these murders and assassination attempts, there is strong evidence of plots by disgruntled, right-wing military Duvaliérists to assassinate Presidents Preval and Aristide. Indeed, during the last week of July 1996, the United States took these threats seriously enough to send troops back to Haiti to calm the political waters and to avert any assassination attempts. At that time, the United States sent approximately two hundred and fifty troops from the Eighty-second Airborne Division, and quietly deployed them around the grounds of the National Palace and on patrols in Port-au-Prince, in humvees armed with machine guns. The combat troops left Haiti on August 1, 1996, after a week of these exercises.[225]

Perhaps the most serious attempt at destabilization by sympathizers of the former military dictatorship occurred on August 19, 1996. Two carloads of heavily armed men (approximately twenty) wearing military fatigues attacked the Port-au-Prince police headquarters, killing a shoeshine boy and wounding a policeman. They also fired a rocket-propelled grenade at the legislative building. Canadian and Pakistani soldiers, part of the UN peace-keeping mission, and Haitian security forces fended off the predawn offensive after an hour-long battle in which the attackers fired automatic weapons and lobbed grenades. Stepped-up UN and police patrols continued throughout the day, with helicopters flying over the downtown area of the city and armored vehicles cruising the streets. Officials erected barriers at the entrances to the National Palace.

The attack came nearly twenty-four hours after the Haitian National Police had arrested nineteen people said to be members of the Mobilization for National Development Party (Mobilisation Pour le Développement National), a rightist political party led by a former presidential candidate, Huber de Ronceray, who also served as a minister under Duvaliér and is an ally of Prosper Avril. The arrests took place at de Ronceray's house, where the men claimed they had gathered to play dominoes. Most of those arrested are former members of FAD'H. These men were arrested on the basis of intelligence reports that they had planned attacks on the National Palace and other government offices. At the time of the attack, they were being held at the police headquarters, but it is not certain whether the attack force intended to free them.[226] Residents of Port-au-Prince's most desperate slums reacted to the crisis by setting up burning tire barricades. In the seaside slum of La Saline, these barricades halted traffic for several hours, until UN troops came to shovel the burning rubber off the road. The people took these actions to show their support for the democratic government.[227]

On August 20, 1996, the day after the attack on the police headquarters in Port-au-Prince, gunmen killed two far-right politicians in a drive-by shooting. Unknown attackers shot Protestant Pastor Antoine Leroy and Jacques Florival of the Mobilization for National Development Party outside Florival's Port-au-Prince home.[228] It is not clear whether the murders had any relationship whatsoever to the previous day's assault at police headquarters.[229] Nevertheless, a newspaper report claimed that American officials had concluded that members of Haiti's U.S.-trained Presidential Security Unit committed the murders.[230] The Presidential Security Unit consists of approximately one hundred men, and it is responsible for the personal security of both President Preval and former President Aristide. The Aristide government, with the assistance of the United States, recruited most of its members. Indeed, the U.S. State Department's

Diplomatic Security Unit assisted in training the Presidential Security Unit. Its members include many people involved in Aristide's Lavalas movement. In contrast, the larger Palace Guard consists primarily of former soldiers from FAD'H that led the 1991 coup, who have been accused by human rights groups of widespread atrocities.[231]

The killings apparently contributed to a hurried one-day trip to Haiti, on August 30, 1996, by Deputy Secretary of State Strobe Talbot and National Security Adviser Anthony Lake. U.S. officials did not then claim, however, that they had independent evidence linking members of the Presidential Security Unit to the killings.[232] Despite the newspaper account that a "congressional source" claimed that evidence linking the security unit to the killings includes eyewitness accounts provided to the U.S. embassy in Haiti, telephone intercepts, and recovered shell casings, no U.S. official could confirm this report.[233]

These speculations are certainly reminiscent of the claims made about the murder of Mireille Durocher de Bertin—that Aristide loyalists murdered her. Those claims have never been proved to be true.[234] Moreover, this issue certainly gives Republicans another opportunity to attack President Clinton's foreign policy initiatives. Indeed, on September 9, 1996, Congressman Benjamin Gilman, chairman of the House International Relations Committee, sent a letter to the secretary of state, demanding that the State Department turn over all correspondence about the murders to his committee.[235] Gilman, a Republican from New York, has been highly critical of the Aristide and Preval governments.[236] In his letter, Gilman threatened to use subpoena power, if necessary, to obtain that correspondence as well as correspondence on related arrests of opposition-affiliated persons and knowledge on the part of President René Preval and other Haitian authorities of police misconduct in these incidents.[237] On September 19, Gilman subpoenaed National Security Council documents that he has been unable to obtain. Apparently, he is trying to determine whether the Clinton administration—in an attempt to spare President Clinton any political embarrassment—concealed the fact that there were death squads operating with official sanction in Haiti.[238] While congressional sources claim that U.S. officials have some evidence linking the Presidential Security Unit to the two murders, they do not claim that Preval had any complicity in the killings. In early September 1996, the Preval government began an investigation into these killings. President Preval has promised to bring all of those implicated in the investigation to trial, even if they turn out to be members of the palace circle.[239]

Under continuing pressure from the Clinton administration, President Preval transferred the two top leaders of his security unit because unnamed congressional sources claim that these two men have been involved in atrocities.[240] On September 12, 1996, Preval transferred Joseph Moïse, head of his security unit, and Milien Romage, his top deputy. The following day, approximately forty armed U.S. agents from the State Department and the Pentagon arrived in Port-au-Prince and rushed to the National Palace, allegedly to protect Preval from any possible retaliation. Simultaneously, approximately seventy armed Canadian agents surrounded the palace. Preval was expected to purge at least a dozen members of his security unit, which he has in fact done. In addition, members of a related force, the 200-member Palace Guard, have also been dismissed.[241] The U.S. security team was expected to remain in Haiti for at least two months. U.S. officials portrayed the American involvement as the response to an urgent request from Preval, and asserted that U.S. agents would not supplant Preval's own security team.[242] Nevertheless, the United States did intervene. During the week of September 11, 1996, James McWhirter, a top State Department security official who had originally helped train the security unit, returned to Haiti to help cull that unit, and the Clinton administration provided Preval with some names of those suspected of crimes.[243] All this happened despite the fact that several sources claim that Preval is not, in fact, in any danger from his security unit. They claim that the Clinton administration sent the troops as a response to the attempt by Republican congressmen to portray the Preval government in disarray. Moreover, these sources claim that Preval never asked the United States to send the troops and that he is confident in the loyalty of his security unit.[244] Indeed, some members of Preval's administration believe that certain U.S. agencies and officials are trying to use this incident to foster animosity between President Preval and Aristide, since many members of the Presidential Security Unit were selected when Aristide was in office and are therefore seen as loyal to him.

In any event, it appears that the United States sees a need to shore up Haiti's security. In addition to sending the forty armed U.S. agents, it recruited American police officers for deployment as part of the UN peace-keeping force in Haiti. At least twenty-five American police officers were scheduled to be sent to Port-au-Prince.[245]

These officers—most of whom were to be Haitian-Americans re-cruited from the New York, Miami, or Boston police forces—were expected to arrive in Haiti some time before the current UN mandate expires on November 30, 1996. As of October 31, 1996, sixteen of them had joined the UN mission to help train Haiti's National Police Force. By January 1997, almost all of the twenty-five officers had arrived in Haiti. Some of the Americans are to be attached to the criminal investigation unit, a unit assigned to investigate recent murder and kidnaping cases with political overtones.[246]

Moreover, in response to the attack at police headquarters and the slaying of the two rightist politicians, fifty troops from the Second Marine Division at Camp Lejeune, North Carolina, arrived in Port-au-Prince on August 21, 1996. The troops were to train for ten days with eighty members of a rapid-reaction unit stationed in Haiti. Embassy officials claimed that the mission was simply a routine rein-forcement of security for 300 American combat engineers building roads, schools, and hospitals in Haiti. The arrival of the Marines nev-ertheless became a symbolic show of force against the threat of more violence in Haiti.[247]

The deployment of U.S. troops to Haiti, however, did not put an end to the increasing political violence. Indeed, on Thursday, August 23, 1996, two days after these troops arrived in Port-au-Prince, gun-men opened fire on Haiti's television station and prominent journal-ists received death threats. In this attack, gunmen fired into the air in front of the Television Nationale building as their car raced by at approximately 3 A.M. They returned an hour later and shot up the facade of the building. The bullets burst a water pipe, shattered the glass front door, and left marks in the second-floor office windows. Fortunately, no one was injured in the attacks. Moreover, that same morning, two prominent journalists—Jean Dominique, the director of the private Radio Haiti-Inter, and Pierre-Louis, anchorman for Television Nationale—received death threats. Similar kinds of press attacks had occurred in the days leading up to the September 1991 coup.[248] Sources suspect that Prosper Avril is the leader of the group of disgruntled soldiers that has been committing these acts of vio-lence.[249]

Another serious incident occurred eight days after the attack on Haiti's television station. On August 31, 1996, a witness saw a man place a bomb under a van on Jean-Jacques Dessalines Boulevard, one of the main thoroughfares of Port-au-Prince. He immediately alerted authorities. Members of the UN peace-keeping force detonated the bomb only a few hours before the area would have been overflowing with Saturday morning shoppers.[250]

On September 13, 1996, in another politically motivated action, vandals attacked a car wash that employs hundreds of homeless youths. According to the manager of the car wash, former soldiers attacked the business because President Aristide had helped found it. The attackers scrawled "Down with Aristide" and "Long Live the Army!" on the walls of the car wash, damaged a water tank and pump, and stole the week's receipts and other items.[251]

Police continue to search for the people who have been involved in these terrorist acts. For example, on September 6, 1996, they arrested Deus Jean-François, a former congressman and leading member of the far-right Mobilization for National Development Party, in Petit-Goave, a small town twenty-five miles west of Port-au-Prince. He is being held on charges of subversive activities.[252]

In addition to plots intended to destabilize Haiti's fragile democracy, crime continues to be a serious concern. Indeed, criminal gangs consisting of former FAD'H members and paramilitary forces have proliferated since Aristide's reinstatement in October 1994. For example, on August 3, 1996, a gang of heavily armed thieves pulled people out of their cars, forced them to the ground, and shot and killed several of them. These criminals also randomly fired their weapons in the air and wounded an unknown number of people who were simply walking down the street.[253]

Unless the former military forces are somehow pacified, acts of violence will become even more common. Indeed, on September 28, 1996, police arrested the head of a demobilized soldier organization and a former member of a paramilitary group hours before these groups had allegedly planned to stage a military coup and assassinate top government officials. They arrested Sergeant Joseph Jean-Baptiste, the leader of the Committee of Soldiers Demands, and Jean Claude, a member of FRAPH, at the residence of Emmanuel Constant, former head of FRAPH. At the time of the arrest, police discovered a cache of automatic weapons and grenades along with a videotape of officials who were marked for assassination, and an audiotape explaining a plan to attack Haiti's poorest slums. Apparently, this group had prepared a documented plan to stage a coup on that very evening. They wanted to create disorder by killing government and police officials, as well as to terrorize the slums.[254]

Haiti's former soldiers are thus still free and armed in Haiti. Many have joined private security companies, personal armies owned or hired by the elite families. With ten private companies, in addition to dozens of private family forces, today there are more private security agents than police officers in Port-au-Prince, and they are better equipped and more experienced than the Haitian police officers.

Many of the former soldiers remain discontented.[255] This group has threatened to use terrorism to force the government to release imprisoned former soldiers and to pay back wages. It claims Aristide violated the Constitution in dissolving the army.[256] One major source of discontent among the former soldiers is financial. Although many former officers have either gone into exile or landed jobs with business people sympathetic to the former regimes, ordinary enlisted soldiers have been unable to collect the pensions, severance pay, and military bank accounts they claim are due them. Cédras and other members of the coup leadership looted these funds when they fled the country. These funds were not earned legally. The military leaders simply took what they wanted and used the national treasury as their personal bank accounts.[257] Some of the former soldiers argue that their military salaries should still be paid because the formal dissolution of the armed forces in accordance with the Constitution is not yet complete, and therefore they are not cashiered, but instead are on an extended leave. This is, of course, a specious argument.[258]

Another source of discontent is the purging of the police. Many of the former soldiers also served as members of the IPSF set up after Aristide's reinstatement, and are furious to see some of their ex-colleagues incorporated into the permanent force, the Haitian National Police, or even into the Palace Guard. The only effort to recycle these former soldiers into productive activities is the job-training course run by the International Organization for Migration, an independent group based in Geneva, Switzerland. The program is funded by the United States and other international donors.[259] More than forty-five hundred former soldiers have enrolled in that six-month program, and they have been training to become mechanics, plumbers, carpenters, welders, or even computer operators while they earn training stipends close to their military salaries. Unfortunately, only 8 percent have been able to find jobs in their new trades after graduation.[260]

Some have suggested that, to alleviate this potential crisis and thus to diffuse the frustration of these discharged soldiers, the government should create jobs, or simply pay off the ex-soldiers. This, however, would be an unpopular and politically costly measure. Indeed, almost two and a half years after the restoration of democracy, the economy is still staggering and unemployment is running at more than 50 percent.[261]

Sporadic waves of violence continue to plague Haiti during its fragile transition period. For example, during a two-week period in February 1997, warring drug gangs in Port-au-Prince killed at least eighteen people. The feud erupted on February 14, following the slaying of a child in unexplained circumstances. On February 26, six people were killed and at least nine people, including a police officer, were wounded when a heavily armed gang attacked the home base of its rival. The gangs have been fighting over turf on which to sell crack cocaine. On February 27, they set a fire that destroyed seventy shacks in the slum of Cité Soleil. Haitian police assisted by UN troops cordoned off the area and removed barricades, restoring calm by afternoon. The weapons used by the drug gangs were stolen from Pakistani and American troops serving with the UN peace-keeping force.[262]

While these problems are not perceived as regime-threatening to President Preval's democratically elected government, they are serious enough to cause concern in Washington. Indeed, these attacks, and the structural problems they reflect, threatened President Clinton's attempt to make his Haiti policy one of the major foreign policy successes in his successful reelection campaign. As an indication of this concern, Deputy National Security Adviser Samuel Berger, Deputy Secretary of State Strobe Talbot, and Attorney General Janet Reno contemplated taking trips to Haiti some time either before or directly after the U.S. presidential election.[263]

These events make it clear that international forces are vital to the security of this fragile democracy. It became crucial that the withdrawal date for the UN peace-keeping force be extended past the November 1996 deadline. Prospects for such an extension proved to be strong. Indeed, on August 29, 1996, the UN agreed to keep a civilian force in Haiti for an additional six months to monitor human rights, help establish an impartial judiciary, and help train police. The 185-member UN General Assembly agreed to the extension without a vote.[264]

The deployment of international forces in Haiti, however, raises another concern. The United States is mounting a parallel security and support system, with the Haitian government's reluctant compliance. The deployment of U.S. troops and security agents underlines the Clinton administration's determination not to let the security situation in Haiti unravel, even if it means operating independently of its allies, or offending them. Indeed, many foreign offi-

cials have privately called these actions "a mini–coup d'état," and
have claimed that this action shows a deep disregard for the pride
and opinion of Haitians and foreign partners.[265] Furthermore, many
Haitians—particularly Aristide—and foreign diplomats maintain
that the United States has consistently misjudged the degree of force
it needs to use in Haiti. They argue that the United States applied
too little force in the initial 1994 phase of the intervention by failing
to disarm the military and paramilitary forces, and is now overcom-
pensating in an effort to prevent Haiti from becoming an embarrassment during Clinton's second term in office.[266] Aristide argues
that these acts of violence—the threats against him and President
Preval, attacks on the National Police headquarters and Parliament,
and the killings of police officers—might have been avoided if American troops had been more aggressive in fulfilling the UN mandate
of total disarmament. He further argues that the need to disarm the
military and paramilitary forces in a legal, nonviolent way remains
crucial to the success of the transition to democracy in Haiti.[267]

One other significant problem is the effort by certain U.S. government officials to create friction in the relationship between Aristide
and Preval. Since Preval's election to the presidency, U.S. and foreign officials have pressured Preval, who lacks Aristide's popular
base of support, to take action to get out from under Aristide's
shadow. Several steps that he has taken suggest that he has followed
this advice. He cleared the government of Aristide's private cabinet,
closed Haiti's lobbying office in Washington, and is now purging the
Presidential Security Unit.[268]

Many Haitians claim that certain elements of the U.S. government, and other foreign officials, have attempted to create a serious
rift between Preval and Aristide. Indeed, on September 16, 1996,
Aristide, in a paid announcement broadcast over Haitian radio stations, did strongly criticize Preval's government. Aristide claimed
that the government was corrupt and disordered. He argued that
the only way to create order is to establish good relations "between
Lavalas in power and Lavalas out of power."[269] Aristide also criticized the privatization plan, calling it "a trap," and "a cigarette lit
at both ends."[270] These comments seem to have created confusion.
Some analysts claim that by this action Aristide is distancing himself
from Preval to prepare for his own return to the presidency in the
year 2000; some say that he is angry by what many see as a U.S.-
engineered effort to reduce his influence; others say it was a call
to unity for his Lavalas movement. Another explanation—one that
meshes nicely with a theory of deliberative democracy—may be

closer to the truth. Aristide's critique can be seen as a very positive step in the transition to democracy. After all, dissent is a hallmark of democracy. Without the ability of a former leader to disagree with, and point out the inadequacies of, a new government, positive changes are less likely to occur. Indeed, President Preval's very positive response to Aristide's criticism proves the point. He agreed that corruption in government is a recurring problem and that the modernization of the state-owned enterprises must be done cautiously. It is clear that Preval's relationship with Aristide remains strong and intimate.[271]

Conclusion

Authoritarianism cannot be overcome simply because people favor democratic methods for resolving conflicts and developing a nation. Powerful social forces block the passage from dictatorship to democracy. In Haiti, these underlying forces are an organic conception of society that leads to a dualistic vision of the social order; corporatism; anomie and unlawfulness; and extreme concentrations of institutional, economic, and social power. These forces are directly related to massive human rights abuses.

As this book amply demonstrates, there is no such thing as an easy fix in the transition to democracy in Haiti. Economic, political, and social stability have not yet been achieved. The corporatist political and social structure has to be transformed to allow the less privileged to enjoy the basic necessities that ensure a life of dignity. Institutional structures, such as an independent judiciary, a representative congressional branch, and limitations on the executive power, must be developed and stabilized. The rule of law and the guarantees of due process have to be consolidated and must become an accepted, basic requirement of social interaction. This is necessary not only to protect human rights and the democratic process, but also to reach a satisfactory level of economic and social development. Moreover, human rights trials are an important step in reaching this goal.

What this means, of course, is that the Haitian people must internalize the importance and legitimacy of a constitutional system based on the rule of law. They must also internalize universal standards of achievement and competition necessary to the proper functioning of a democracy. The belief in the overpowering significance of status and connections, which severely cripples the transition to democracy, must be defeated.

In the long run, nothing positive can be achieved in Haiti without the establishment of a deliberative democracy—a democracy that allows for equal participation and rational discourse among all segments of the population. This discourse, in turn, is essential for the creation of a moral consciousness of humanity that recognizes the value of human rights and abhors any notion that disregards them. Moreover, the view of democracy that I have defended in this book—based on the epistemic value of democratic decision making and discussion—is the theory best suited to the creation of a moral consciousness so necessary to the development of an environment free from fear and death.

A deliberative democracy can be conceived as an ongoing order characterized by a certain principle of justification—a principle of democratic legitimacy. This principle requires a continuous order of mutually assured and encouraged autonomy in which political decisions are manifestly based on the judgments of members who are free and equal persons. It requires that the expression of self-governing capacities operate both within the formal institutions of politics and in the affairs of daily life. The democratic order must also satisfy the conditions of equal freedom and autonomy that give it definition.

This democratic conception suggests possible solutions, or roads to follow, in resolving the seemingly intractable problems in Haiti: one way to attack the country's political, economic, and social problems is through a radical change in institutional structure. The dominant constitutional tradition in the rich industrial countries, such as the United States, relies upon arrangements and practices tending to use the fragmentation of power and the promotion of impasse as a safeguard of freedom, and to maintain political society at relatively low levels of political mobilization. In the real conditions of a nation like Haiti, however, which is attempting to make the transition to democracy, structural reforms require at least two sets of institutional innovations.

First, a merger of the electoral characteristics of presidential regimes is needed, posing a periodic threat to oligarchic control of political power. There must be a facility for rapid resolution of impasse through priority accorded to programmatic legislation, liberal resort to plebiscites and referenda, and perhaps the vesting of power in all branches of government to provoke anticipated elections in the face of impasses over the direction the country should take. Second, measures must be taken to heighten the level, and to broaden the scope, of political mobilization in society, especially through strengthening the parties (districts and lists), public financing of campaigns, increased free access to television and radio, and the breakup of the broadcasting "cartel." Direct democracy must be encouraged at all levels of society.

In the organization of civil society, the prevailing legal tradition in the rich industrial democracies relinquishes the self-organization of civil society to private contract. The integrity of economic and political institutions, such as those that I have described here, however, requires a civil society both strongly organized and independent from governmental tutelage in this organization.[1]

The macropolitics of institutional change remains inadequate to the aims of democratization and practical experimentalism unless complemented by a micropolitics confronting the logic of habitual social interactions in Haiti. Indeed, as discussed above, the history of Haiti is permeated by a duel social, political, and economic structure that stubbornly impedes any progress toward positive change.

The typical elements of this logic are similar to those that are prevalent in many developing nations. There is a predominance of patron-client relations, with their pervasive mingling in the same associations and encounters of exchange, power, and sentimental allegiance. There is frequently an oscillation between rule formalism and personal favoritism, and each creates the opportunity and the need for the other. There is also a stark contrast between the treatment of *insiders* (anyone with whom, by virtue of the role you occupy, you have a preexisting relationship) and *outsiders* (everyone else), and the consequent shortage of impersonal respect and reliability.

A "transformative" politics—a democratic system—capable of challenging and changing both the established arrangements of the economy and the polity and the intimate habits of sociability must appeal to each of the (at least) two parts of the Haitian nation that it wishes to unite. In this task, those who yearn for democracy must combine a strategic approach to the satisfaction of recognized material interests with the visionary invocation of a reordered society. In Haiti, a nation trapped in these impoverished visions, nothing is more important than to encourage the belief in the Haitian people that structural change is possible.

Haiti's democracy remains fragile, its new security structures are inexperienced and untested, and economic renewal is, at best, tentative. Nevertheless, there is also cause for hope and optimism. That hope rests ultimately with the Haitian people. Almost three years after the American-led intervention, the economy is looking stronger, and the political and security situations in Haiti have improved dramatically on those of the days directly after the reinstatement of President Aristide.[2] These improvements have advanced to a point that permits a more modest international presence in Haiti—one that will help to ensure a smooth and sure transfer of key functions enabling Haitians to assume responsibility for their own future.

Many brave and dedicated Haitian people are struggling daily to create and perpetuate a constitutional democratic system of government. In the vanguard of this effort is a core group of peasants, intellectuals, lawyers, and government officials who are attempting to implement the necessary changes in this society. These individuals clearly understand the incredibly difficult obstacles they face and the various solutions to these issues. They have not been remiss about taking action to effect these changes, even in the face of very credible threats of physical harm to themselves and their families. Their work and actions are nothing short of heroic.

President Aristide stands out as the one figure in Haiti who represents the best of his generation. Notwithstanding the tremendous amount of criticism and threats that he has faced, he remains a very charismatic figure who symbolizes the hopes of the Haitian poor and disenfranchised for a better life—one free from violent repression. There are many people in Haiti who believed, and still believe, that he should have been allowed to serve an additional three years to make up for his time in exile. Still others would have liked him to be president for as long as he wished.

Even with all of this pressure, and in the face of cynical disbelief by some, President Aristide set in motion the presidential election process that led to a peaceful passage of power in accordance with the provisions of the Haitian Constitution, after the expiration of his five-year term. By this act, he stressed the importance of establishing the constitutional precedent of a legitimate transfer of power for the future of Haitian democracy over his personal beliefs or those of his most ardent supporters. He made the point, in action, that, in a democracy, the second presidential election is perhaps even more important than the first. Indeed, President Aristide's demonstrated commitment to constitutional rule will be a fundamental principle of future political life in Haiti. This stands in stark contrast to Haiti's long history of military governments and dictators who cared nothing for democracy or the welfare of the Haitian people.

His quest for democracy and for a better life for the Haitian people has not ceased on his departure from public office. As a private citizen, he has created the Aristide Foundation for Democracy, an organization that is attempting to help create the conditions for democracy in his country. To bring real change, democracy in Haiti must go beyond the polling places. It must become a daily practice. The goal of his foundation is to ensure that all sectors of Haitian society are able to participate actively in the democratic life of the nation. Democracy must include those at the margins of society—street children, market women, landless peasants, *restaveks* (children living in Haitian households as unpaid domestic laborers), and the urban poor.

The foundation is dedicated to opening up avenues of democratic participation for those who traditionally have had no voice in public affairs. It seeks to echo and amplify the voices of the Haitian people on national and international levels, and it strives to foster dialogue across class and social lines.

To put it another way, the Foundation seeks to create what I have referred to as a deliberative democracy. In an attempt to create the conditions under which democratic participation is possible for all Haitians, the Aristide Foundation works in three major areas: creating forums for dialogue; supporting literacy programs; and fostering community-based economic initiatives. Aristide has also created a new grass-roots movement—the Lavalas Family—to democratize Haiti's democracy. The purpose of this movement is to incorporate the vast majority of Haitians, particularly those living in the rural areas of Haiti, into the decision-making process of government. It is an attempt to make democracy come alive for all of the Haitian people.[3]

To a large extent, the question of whether Haiti continues down the path to a better future or slides back to the Haiti of old is now in the hands of the new government. It must act quickly and decisively to maintain the gains made with the restoration of democracy and to revive the momentum of that magic moment. In this struggle it will continue to need the help of the international community. The people of Haiti still have enormous sacrifices to make to bring their country into the twenty-first century as a viable democracy, but it cannot be doubted that they have made enormous strides in their slow but ineluctable journey from "misery to poverty with dignity."

Notes

Most of the newspaper and law review articles cited in this book are available online through LEXIS/NEXIS or WESTLAW.

PROLOGUE

1. According to people who traveled on the other two planes, the passengers on those flights were equally excited but more restrained.

2. One of the first people I saw as I entered the National Palace was Ira J. Kurzban, at that time the chief lawyer for Aristide's government. I was overjoyed to see him. He has been the driving force behind the almost twenty years of Haitian refugee litigation and is the person who first asked me to work with Haitian refugees. He had been in Haiti for approximately two weeks, preparing the way for Aristide's return.

President Aristide later appointed Mr. Kurzban as chief counsel for the Republic of Haiti in the United States. In that capacity, he has been involved in almost every aspect of Haitian government activity, including economic, cultural, social, and political matters. President Preval has retained Mr. Kurzban in the same capacity.

3. After his return to Haiti, and during the remainder of his term in office, approximately sixteen months, President Aristide lived in four offices at the National Palace, except when he managed to travel to his personal residence in Tabarre, on the outskirts of Port-au-Prince, almost every other week. He had no personal rooms in the palace. There was his formal office; an adjacent office behind that, where he often met more informally with his staff and his cabinet, and where he had a large, glass-topped desk; his inner private office; and the presidential staff's inner office. The residential floor of the palace, decorated in chromes and beiges in the 1980s by Michele Bennett-Duvaliér—then the wife of Jean-Claude Duvaliér—remained destroyed for many months after Aristide's return. It was not fully renovated until the last weeks of his term. Aristide often slept in his private office on a pull-out couch. Moreover, for many months after Aristide's reinstatement, there was no bathtub or shower in the bathroom. Instead, he used the sink.

4. Haitians nudged each other as the flowery metaphors and the folk sayings poured forth—sayings like, "many hands make a light burden," and "you can't eat okra with one finger."

5. The United States, of course, was also directly responsible for putting these men into power in the first place. See chapter 8, "Security and U.S. Involvement in Haiti."

6. Lavalas is a Creole word meaning downpour, flash flood, deluge,

tempest, or avalanche. The reason the name is so powerful is that Haiti's storms are so powerful. But it has other resonances as well: "Nou se lavalas, n'ap pote ale" (We are the flood, we will sweep everything away). These were the lines that inspired Aristide to choose the name Lavalas—lines from a 1987 song written and sung by militant peasant groups in Haiti's starving Northwest Province.

7. I first met President Aristide in late 1991, after his ousting by the coup leaders. I have been an attorney and adviser to his government since that time. One of his advisers introduced me to him because of my extensive experience in the legal representation of Haitian refugees. Since 1977, I have worked with Ira Kurzban, the lawyer who has spearheaded this litigation, and other lawyers on every major Haitian refugee case filed in the United States. The list of cases is long and complicated.

Since 1994, when President Aristide was reinstated to office, I have been in charge of investigating and helping to prosecute those who committed massive human rights abuses during the coup regime era (1991–94). I continued this role into the early part of President Preval's term. In this capacity, I have helped organize a staff of investigators and lawyers, worked directly with the UN Mission in Haiti (UNMIH), U.S. government officials, and Haitian government officials. I have also worked with Haitian lawyers and judges. These experiences have given me access to information otherwise unavailable to the public and have helped shape my vision of Haiti and the transition process.

8. The Multi-National Force (MNF) was in Haiti only until March 1995. At that time, the UNMIH took over. The UN peace-keeping force was originally scheduled to leave Haiti on February 7, 1996, but the UN Security Council voted to extend the mandate through June 30, 1996. On June 28, 1996, however, the Security Council voted once again to extend the peace-keeping forces' presence until November 30, 1996. Don Bohning, "A Sigh of Relief in Haiti after U.N. Mission Is Extended," *Miami Herald,* June 30, 1996, A1. While the UNMIH changed its title to "UN Support Mission in Haiti," it did not change its task of supporting the Haitian National Police. The request by the Preval government for the extension came as a result of the several police killings and high-profile crimes, including murder, robbery, and kidnaping, that have occurred since March 1996. The number of soldiers in the UN peace-keeping force has been reduced, however, by 600, leaving 1,300 soldiers; the number of civilian police advisers will not change. See ibid., A1, A4. On December 6, 1996, the UN Security Council approved an extension of the UNMIH through May 31, 1997. "Security Council Extends Mission in Haiti until May 31," *New York Times,* December 6, 1996, A5. On April 5, 1997, the UN renewed that extension until July 31, 1997. "Haiti," *Miami Herald,* April 5, 1997, A20.

9. In Haiti, *borlette* (lottery) tickets are sold at little stalls called *borlettes* (banks). There is simply no other kind of bank for 98 percent of the population—the common people. Moreover, virtually every deposit they make at the bank is a major gamble. The *borlettes* are operated in chains; each chain is owned by one person. The *borlettes* have a checkered history. During François (Papa Doc) Duvaliér's reign of terror, the *borlette* was run for the profit

of Papa Doc's supporters. They were told, sometimes by Papa Doc personally, which number would win (in Haitian parlance, they were told which
balls would fall). Today, the *borlettes* are not as corrupt as they were under
Duvaliér's rule, but there still is occasional corruption.

10.   Some parts of Haiti—small rural areas—are still controlled by paramilitary groups and other antidemocratic forces.

11.   Serious threats of violence by the deposed military raise this issue.
Top U.S. military officials in Haiti have repeatedly warned several former
Duvaliér-era officials to stop plotting the overthrow of Presidents Aristide
and Preval. Moreover, political violence occurred throughout President
Aristide's entire term of office and continues during President Preval's term.
For example, on February 24, 1995, the Aristide government issued warn-
ings of a plot to disrupt through violence the pre-Lenten carnival that takes
place at the end of February. Don Bohning and Christopher Marquis, "U.S.
Warns of Plot against Aristide," *Miami Herald,* February 24, 1995, A1. See
chapter 8, "Security and U.S. Involvement in Haiti."

Threats consistently occur. Political assassinations continue. On November 7, 1995, for example, paramilitary forces allied with the de facto regime
assassinated two newly elected members of Parliament. During Preval's
term, these same forces murdered at least nine police officers in a few short
months. On July 19, 1996, gunmen assassinated former Sergeant Andre
Pierre Armand, the outspoken leader of an organization for disgruntled former soldiers—the Association of Unjustly Discharged Soldiers. Armand had
numerous enemies among former servicemen, some of whom had threatened to start a guerilla war over unpaid wages and pensions. Approximately
one week before his assassination, Armand had denounced these servicemen's plans to assassinate Aristide and President Preval, and claimed
that some political parties had stockpiled arms. "In Haiti, Leader of Disgruntled Ex-Soldiers Slain," *Miami Herald,* July 24, 1996, A4. For an analysis of
public security issues, see chapter 8, "Continuing Security Concerns."

12.   See Larry Rohter, "Army Leaders Forced Out by Aristide," *New York
Times,* February 22, 1995, A5.

13.   President Aristide originally asked Michael Ratner and me to help
oversee the prosecutions of those responsible for the murders. In this role,
we have organized an international team of lawyers, forensic experts, and
investigators to work on these cases with the appropriate Haitian government officials. As of February 1997, massive amounts of information have
been gathered, witnesses have been interviewed, several *ordonnances* (indictments) have been issued, and at least one person has been tried, convicted, and sentenced for committing a political assassination. See chapter
8, "Prosecutions: The Zimbabwe Trial," "Prosecutions: The Jean-Ronique
Antoine and Robert Lecorps Trial," "Other Steps toward Justice."

14.   As of February 22, 1995, approximately seven hundred adults and
three hundred unaccompanied children remained incarcerated at the Guantanamo Bay Naval Base. Cheryl Little, interview by author, Miami, Florida,
February 22, 1995 (Little is an attorney with Florida Rural Legal Services
who represents many of these Haitian detainees). Many of these children
believed that they would never leave Guantanamo and became seriously

depressed. Others had serious physical problems. See Mireya Navarro, "Many Haitian Children View Camps' Limbo As Permanent," *New York Times*, May 1, 1995, A5. By July 1995, the United States had returned almost all of the refugees to Haiti, and after a protracted legal and political battle by Haitian refugee advocates, the U.S. government allowed a small number of children to enter the United States.

15. Haitian Refugee Center v. Christopher, 43 F.3d 1431, 1432 (11th Cir. 1995) (citing Haitian Refugee Center v. Christopher, No. 95-0022-CIV-MOORE (S.D. Fla. 1995)).

16. Ibid., 1433.

17. Since the 1970s, numerous lawsuits have been litigated over this illegal treatment of Haitian refugees, and several of these cases have reached the U.S. Supreme Court. For an analysis of the history of the approximately twenty years of Haitian refugee litigation, see Irwin P. Stotzky, "America's Unwanted Burden: Haitian Refugees and the Rule of Law," 1996 (on file with Irwin P. Stotzky).

CHAPTER ONE

1. Although Haiti enjoyed relative political stability under Jean-Pierre Boyer (1818–43), his methods were certainly not always just. See David Nicholls, *From Dessalines to Duvalièr: Race, Colour, and National Independence in Haiti* (Cambridge: Cambridge University Press, 1979), 67–82; see also Michel-Rolph Trouillot, *Haiti, State against Nation: The Origins and Legacy of Duvaliérism* (New York: Monthly Review Press, 1990), 47–50.

2. The occupation of Haiti by the United States may have stabilized the currency and briefly reduced administrative corruption, but the overall effect of the occupation severely damaged Haiti in a variety of ways. Trouillot, *Haiti, State against Nation*, 102–8.

3. See, e.g., Charles R. Foster and Albert Valdman, eds. *Haiti—Today and Tomorrow: An Interdisciplinary Study* (Lanham, Md.: University Press of America, 1984), 255–56; Trouillot, *Haiti, State against Nation*, 100–4; Amy Wilentz, *The Rainy Season: Haiti since Duvalièr* (New York: Simon & Schuster, 1989), 77; Jonathan Power, "Haiti Still Has a Chance to Survive," *Calgary Herald*, November 1, 1993, A4. For a more detailed account of the American occupation of Haiti, see Hans Schmidt, *The United States Occupation of Haiti 1915–1934* (New Brunswick, N.J.: Rutgers University Press, 1971).

4. Indeed, Haiti and the Dominican Republic have been at odds since the beginning of the nineteenth century, when France acquired Santo Domingo from Spain in 1795 by the Treaty of Basel. French control over the island had already been disrupted by the slave revolt in 1791. In 1801, Toussaint Louverture, after establishing his authority in Saint-Domingue, occupied Santo Domingo. He promulgated a constitution, which proclaimed him (as governor-general) sovereign over the whole island of Hispaniola, where Haiti and the Dominican Republic are situated. This constitution gave subsequent Haitian rulers the so-called legal basis for their attempts to regain possession over the eastern part of the island. After the French withdrawal from Saint-Domingue in November 1803, Toussaint's successors, Generals Jean-Jacques Dessalines and Henri Christophe, attempted to expel the

French who still remained in Santo Domingo. But the French brought in reinforcements and forced the Haitians to retreat. While retreating, the Haitians looted and slaughtered Dominicans, which became the basis for indictments by Dominican historians of Haitian "barbarism."

In 1821, President Jean-Pierre Boyer of Haiti, responding to overtures from some Dominicans, invaded the Dominican Republic, and by February 1822 had conquered the entire island. He reasserted the principle of the indivisibility of the island. This invasion began a 21-year period in which Haitians took over most of the administrative posts in Santo Domingo and ruled with an authoritarian hand. Boyer abolished slavery, but revived forced labor. He closed the university and left many churches without priests. In February 1844, the Dominicans revolted and won their independence from Haiti. Hostilities between Haiti and the Dominican Republic continue through today. See, e.g., Raymond W. Logan, *Haiti and the Dominican Republic* (New York: Oxford University Press, 1968), 145; Cathy Maternowska, continuing interview by author, November 8, 1993, to August 1, 1995 (Maternowska, an anthropologist who lived in Haiti from 1985 to 1993, worked extensively with the poor of Haiti and was instrumental in the preliminary attempts by the Aristide government to reform the nation).

5.   This phrase has often been used by the enemies of democracy inside and outside of Haiti to refer derogatorily to Haitians as irrational. It suggests that the Haitian political dilemma is immune to rational explanation and therefore to solutions that could be both just and practical. Even those people who claim to believe in democracy, and who should know better, sometimes hide behind this mask of irrationality. For example, Robert Malval, former prime minister of Haiti, claimed that the civilian military leaders behind the coup were simply not rational. *Morning Edition,* National Public Radio, November 1, 1993. This phrase has also been used to refer to positive aspects of Haitian culture.

6.   Schmidt, *Occupation,* 19–41.

7.   It is also worth noting that the historical aspects of Haitian life and class structure are intimately related. A very difficult task awaits the Haitian people. Modifying the barriers created by class structure necessitates fundamental changes in Haitian culture, politics, social relations, and economic development. To make matters even more difficult, all of these factors must be developed simultaneously.

8.   See Sidney W. Mintz, "Can Haiti Change?" *Foreign Affairs* 74 (1995): 73–86.

9.   See ibid.; Schmidt, *Occupation.*

10.   This dual strategy was set up during the presidencies of Alexandre Pétion (1807–18) and Jean-Pierre Boyer (1818–43). For analysis of these points, see Trouillot, *Haiti, State against Nation,* passim. For many of the points expressed in this section of the book, see Michel-Rolph Trouillot, "Haiti's Nightmare and the Lessons of History," *NACLA Report on the Americas* 27 (January/February 1994): 46–53.

11.   See Trouillot, *Haiti, State against Nation,* passim.

12.   See ibid. Under the Aristide and Preval governments, taxes on the elites and the middle class are finally beginning to be collected. For example,

those who import automobiles are now sometimes required to pay the import tariffs. Nevertheless, tax collection remains sporadic and inconsistent. Corruption of public officials is a continuing problem. For example, on October 13, 1996, Max Penn, who headed the State Audit Office under the military regime from 1991 to 1994, was charged with complicity in the theft and sale of government-owned vehicles. "Former Audit Official Charged in Vehicle Sales," *Miami Herald,* October 15, 1996, A9.

On October 15, 1995, police arrested Reynold Georges, a right-wing politician and colleague of Max Penn, while he visited Mr. Penn at the Petionville police station. Police arrested Mr. Georges on charges of criminal conspiracy and subversive activities aiming at the destabilization of public authority. "Police Arrest Far-Right Politician," *Miami Herald,* October 16, 1996, A8. Mr. Georges is also suspected of being involved in public corruption.

13.   U.S. physician Jonathan Brown, who visited Haiti in the 1830s, was highly critical of all aspects of Haiti—its politics, its culture, its social structure, and its people. Indeed, his racist views included the belief that Haiti would be a worthless nation but for its rich soil, which, he believed, saved Haiti from political dissolution. Jonathan Brown, M.D., II, *The History and Present Condition of St. Domingo* (London: Frank Cass & Co. 1971), 259–89.

14.   Historians regard the legislative elections of 1870 in Port-au-Prince as one of the few legitimate electoral victories of nineteenth-century Haiti. Yet, in 1870, fewer than a thousand Port-au-Prince residents had the right to vote. Léon-François Hoffmann, continuing interview by author, January 1993 to July 1996. See Jean-Bertrand Aristide with Christophe Wargny, *Aristide: An Autobiography,* translated by Linda M. Maloney (Maryknoll, N.Y.: Orbis Books, 1993), passim.

15.   For an intriguing discussion of Haitian culture, see Léon-François Hoffmann, "Haitian Sensibility," in *Hispanic and Francophone Regions,* vol. 1 of *A History of Haitian Literature in the Caribbean,* edited by A. James Arnold (Philadelphia: J. Benjamins, 1994), 365–78.

16.   The Aristide and Preval governments have attempted to make the Creole language the official language in schools and in courts.

17.   Hoffmann, "Haitian Sensibility," 368.

18.   Ibid., 368.

19.   Ibid., 372.

20.   See Trouillot, *Haiti, State against Nation;* Michel-Rolph Trouillot, "L'État Prédateur, Nicaragua Aujourd'hui," *Été* 76–77 (1991): 25–27; Michel-Rolph Trouillot, "État et duvaliérisme," in *La République haïtienne: État des lieux et perspectives,* edited by Gérard Barthélemy and Christian Girault (Paris: Karthala, 1993), 189–92.

21.   Schmidt, *Occupation,* 64–107.

22.   The army's dominant factions imposed the presidency of François "Papa Doc" Duvaliér.

23.   See George DeWan, "Reigns of Terror," *Newsday,* October 26, 1993, 24; "Haiti Coup Leader Sentenced to Life," *New York Times,* July 31, 1991, A3. See Bernard Diederich and Al Burt, *Papa Doc: Haiti and its Dictator* (Port-

au-Prince: Éditions H. Deschamps, 1986), passim; James Ferguson, *Papa Doc, Baby Doc: Haiti and the Duvaliérs* (Oxford: Basil Blackwell, 1987), 30–59.

24. DeWan, "Reigns of Terror."

25. Ibid., 25 (estimating the number as up to 60,000, with millions more exiled); see also Ferguson, *Papa Doc, Baby Doc,* 57.

26. Trouillot, *Haiti, State against Nation,* 213–14, 226.

27. Ibid., 175–77.

28. On January 22, 1971, the official gazette, *Le Moniteur,* carried the amendments that were to be voted on in the national referendum. One of the amendments included lowering the minimum age for the presidency from forty to eighteen. The ballot stated that Jean-Claude had been chosen to succeed his father and listed two questions plus the answer: "Does this choice answer your aspirations? Do you ratify it? Answer: yes." *Le Moniteur,* January 22, 1971. The official count was 2,391,916 in favor and, of course, not a single vote opposed. See, e.g., Diederich and Burt, *Papa Doc,* 397.

29. Ferguson, *Papa Doc, Baby Doc,* 60–89. The popular will had been expressed in other ways prior to 1990. In 1984, for example, there were food riots in Gonaives, where the masses attacked the warehouses of nine charitable organizations. This was the first mass demonstration against the regime. The 1987 Constitution was another expression of the popular will. Maternowska, continuing interview.

30. For a discussion of the emerging Haitian peasant movement, see Robert E. Maguire, "Haiti's Emerging Peasant Movement," *Cimarrón: New Perspectives on the Caribbean* 2(3) (1990): 28–44.

31. At least five different governments ruled the country until the election of Aristide. See, e.g., *Special Economic and Disaster Relief Assistance to Haiti: Note by the Secretary-General,* at 10, U.N. Doc. A/45/870/ADD.1 (1991) (hereafter cited as UN Report on Mission).

32. Maternowska, continuing interview.

33. Steven Forester, "Haitian Asylum Advocacy: Questions to Ask Applicants and Notes on Interviewing and Representation," *New York Law School Journal of Human Rights* 10 (1993): 357; see Lawyers Committee for Human Rights, *Paper Laws, Steel Bayonets: Breakdown of the Rule of Law in Haiti* (New York: Lawyers Committee for Human Rights, 1990), 3–10.

34. A provisional government, the National Governing Council, assumed control after Baby Doc went into exile. Leslie Manigat was the first person then to serve as president through an election marred by massive fraud and abstention. After he attempted to assert civilian control over the military, he was overthrown. General Henri Namphy then declared himself leader and served from June through September 1988, placing Haiti under strict military control. Lawyers Committee, *Paper Laws.*

35. See Americas Watch et al., *Haiti: The Aristide Government's Human Rights Record* (New York: Human Rights Watch, 1991).

36. See, e.g., Howard W. French, "Haitians Overwhelmingly Elect Populist Priest to the Presidency," *New York Times,* December 18, 1990, A4; Lee Hockstader, "Haiti's Army Chiefs Defend Overthrow; OAS Delegation Holds 2nd Day of Talks," *Washington Post,* October 6, 1991, A29.

37.   See, e.g., Human Rights Watch, *Human Rights Watch World Report 1992: Events of 1991* (New York: Human Rights Watch, 1992), 258–59; Forester, "Asylum Advocacy," 359; Don A. Schanche, "Populist Priest Wins in Haiti, Is Backed by U.S.," *Los Angeles Times*, December 18, 1990, A1. Aristide actually received even greater popular support. Approximately four hundred thousand votes in his favor had to be nullified because the ballots were so complex that many of the illiterate people could not understand how to cast their votes. These people were, of course, Aristide supporters. Maternowska, continuing interview.

38.   See, e.g., Council of Freely Elected Heads of Government, *The 1990 General Elections in Haiti* (Washington, D.C.: National Democrat Institute for International Affairs, 1991), 87, 92. Similarly, both the UN and the OAS took leading roles in post-coup efforts to restore democracy in Haiti. Even with the restoration of the democratically elected Aristide government, the efforts of the international community to create a democracy in Haiti have not been entirely successful. See Peter Hakim, "Saving Haiti from Itself: How a New OAS Effort Can Build Democracy," *Washington Post*, May 31, 1992, C1; see also Barbara Crossette, "Accord on Ending Haiti Crisis Reported," *New York Times*, November 16, 1991. The same organizations provided tremendous help in monitoring the 1995 elections. See chapter 8, "Elections."

39.   For a useful account of the 1990 elections in Haiti, see Council of Heads of Government, *General Elections in Haiti*; UN Report on Mission.

40.   Approximately 70 percent of Haiti's population is illiterate and desperately poor. See, e.g., Howard W. French, "Haiti's Split Seen at a Swearing-In," *New York Times*, June 21, 1992, sec. 1, p. 13; cf. "Haitian Vote, So Bloody Before, Is Peaceful," *St. Louis Post-Dispatch*, December 17, 1990, A1 (citing the illiteracy rate as high as 80 percent).

41.   Pamela Constable, "For the U.S. No Choice but Optimism after Haiti Vote," *Boston Globe*, December 23, 1990, 4. See "Haitian Vote," A1.

42.   Kenneth Roth, "Haiti: The Shadows of Terror," *New York Review of Books*, March 26, 1992, 62–63 (pointing out that Raul Cédras, whom Aristide selected to head the army, was credited with supervising the relatively peaceful December 1990 elections). This behavior directly contradicts claims by apologists for the military during the coup period and the reign of terror that followed it, that the army was nothing more than a coalition of competing gangs and that the military hierarchy was unable to control the actions of its subordinates.

43.   See, e.g., Howard W. French, "Troops Storming Palace, Capture Plotters and Free President," *New York Times*, January 8, 1991, A1; "High Abstention in Second-Round Polls; At Stake Is Who Will Be Aristide's Prime Minister," *Latin American Weekly Report*, January 31, 1991, 10.

44.   This reign of terror resulted in the deaths and torture of thousands of innocent people. See note 54 below. The coup itself resulted in the death of at least thirty people. See, e.g., "Haitian President Is Ousted; At Least Thirty Reported Killed as Army Troops Mutiny," *Chicago Tribune*, October 1, 1991, 4.

45.   Ira J. Kurzban, continuing interview by author, November 8, 1993,

to November 1996 (Kurzban is attorney and adviser to President Aristide); President Jean-Bertrand Aristide, continuing interview by author, November 8, 1993, to November 1996.

46. This was his inaugural address. *Haiti Progress,* a Haitian-language daily newspaper in New York, published his address in full on February 1, 1971. A copy of the address cannot be obtained because the newspaper did not keep copies of it.

47. Kurzban, continuing interview; President Aristide, continuing interview.

48. Roth, "Haiti: Shadows," 62; Kurzban, continuing interview; President Aristide, continuing interview.

49. Kurzban, continuing interview; Maternowska, continuing interview; President Aristide, continuing interview.

50. Americas Watch et al., *Haiti;* Kurzban, continuing interview; Maternowska, continuing interview; President Aristide, continuing interview.

51. Aristide replaced section chiefs with unarmed "communal police agents." They were under the supervision of the local judiciary. This action was in line with the requirement of the 1987 Constitution of putting the police force under civilian control and thereby separating it from control of the army. Americas Watch Committee, *Silencing a People: The Destruction of Civil Society in Haiti* (New York: Human Rights Watch 1993), 104.

52. Kurzban, continuing interview; Maternowska, continuing interview; President Aristide, continuing interview.

53. Roth, "Haiti: Shadows," 62–63; Kurzban, continuing interview; Maternowska, continuing interview; President Aristide, continuing interview.

54. The Platform of Haitian Organizations for the Defense of Human Rights (La Plate-Forme des Organismes Haïtiens de Défense des Droits Humains) documented 1,021 cases of extrajudicial executions from October 1991 to August 1992 and estimates the number of cases could be as high as 3,000. Memorandum to the OAS Commission to Haiti, August 17, 1992, 3. Perhaps several thousand more Haitians have been murdered since that time, and thousands have been illegally arrested, detained, and tortured. Indeed, recent estimates suggest that at least 5,000 and perhaps as many as 6,000 people were executed between the occurrence of the 1991 coup and the reinstatement of the Aristide government. A knowledgeable observer in Haiti estimates that between 200,000 and 400,000 people were also forced into hiding from the time the coup occurred until Aristide's reinstatement. Some people were so frightened of the attachés that they remained in hiding for months after Aristide's return. Kurzban, continuing interview; Maternowska, continuing interview; President Aristide, continuing interview.

Unfortunately, Aristide's reinstatement to office did not totally stop the violence. For example, during the week of March 25, 1995, approximately twenty-five people were murdered in Port-au-Prince alone. Many of these were political murders. On March 29, 1995, a prominent coup supporter was assassinated, and unsubstantiated allegations made by U.S. officials suggest that the interior minister may have ordered the killing. Further investigation suggests, however, that either paramilitary forces or criminals involved in the drug trade were behind the murder. Political murders of

Aristide supporters continued throughout President Aristide's final months in office, and into President Preval's term. The renewed violence makes it clear that, while the approximate eight-month U.S. military occupation, the several-month MNF occupation, and the close to two-year UN peace-keeping force occupation may have subdued turbulence in Haiti, they have clearly not eliminated the notorious culture of political murder and paramilitary terror. See "Haiti, after Six Months," *New York Times*, March 31, 1995, A30; see also chapter 8, "Continuing Security Concerns."

55. See, e.g., "Haitian Troops Threaten Assembly," *St. Louis Post-Dispatch*, October 8, 1991, A1.

56. Kurzban, continuing interview; Maternowska, continuing interview; President Aristide, continuing interview. The systematic seizure and torture of other democratically elected officials ensued as well. See, e.g., Evans Paul, "A Mayor in Hiding Speaks Out," *Miami Herald*, November 3, 1991, C1.

57. "Macoutes Stand to Reap Benefit as Haiti Gives Political Pardons," *Florida Sun-Sentinel*, December 26, 1991, A10; Kurzban, continuing interview; Maternowska, continuing interview; President Aristide, continuing interview.

58. Kurzban, continuing interview; Maternowska, continuing interview; President Aristide, continuing interview.

59. Kurzban, continuing interview; Maternowska, continuing interview; President Aristide, continuing interview.

CHAPTER TWO

1. For a step-by-step description of the attempt by the OAS to enforce the "Santiago Commitment to Democracy and the Renewal of the Inter-American System" in Haiti, see Stephen J. Schnably, "The Santiago Commitment as a Call to Democracy and Human Rights in the United States: Evaluating the OAS Role in Haiti, Peru, and Guatemala," *University of Miami Inter-American Law Review* 25 (1994): 393–587. For an interesting catalogue and analysis of events that took place in Haiti between 1991 and 1995, see Roland I. Perusse, *Haitian Democracy Restored: 1991–1995* (Lanham, Md.: University Press of America, 1995).

2. The problem is even more complex than it first appears. Certain factions of the U.S. government have always had reservations about Aristide. Indeed, President Clinton's goal of restoring Aristide to power was long undermined by officials in the defense establishment—the CIA, Pentagon, and State Department. Early in Aristide's exile, the CIA distributed a report that branded Aristide as mentally unstable, claiming that he had spent time in a mental hospital in Canada. Senator Jesse Helms, basing his conclusion on this CIA report, referred to him as a "psychopath" and a "demonstrable killer." See Christopher Marquis, "What Next for U.S. on Haiti? The Options Aren't Good," *Miami Herald*, October 30, 1993, A28. The report was a sham. The Cable News Network (CNN) found no record of Aristide being treated for mental depression in Canada, and the report was revealed to be based on unconfirmed information supplied by the very people who overthrew him. The CIA has even admitted that it has been paying individuals in the

Haitian military leadership for this kind of information since the early 1980s. Tim Weiner, "Key Haiti Leaders Said to Have Been in the C.I.A.'s Pay," *New York Times*, November 1, 1993, A1. Even more disturbing is the CIA analysts' portrait of Cédras, who was praised as a member of "the most promising group of Haitian leaders" to emerge since 1986. Christopher Marquis, "Clinton Goal to Return Aristide to Power Undercut by Aides," *Miami Herald*, November 4, 1993, A19. The CIA was and is intentionally engaged in the character assassination of Aristide. Other government departments, in subtle and not so subtle ways, bought into this disparagement of Aristide and his government. For example, when Les Aspin served as secretary of defense, he objected both to sending troops to Haiti and to committing them armed only with handguns. Senior Pentagon officials constantly questioned whether we should help at all in reinstating Aristide to power. This skepticism toward Aristide was essentially the legacy of the Bush State Department, and it repeatedly undercut Aristide's chances of returning to Haiti and establishing a democracy. Jill Smolowe, "With Friends Like These," *Time*, November 8, 1993, 44–45. The Clinton administration seems to have followed this skeptical approach, particularly in negotiating Aristide's return and in dealing with his government since his restoration. Other parts of the defense establishment have also expressed misgivings about the Aristide government. See chapter 3.

Certain U.S. government agencies and officials continued to spread false and unsubstantiated information about Aristide and his government after he had been reinstated. Throughout Aristide's term and into President Preval's, certain journalists floated rumors that Aristide's people were involved in murders. For example, in 1996, syndicated columnist Robert Novak reported that U.S. military intelligence sources had said that, since October 1, 1994, there had been at least eighty politically motivated killings "traceable to close associates" of Aristide. The U.S. embassy in Port-au-Prince says there is no evidence to support these allegations. It estimates the number of politically motivated deaths to be ten, not eighty. More important, these people were probably victims of supporters and members of the former de facto government. Some recent examples of suspected political murders include Fresnel Lamarre, who was killed in early May 1995. Lamarre was a leading suspect in the September 1993 assassination of Antoine Izméry, an outspoken Aristide ally. Shortly after Lamarre's death, Clerveau Bonaparte, one of his friends, was killed in his car by gunmen who shot him forty times at close range. Haitian police officials and diplomats have speculated that Lamarre and Bonaparte may have been targeted by those who commissioned Antoine Izméry's killing. Colonel Michael Ange Hernan was shot and killed as he walked out of a clinic on May 24, 1995. He was formerly in charge of administering pensions for the army. Police officials suggest he may have been killed by disgruntled soldiers from Haiti's disbanded army. Michael Gonzales, director general of the airline Haiti Air, was killed on May 22, 1995, by gunmen riding motorcycles as he and his daughter drove past Aristide's private residence. The case clearly has Haitian officials stumped. Sandra Marques, "Leaked Report Shows Internal U.S. Discord Over Haiti Policy," *Miami Herald*, August 17, 1995, A18. A French member of the UN peace-keeping force in Haiti was shot in the head and critically wounded by an unidentified assailant. Marshall Christian Marginier, a member of the CIVPOL in the western town of Petit Goave, was preparing to go to bed when he was shot from about ten yards away. The attackers left a tract stating that President Jean-Bertrand Aristide had not kept his promise to pay Haiti's newly demobilized soldiers. "U.N. Peacekeeper Shot by Unknown Assailant," *Miami Herald,* September 2, 1995, A23. In November 1995, two newly elected members of Parliament were attacked by gunmen, and one died. The one who died was President Aristide's cousin. The attack was a clear warning to the Aristide government. Political murders continue into President Preval's term. See chapter 8, "Security and U.S. Involvement in Haiti."

3. *Support to the Democratic Government of Haiti,* M.R.E. Res. 1/91, OAS Ad Hoc Meeting of Ministers of Foreign Affairs, OEA/Ser.F/V.1, OAS Doc. MRE/RES (1991).

4. The Aristide government had long been urging a total trade embargo, including a boycott of travel into and out of Haiti. The United States, however, consistently and persistently refused to impose a total embargo. John Donnelly, "Haitian Army Leaders Snub Negotiations," *Miami Herald,* November 6, 1993, A1. Several months before the return of the democratically elected government, the boycott became more intense and more effective. U.S. officials finally agreed to take further action, even taking cues from an adviser to Aristide, who—among other things—suggested peppering Haiti with radio transmissions of speeches by President Aristide in the hope of creating enough hostility in the citizenry to force the military leaders to step down. The United States provided President Aristide with the technology to send weekly addresses to the Haitian people. Haitian exiles in Montreal went even further by calling for a volunteer force of exiles to invade Haiti, and urging President Aristide to seek help from Canada and the United States to arm, train, and finance their group. "Haiti Envoy Flies to U.S. for Meetings," *Miami Herald,* November 7, 1993, A26.

Unfortunately, the effects of the series of international embargoes during Aristide's forced exile seemed to cause more hardship for the Haitian people than for the intended victims, the military leaders, and their supporters. See, e.g., Kenneth Freed, "Next Step; Haiti: A Society Burning with Sorrow," *Los Angeles Times,* October 26, 1993, 1 (estimating that more than ten thousand people have starved to death since the first international embargo went into effect in October 1991); see also Howard W. French, "Study Says Haiti Sanctions Kill Up to 1,000 Children a Month," *New York Times,* November 9, 1993, A1 (estimating that, as a result of the latest embargo, an additional thousand Haitian children were dying each month). It appears that these estimates were highly overstated.

5. *Protocole entre le Président Jean-Bertrand Aristide et la Commision parlementaire de négociation en vue de trouver une solution définitive à la crise haïtienne,* February 23, 1992, reprinted in Annexe I to *Lettre datée du 10 mars 1992, adressée au Secrétaire général par le Représentant permanent d'Haïti auprès de L'Organisation des Nations Unies,* A/46/891, S/23691 (March 11, 1992) (hereafter cited as *Protocol of Washington*).

6. See *Protocole d'Accord Entre le Président Jean-Bertrand Aristide, et le Premier Ministre Désigné, René Theodore, sous les Auspices de L'Organisation des États Américains (OEA)*, February 25, 1992, translated in *Report on the Situation of Human Rights in Haiti Submitted by Mr. Marco Tulio Bruni Celli, Special Rapporteur, in Accordance with Commission Resolution 1992/77*, U.N. ESCOR, Comm'n on Hum. Rts., U.N. Doc. E/CN.4/1993/47 (1993), Annexe II, and in Organization of American States, *Report on the Situation of Human Rights in Haiti*, OEA/Ser.L/V/II.83, Doc. 18, at 55 (March 9, 1993) (hereafter cited as *1993 Bruni Celli Report*).

7. Ibid.

8. *Protocol of Washington*, art. V.1 ("une amnistie générale, hormis les criminels de droit commun"). The United States read this amnesty phrase to include the coup leaders. The particular concern of the United States seemed to be the protection of General Raul Cédras. Aristide, of course, claimed Cédras to be a common criminal and thus subject to trial. See, e.g., Barbara Crossette, "Ousted Leader Signs Pact with Old Rival," *New York Times*, February 26, 1992, A3. This obviously correct position led several diplomats close to the OAS mission to express impatience with Aristide, see, e.g., Howard W. French, "Two Rights Groups Protest Offer of Amnesty in Haiti," *New York Times*, April 16, 1993, A7, and to praise Cédras as a "moderate" and a "positive force." See Christopher Marquis, "Aristide Vows Not to Return until Army Chief is Ousted," *Miami Herald*, January 21, 1992, A11.

9. "Haiti's President Won't Step Down," *Miami Herald*, March 7, 1992, A6.

10. Don Bohning, "Hopes Fade for Haiti Accord," *Miami Herald*, March 19, 1992, A24; "OAS Must Set Haiti Free," *Miami Herald*, March 27, 1992, A20.

11. See J. P. Slavin, "Court Rejects Pact for Aristide's Return," *Washington Post*, March 28, 1992, A16.

12. *1993 Bruni Celli Report*, 7.

13. "Chamber Plan Offers Aristide No Guarantee," *Miami Herald*, May 21, 1992, A27; Lee Hockstader, "Premier Nominated in Haiti; Police Break Up Funeral; International Backing for Appointee Seen Unlikely," *Washington Post*, June 3, 1992, A23; J. P. Slavin, "Haiti Plans to Form New Government," *Miami Herald*, June 11, 1992, A23.

14. Howard W. French, "Rival of Haiti's Ousted President Is Installed as the Prime Minister," *New York Times*, June 20, 1992, 3; see also "Deputies Ratify Aristide Rival as Haiti's New Prime Minister," *Miami Herald*, June 11, 1992, A23; Hockstader, "Premier Nominated in Haiti." Bazin, the apparent choice of the United States to become president of Haiti in 1990, ran a distant second in the 1990 presidential election, much to the chagrin of U.S. officials.

15. *Restoration of Democracy in Haiti*, OAS Ad Hoc Meeting of Ministers of Foreign Affairs, OEA/Ser.F/V.1, para. 2, OAS Doc. MRE/RES.3/92 (1992), reprinted in *Foreign Policy Bulletin* 3 (July–August 1992): 82–83.

16. Ibid., paras. 5a, 5e. Although the United States announced it would comply with the OAS request, it clearly did not enforce the order to bar ships that had violated the embargo. See "Bush Backs OAS in Denying Use

of United States Ports to Vessels Trading with Haiti," *Weekly Compilation of Presidential Documents* 28(22) (June 1, 1992): 941. See David Adams, "Embargo Fails to Seal Off Haiti," *San Francisco Chronicle*, March 18, 1993, A14; Kenneth Freed, "In Haiti, Slipping through Embargo's Net," *Los Angeles Times*, July 12, 1992, A5.

17. See Howard W. French, "U.S. Presses Ousted Haitian Chief to Negotiate a Return from Exile," *New York Times*, June 27, 1992, sec. 1, p. 2; Christopher Marquis, "U.S. to Aristide: Negotiate," *Miami Herald*, June 24, 1992, A1.

18. See Christopher Marquis, "Make Deal, U.S. Tells Aristide," *Miami Herald*, July 25, 1992, A9.

19. See J. P. Slavin, "Haiti Agrees to Allow Team of Observers," *Miami Herald*, September 10, 1992, A28.

20. See *1993 Bruni Celli Report*, 10–11; Barbara Crossette, "Haiti Detains 150 Returned by the U.S.," *New York Times*, August 15, 1992, sec. 1, p. 3; "Haitian Factions Hold Talks in Washington," *New York Times*, September 2, 1992, A7; Christopher Marquis, "Aristide Names Panel to Discuss Haiti Solution," *Miami Herald*, July 8, 1992, A6; "OAS Team, Haitians to Try to Solve Crisis," *Miami Herald*, August 19, 1992, A5; Marjorie Valbrun, "Aristide Set to Negotiate His Return," *Miami Herald*, July 4, 1992, B1.

21. See Barbara Crossette, "Gains Are Reported in Talks on Haiti," *New York Times*, September 7, 1992, sec. 1, p. 5; "Haiti Agrees to Accept Human Rights Observers," *New York Times*, September 14, 1992, A8; Christopher Marquis, "Ex-Jamaican Chief May Try to Broker End to Haiti Crisis," *Miami Herald*, September 17, 1992, A20. Reportedly, Aristide supported a mission of 500 members, but the Haitian army would not allow Bazin to agree to such a large number. See *1993 Bruni Celli Report*, 11.

22. See Christopher Marquis, "Clinton, Bush Aides Back Haiti Efforts," *Miami Herald*, January 7, 1993, A21.

23. The UN General Assembly and the OAS condemned the elections. G.A. Res. 47/20, U.N. GADR, 47th Sess., U.N. Doc. A/RES/47/20 (1992).

24. See Howard W. French, "Visiting U.S. General Warns Haiti's Military Chiefs," *New York Times*, January 9, 1993, sec. 1, p. 5.

25. See Don Bohning, "Haiti Observers a Glimmer of Hope," *Miami Herald*, February 18, 1993, A20.

26. See Don Bohning, "U.S. Names Special Haiti Advisor," *Miami Herald*, March 12, 1993, A7.

27. See Don Bohning, "U.N. Envoy Leaves Haiti; Crisis Persists," *Miami Herald*, April 17, 1993, A9.

28. See Pamela Constable, "U.S. Readies for Return of Aristide; $1 Billion in Aid, Foreign Advisers Envisioned for Haiti," *Boston Globe*, April 8, 1993, 1; Howard W. French, "Haiti Talks Stall Over Amnesty for Coup Leaders," *New York Times*, April 7, 1993, A11; Kurzban, continuing interview.

29. See Howard W. French, "Two Rights Groups Protest Offer of an Amnesty in Haiti," *New York Times*, April 16, 1993, A11. Americas Watch

and the National Coalition for Haitian Refugees criticized UN and U.S. support for a blanket amnesty as contrary to international law. Ibid.

30. The OAS/UN joint envoy, Dante Caputo, brokered the deal. This effort was a very significant one. It represented one of the first resolution efforts with direct interhemispheric involvement. See Don Bohning, "Haiti Talks Once More at Crossroads," *Miami Herald*, April 15, 1993, A20; Howard W. French, "Haiti Army Spurns Offer of Amnesty by Exiled President," *New York Times*, April 17, 1993, A1; Marquis, "Clinton, Bush Aides Back Haiti Efforts."

31. See Agreement between President Jean-Bertrand Aristide and General Raul Cédras, July 3, 1993, reprinted in *The Situation of Democracy and Human Rights in Haiti: Report of the Secretary General*, A/47/975, S/26063, 2–3 (July 12, 1993); see also Howard W. French, "Haitian Military Is Said to Accept Plan to End Crisis," *New York Times*, July 3, 1993, A1. The joint envoy negotiated primarily with Cédras. See Howard W. French, "Haiti's Military Leaders Reported Unyielding at Talks," *New York Times*, June 29, 1993, A3. Aristide had limited input into the plan's terms, and, after securing Cédras's agreement, officials presented the plan to Aristide, leaving him virtually no choice but to accept it. See Howard W. French, "Haiti Negotiations are Reported at a Critical Stage," *New York Times*, July 1, 1993, A9; Christopher Marquis, "Haiti Talks: Distrust and Hope—Transition of Power Discussed," *Miami Herald*, June 28, 1993, A1 ("Caputo focused his energies on Cédras Sunday, spending at least six hours with the general throughout the day, in comparison with a one-hour morning session with Aristide"); see also Christopher Marquis, "Aristide Balks at Haiti Plan," *Miami Herald*, July 3, 1993, A1 (UN Secretary-General Boutros-Ghali indicates to Aristide, "don't think, just sign"); Elaine Sciolino, "Haiti's Man of Destiny Awaiting His Hour," *New York Times*, August 3, 1993, A1, A5 (reports that Aristide was told not to examine the agreement, but to just sign it). Lawyers and advisers to Aristide were furious about this treatment and the pressure exerted, on Aristide alone, by the United States and the international community. Kurzban, continuing interview.

32. Governors Island Agreement, July 4, 1993, paras. 2, 3 (on file with Irwin P. Stotzky). It was also understood that Aristide would name a consensus prime minister. In addition, the confirmation of the prime minister would not take place until the matter of the election of nine new members to the Parliament in sham elections conducted by the military in January 1993 had been resolved.

33. Ibid., para. 4.

34. Ibid., para. 9.

35. Ibid., para. 8.

36. See Sciolino, "Haiti's Man of Destiny Awaiting His Hour," A1.

37. Governors Island Agreement, para. 7.

38. Ibid., para. 5C.

39. Ibid., para. 5B.

40. Ibid., para. 6.

41. New York Pact, para. 2, reprinted in *Report on the Situation of Human*

Rights in Haiti, Inter-Am. C.H.R., OEA/Ser.L/V/II.85, Doc. 9 rev. (1994). The New York Pact also described the steps necessary to remove the members of Parliament who had taken office after the January 1993 election. Ibid., para. 4(viii).

42. Ibid., paras. 3, 4.

43. See Harold Maass, "Haitian Premier Swears in New Cabinet," *Miami Herald,* September 3, 1993, A16; "Premier Vows to Help Heal Haiti's Torment," *Miami Herald,* August 31, 1993, A1.

44. S.C. Res. 867, U.N. SCOR, 3282d mtg., U.N. Doc. S/RES/867 (1993); see also Paul Lewis, "U.N. Votes to Send Team to Assess Cost of Haitian Mission," *New York Times,* September 1, 1993, A7; "U.N. Wants Units in Haiti Fast," *Miami Herald,* September 24, 1993, A5.

45. See Christopher Marquis, "U.S. Sending Troops to Haiti for U.N. Nation-Building Plan," *Miami Herald,* September 28, 1993, A28; Frank J. Prial, "U.N. Lifts Haitian Oil Embargo as Junta Prepares to Step Aside," *New York Times,* August 28, 1993, A1; "U.N. Advance Mission Will Head to Haiti to Help Reform Police," *Miami Herald,* September 1, 1993, A12.

46. See "U.N. Ready to Reform Haitian Police Force," *Miami Herald,* September 26, 1993, A29.

47. See Steven A. Holmes, "U.N. Force to Rely on Haitians to Keep Order," *New York Times,* October 1, 1993, A5; "U.S. Dispatching 600 on Haiti Assignment," *New York Times,* September 29, 1993, A5.

48. See Human Rights Watch/Americas and National Coalition for Haitian Refugees, "Terror Prevails in Haiti," 6(5) (April 1994): 5. Although attachés never had, and today certainly do not have, any legally recognized status, they were, and remain, perhaps the most significant factor in "policing" many areas in Haiti. OAS/IACHR *Report on the Situation of Human Rights in Haiti,* OEA/Ser.L/V/11.85, Doc. 9 rev., February 11, 1994, at 73. In their heyday, attachés and other paramilitary groups were armed and dressed in civilian clothes; some had identification cards issued by the army. With the cooperation of the Haitian military, attachés operated as death squads that frequently descended on poor neighborhoods at night to carry out violent attacks with impunity. These actions, of course, created a climate of terror in Haiti.

They initiated, and were directly involved in, several public violent attacks against members of the Aristide government and its supporters. For example, on September 11, 1993, just over a month before the assassination of Guy Malary, then the minister of justice, a group of attachés, together with a member of the Haitian military, forced prominent Haitian businessman and pro-Aristide figure Antoine Izméry from a church in Port-au-Prince during a mass and shot him twice in the head at point-blank range as he knelt in the street. HRW/Americas, "Terror," 13. (Izméry had organized the mass to commemorate the fifth anniversary of the burning of Aristide's former church and the murder of thirteen members of the congregation by armed men.) Izméry's killers entered and departed the scene protected and escorted by police vehicles operated by uniformed police officers. The OAS/UN International Civilian Mission (ICM) concluded that the Izméry murder "could not have been carried out without the complicity, if not the direct participation, of highly-placed members of the Haitian armed forces [FAD'H]." OAS/UN International Civilian Mission in Haiti, *Report on the Assassination of Antoine Izmery*, November 18, 1993, at 17 (hereafter cited as OAS/UN Report).

In addition, on September 2, 1993, attachés seized and occupied City Hall at Port-au-Prince during a ceremony for the reinstatement of Evans Paul as mayor. Attachés announced to local Radio Metropole that they did not recognize Robert Malval as prime minister or Evans Paul as mayor and threatened to kill anyone attempting to enter the building. The ceremony was rescheduled for September 8 in front of City Hall, where, on that date, several hundred people gathered. Over two hundred attachés, who had been occupying the building, withdrew following police orders, then regrouped around the building, where they fired off rounds of automatic gunfire and attacked passers-by with batons and knives. Despite the presence of the police, no attempt was made to prevent the violence. Mayor Paul's pleas to Colonel François to provide police security were ignored. Three civilians were shot to death and thirty-one others were injured, including Hervé Denis, the minister of information and culture. Ibid.

On October 11, 1993, just days before the Malary killing, attachés were also involved in a violent demonstration, which forced the USS *Harlan County* to abort docking at the harbor in Port-au-Prince. HRW/Americas, "Terror," 36. Armed members of FRAPH, demonstrators, and attachés yelled insults at foreign journalists on the scene, and then violently attacked them and the car of the U.S. chargé d'affaires. This violence occurred in plain view of ICM monitors and in the presence of a large number of uniformed police who did not intervene. *The Situation of Democracy and Human Rights in Haiti, Report by the Secretary-General,* A/48/532/Add.1, at 7 (New York UNIPUB, November 18, 1993) (hereafter cited as UN/Secretary-General Report).

49.   See, e.g., Joseph B. Treaster, "Drug Flow through Haiti Cut Sharply by Embargo," *New York Times,* November 4, 1993, A10. Indeed, the military built a modern paved highway into the Dominican Republic to help avoid the embargo and to aid in its drug trade. See, e.g., French, "Haitian Military Is Said to Accept Plan to End Crisis."

50.   Howard W. French, "Haitians Block Landing of U.S. Forces," *New York Times,* October 12, 1993, A1. The UN/OAS observers were eventually evacuated after Justice Minister Guy Malary was gunned down, and after other cabinet members received death threats. See John Donnelly and Harold Maass, "Aristide Aide Assassinated," *Miami Herald,* October 15, 1993, A1; Andres Oppenheimer and Christopher Marquis, "Big Guns to Enforce Embargo," *Miami Herald,* October 16, 1993, A1; Garry Pierre-Pierre, "Rights Monitors Are Pulled Out of Haiti," *New York Times,* October 16, 1993, A4.

51.   See Don Bohning et al., "Mob to Americans: 'Go Home!'" *Miami Herald,* October 12, 1993, A1; French, "Haitians Block Landing."

52.   *Note by the President of Security Council,* U.N. SCOR, 3289th mtg., U.N. Doc. S/26567 (1993) (hereafter cited as *Note by the President of Security Council*); see Steven A. Holmes, "U.S. and U.N. Tell Haiti Military Must Cooperate," *New York Times,* October 12, 1993, A12; Christopher Marquis and Rob-

ert A. Rankin, "Let Troops Land or Face U.N. Action, Haiti Told," *Miami Herald*, October 12, 1993, A6.

53.   John Donnelly and Harold Maass, "U.S. Ship Retreats from Haiti," *Miami Herald*, October 13, 1993, A1; Steven A. Holmes, "Bid to Restore Haiti's Leader Is Derailed," *New York Times*, October 13, 1993, A1.

54.   See Howard W. French, "Tension is Rising as Haiti Military Tightens Its Grip," *New York Times*, October 17, 1993, A1; see also Paul Lewis, "U.N. Backs Use of Ships to Enforce Haiti Embargo," *New York Times*, October 17, 1993, A15.

55.   *Note by the President of Security Council.* Clinton ordered U.S. warships to move within three miles of Haiti's coast, and some officials hinted at the use of force to restore Aristide. On the use of helicopters and boats, see Marquis and Rankin, "Let Troops Land." On the refusal to rule out force, see "U.S. Not Ruling Out Use of Force, U.S. Envoy Says," *Miami Herald*, October 18, 1993, A6; see also Steven A. Holmes, "Clinton Warns North Korea against Building Atom Bomb," *New York Times*, November 8, 1993, A6 (mentioning President Clinton's refusal to rule out force to restore Aristide).

56.   Specifically, the United States froze the assets of forty-one individuals and thirty-four organizations that were obstructing the restoration of democracy in Haiti. See Christopher Marquis, "Clinton Freezes U.S. Assets of Haitians in Homeland," *Miami Herald*, June 23, 1994, A16; Christopher Marquis, "U.S. Blocks Assets of Aristide Opponents," *Miami Herald*, October 23, 1993, A24.

57.   The UN sanctions focused on the ban of petroleum and weapons, while U.S. and OAS sanctions covered all trade. See Ron Howell, "U.S. Boards Ship Off Haiti; Sanctions Begin, Poor Express Pain," *Newsday*, October 20, 1993, 7; see also David Hancock, "Customs Expects Traders to Take Trade Ban Seriously," *Miami Herald*, October 20, 1993, A13; Andres Oppenheimer and Christopher Marquis, "Clinton Tightens Haiti Sanctions," *Miami Herald*, October 20, 1993, A1.

58.   Only under significant U.S. pressure did Joaquin Balaguer, president of the Dominican Republic, agree to take steps to enforce the international embargo. See Susan Benesch and Christopher Marquis, "Fuel Still Flows to Haiti from Dominican Republic," *Miami Herald*, May 22, 1994, A26; John Kifner, "Balaguer Says He'll Enforce Curbs On Haiti," *New York Times*, May 30, 1994, sec. 1, p. 4.

59.   See John Donnelly, "New Round of Talks Tentatively Set," *Miami Herald*, November 4, 1993, A19; Tim Johnson, "Haitian Army Snubs U.N. Request to Revive Talks," *Miami Herald*, November 2, 1993, A10; Garry Pierre-Pierre, "Haitian Talks End on a Hopeful Note," *New York Times*, November 4, 1993, A10.

60.   Garry Pierre-Pierre, "Effort to Save Haitian Talks Fails as Military Leaders Shun Meeting," *New York Times*, November 6, 1993, sec. 1, p. 1.

61.   See Steven A. Holmes, "Premier of Haiti Is Seeking Talks to End Impasse," *New York Times*, December 7, 1993, A3; Christopher Marquis, "Malval Seeks to Launch Dialogue to Restore Aristide," *Miami Herald*, December 7, 1993, A18; see also "Aristide's Plight: Out of Sight Out of Mind," *COHA's Washington Report on the Hemisphere*, December 14, 1993, 3.

62.   Steven A. Holmes, "U.S. Disenchantment with Aristide Growing," *New York Times*, December 18, 1993, A7.

63.   Christopher Marquis, "Clinton Vows to Reassess Haiti Policy," *Miami Herald*, January 7, 1994, A1; see also Steven Greenhouse, "U.S. Aides Say They Still Back Aristide," *New York Times*, January 7, 1994, A10.

64.   Marquis, "Clinton Vows."

65.   The change in the focus of the conference resulted from the position that the refugee topic would have been embarrassing for the United States in light of Clinton's policy of forcibly repatriating Haiti's boat people. "Aristide Bows to U.S. On a Haiti Conference," *New York Times*, January 8, 1994, sec. 1, p. 6.

66.   See "Aristide Agrees to Have Army at Meeting," *Miami Herald*, January 8, 1994, A20; Steven Greenhouse, "U.S. Sees a Ray of Hope in Haiti Talks," *New York Times*, January 14, 1994, A6; Christopher Marquis, "Aristide Convenes Talks in Miami Amid Controversy," *Miami Herald*, January 14, 1994, A20; Christopher Marquis, "Legislators Prod U.S. on Haiti," *Miami Herald*, January 16, 1994, A1.

67.   See Ron Howell, "New Prime Minister Sought for Haiti," *Newsday*, January 17, 1994, 13.

68.   Howard W. French, "Aristide Seeking to Rally Support," *New York Times*, January 18, 1994, A10.

69.   Ibid.; Christopher Marquis, "Aristide Makes Plea for Unity as Miami Conference Ends," *Miami Herald*, January 17, 1994, A8. On March 4, 1993, Aristide finally gave the U.S. government the six months notice required to terminate the 1981 agreement on which the United States legitimized its policy of interdicting Haitian refugees. He did not adopt most of the other recommendations. On April 21, 1995, Aristide refused to sign a new agreement with the United States allowing it to intercept and repatriate Haitian boat people in international waters. See "Haiti to End Agreement," *Miami Herald*, April 22, 1995, A16.

70.   See "U.S. Tells Aristide to Bend on Plan," *New York Times*, February 23, 1994, A1; see also Christopher Marquis, "A New Try at Haiti Solution, Aristide's OK Awaited," *Miami Herald*, February 14, 1994, A1.

71.   See Steven Greenhouse, "Which Way Forward on Haiti?" *New York Times*, March 9, 1994, A8. The proposal touted by U.S. and UN officials as a homegrown plan to restore democracy in Haiti was actually devised by U.S. officials, a State Department adviser acknowledged. The U.S. government, it turns out, sketched out the proposed political settlement, hand-picked the negotiators, and indirectly covered their expenses to Washington. See Christopher Marquis, "Haitian Proposal Was Made in U.S.A.," *Miami Herald*, March 9, 1994, A4; "The State Department's Haiti Parliamentary Plan," *COHA's Washington Report on the Hemisphere*, March 7, 1994, 3.

72.   "New Haiti Plan Awaits Action from Aristide," *Dallas Morning News*, February 14, 1994, A13. The plan called on the president to name a new prime minister as a first step to overall settlement. The onus was on the military to act first and resign. Ibid.

73.   Ibid.; see also "U.S. and U.N. Put Heat on Aristide," *Latin American Weekly Report*, March 3, 1994, 94.

74.   See "Aristide Unbending in Talks with U.N. Chief," *New York Times,* March 6, 1994, sec. 1, p. 6. UN Secretary-General Boutros Boutros-Ghali failed to convince Aristide to accept a U.S.-backed plan to end the country's political crisis. See "Aristide Won't Bend on U.S. Plan," *Miami Herald,* March 6, 1994, A26.

75.   *Aristide against Plan; Protests Outside UN; Tightening of Sanctions Considered,* BBC Summary of World Broadcasts, March 9, 1994. According to Aristide, the previous pact signed at the Governors Island in New York was the only viable framework for the restoration of democracy in Haiti. President Aristide, continuing interview.

76.   Greenhouse, "Which Way Forward?" Lawrence Pezzullo, President Clinton's special adviser on Haiti, claimed that, although the plan was not foolproof, it represented the best chance of restoring President Aristide to power. Ibid.

77.   "An Urgent Message to President Clinton," *New York Times,* March 23, 1994, A11; "Black Caucus Urges Tougher Haiti Policy," *New York Times,* March 23, 1994, A13; Christopher Marquis, "Clinton, Caucus at Odds," *Miami Herald,* March 24, 1994, A18; Tony Pugh, "Black Caucus Steps Up Haiti Democracy Campaign: Lawmakers Urge New U.S. Policy," *Miami Herald,* March 19, 1994, A1.

78.   See Steven Greenhouse, "Aristide Cool to U.S. Shift in Haiti Policy," *New York Times,* March 30, 1994, A11; Steven Greenhouse, "U.S. Again Shifts Its Policy on Haiti," *New York Times,* March 27, 1994, A4.

79.   See Susan Benesch, "Sanctions Worsen Hunger in Haiti," *Miami Herald,* June 18, 1994, A1 (sanctions impede humanitarian aid workers' efforts to feed the starving); Yves Colon, "Haiti's Middle Class Becoming Poor," *Miami Herald,* June 27, 1994, A9 (sanctions barring trade with Haiti are choking the middle-class businessmen, while the rich go on with their lives as before); Carl Hiaasen, "Haiti's History Holds Ominous Tale for U.S.," *Miami Herald,* June 12, 1994, B1 (tightening the embargo inflicts more misery on Haiti's poor).

80.   The political pressure exerted against the Clinton administration by human rights groups was especially intense. The actions of one of the most prominent human rights activists, Randall Robinson, the executive director of TransAfrica, seem to have been very effective in persuading Clinton to change his refugee policy. In the midst of heavy media coverage, Robinson fasted for several weeks until the Clinton administration, apparently embarrassed by Robinson's actions, stopped repatriating Haitian refugees without first giving them a preliminary interview about their asylum claims. See Bob Herbert, "Fasting for Haiti," *New York Times,* May 4, 1994, A23.

81.   "Clinton Grants Haitian Exiles Hearing at Sea," *New York Times,* May 8, 1994, sec. 1, p. 1.

82.   See Steven Greenhouse, "Haitians Taking to the Sea In Droves, Alarming the U.S.," *New York Times,* June 28, 1994, A1. See prologue.

83.   The refugee crisis was a major concern because the United States harbors a traditional hostility toward refugees. That hostility may be due, in part, to the following factors: the cost of processing, holding, and admitting refugees; racial discrimination; a growing fear that immigrants will take cov-

eted jobs. See A. M. Rosenthal, "Fear of Compassion," *New York Times,* June 25, 1993, A31; see also Doris Meissner, "How the Administration Sees It: Help On Immigrants Coming," *Miami Herald,* June 22, 1994, A13.

84.   See Marianne Means, "Cuba Holds a Lesson on Haiti," *Miami Herald,* June 5, 1994, C3 (early on, some high-ranking Democrats and Clinton foreign-policy advisers advocated invasion).

85.   The Congressional Black Caucus introduced a bill to tighten the economic embargo and sever the commercial air links between the United States and Haiti. Steven A. Holmes, "With Persuasion and Muscle, Black Caucus Reshapes Haiti Policy," *New York Times,* July 14, 1994, A10. Senator Bob Graham, a vocal proponent of more drastic change, firmly believed that economic sanctions would not work, and advocated invasion. Susan Benesch, "Graham: Be Ready For Haiti Invasion," *Miami Herald,* June 20, 1994, A8.

Despite some congressional approval, there appeared to be a growing disapproval of any form of U.S. military intervention among most of Congress and the American public. See Steven Greenhouse, "U.S. View of Sanctions: Turn Up Heat Half Way," *New York Times,* July 3, 1994, sec. 1, p. 12; see also Steven Greenhouse, "U.S. Shifts Stress to Haiti Sanctions," *New York Times,* June 9, 1994, A3.

Additionally, the Caribbean leaders failed to take a firm stance on the invasion issue; although some publicly attacked the idea, most reportedly gave private support to military intervention in the event that sanctions failed. Steven Greenhouse, "A Haiti Invasion Wins Hemisphere Support," *New York Times,* June 13, 1994, A10.

86.   Susan Benesch, "Haiti Bets against U.S. Invasion," *Miami Herald,* June 4, 1994, A1.

87.   See Greenhouse, "U.S. Shifts Stress"; Greenhouse, "U.S. View of Sanctions"; see also "Clamp Total Embargo on Haiti, U.S. Urges United Nations," *Miami Herald,* April 30, 1994, A10.

The United States tightened the embargo by banning both commercial flights and financial transactions of over $50 between Haiti and the United States. See Christopher Marquis, "Haitian Flights to Halt in 2 Weeks," *Miami Herald,* June 11, 1994, A1; see also Andres Viglucci and Lori T. Yearwood, "In South Florida, Haste—and Dread," *Miami Herald,* June 11, 1994, A1. Meanwhile, the United States continued negotiations aimed at convincing Cédras and his top two military leaders to resign. See "U.S. Trying to Induce Leaders to Leave Haiti," *Miami Herald,* June 20, 1994, A8.

88.   See Elaine Sciolino, "Clinton's Haiti Problem: What Price Democracy?" *New York Times,* July 7, 1994, A8; see also James McCartney, "Clinton's Latest Haiti Gambit is Pure Political Response," *Miami Herald,* July 11, 1994, A17 (stating Clinton's policy toward Haiti changes from week to week).

89.   On June 12, in what many considered a blatant act of defiance, the de facto Haitian government declared a state of emergency whereby the government had the right to set curfews and restrict the movements of its citizens, purportedly to guarantee peace and order. Susan Benesch, " 'An Act of Defiance' in Haiti," *Miami Herald,* June 13, 1994, A1; "Haiti Declares an Emergency," *Miami Herald,* June 13, 1994, A4. In early July, the Haitian

military's aggression toward UN human rights observers culminated in an order to leave the country. See "Armed Men Stop U.N. Cars, Smash Radios, Seize Handgun," *Miami Herald,* June 9, 1994, A17; see also Susan Benesch and Christopher Marquis, "Haiti Orders Rights Team to Go Home," *Miami Herald,* July 12, 1994, A1; Garry Pierre-Pierre, "Haiti Orders Out Foreign Monitors of Human Rights," *New York Times,* July 12, 1994, A1.

In another incident, Haitian police fired on a boat of refugees; thirty of them drowned. "30 Drown as Haitian Police Fire on Refugees," *New York Times,* July 1, 1994, A6. Unfortunately, the atrocities continued. In yet another violent act of defiance, the bodies of twelve young men were dumped in the streets; police were suspected to be responsible for their murders. Susan Benesch and Tim Johnson, "12 Slain as Haiti Descends 'Into Hell,'" *Miami Herald,* July 14, 1994, A1.

90. The powerful police chief, Lieutenant Colonel Joseph Michel François, allegedly met with his most trusted commanders and stated that Cédras should step down. Howard W. French, "Split Reported in Haiti's Army, With Chief Urged to Quit," *New York Times,* June 27, 1994, A2. François's brother, a Haitian diplomat, publicly announced that Cédras must go. Garry Pierre-Pierre, "Haiti Official Seen as Ready to Step Down," *New York Times,* June 15, 1994, A3.

91. See Rosenthal, "Fear of Compassion."

92. Michael R. Gordon, "In Shift, U.S. Will No Longer Admit Haitians at Sea," *New York Times,* July 6, 1994, A1.

93. Originally, Panama, Suriname, Dominica, St. Lucia, and the Turks and Caicos Islands agreed to allow the Clinton administration to process Haitian refugees on their soil. However, three days after making this offer, Panamanian president Guillermo Endara rescinded it. Michael R. Gordon, "Panama Refuses to Take Haitians; A Rebuff for U.S.," *New York Times,* July 8, 1994, A1.

94. Douglas Jehl, "Clinton Seeks U.N. Approval of Any Plan to Invade Haiti," *New York Times,* July 22, 1994, A1.

95. See Richard D. Lyons, "U.N. Authorizes Invasion of Haiti to be Led by U.S.," *New York Times,* August 1, 1994, A1.

96. See Larry Rohter, "Last Flight Out of Haiti Strands Some," *New York Times,* July 31, 1994, 10; see also Susan Benesch and Tim Johnson, "Haitians Wait for an End to the Stalemate," *Miami Herald,* July 31, 1994, A1.

97. See Tim Johnson, "State of Siege Declared in Haiti: Repel Any Invasion, Acting President Says," *Miami Herald,* August 2, 1994, A1.

98. See "Attack Forces U.S. Closer to Invasion," *Times-Picayune* (New Orleans), August 3, 1994, A1 (amid signs of attacks on civilians, Haitian military threatens to crack down on "enemies of the state"); see also Tim Johnson, "Haitian Who Criticized Regime Pays in Blood," *Miami Herald,* August 3, 1994, A1 (gunmen wound former Haitian Senator Reynold Georges, who recently spoke out against the military).

99. Douglas Jehl, "Clinton Addresses Nation on Threat to Invade Haiti: Tells Dictators to Get Out," *New York Times,* September 16, 1994, A1; Christopher Marquis, "Clinton: 'Your Time Is Up,'" *Miami Herald,* September 16, 1994, A1.

100.   Douglas Jehl, "Holding Off, Clinton Sends Carter, Nunn, and Powell to Talk to Haitian Junta," *New York Times,* September 17, 1994, A1; Christopher Marquis, "A Final U.S. Reach for Peace," *Miami Herald,* September 17, 1994, A1.

101.   "What They Signed," *Miami Herald,* September 19, 1994, A8 (reproducing text of September 18 agreement); see Susan Benesch et al., "Back from the Brink," *Miami Herald,* September 19, 1994, A1.

102.   "What They Signed."

103.   Ibid. In a speech to the UN on September 26, 1994, President Clinton announced that the United States would suspend all unilateral sanctions against Haiti "except those that affect the military leaders and their immediate supporters." See Christopher Marquis and Peter Slevin, "U.S. Lifts Haiti Sanctions," *Miami Herald,* September 27, 1994, A18; "President's Words: Fight between Hope and Fear," *New York Times,* September 27, 1994, A6 (excerpts of speech). On September 29, the UN Security Council voted to terminate sanctions on the day after President Aristide returned to Haiti. S.C. Res. 944, U.N. SCOR, 49th Sess., 3430th mtg. para. 4, U.N. Doc. S/RES 944 (1994).

104.   The Carter Agreement became void once televised military violence in Haiti forced the United States to adopt a harder line with the Haitian army. Only then was President Aristide able to return to Haiti. If not for this change of circumstance, Aristide might well still be in Washington, or the United States would have had to invade Haiti. Thus, many Haitians recall the Carter Agreement as an act of treachery, not heroism.

105.   Larry Rohter, "3,000 U.S. Troops Land without Opposition and Take Over Ports and Airfields in Haiti," *New York Times,* September 20, 1994, A1; Peter Slevin et al., "Troops Enter Haiti without Firing a Shot," *Miami Herald,* September 20, 1994, A1.

106.   See "Perry: Haiti Showing 'Significant Progress,'" *Miami Herald,* October 9, 1994, A23.

107.   One such incident took place on September 20, 1994, after which the United States changed the rules of engagement of its soldiers to permit limited intervention in such cases. See Yves Colon et al., "U.S. Troops Watch Helplessly as Police Attack Demonstrators," *Miami Herald,* September 21, 1994, A1; Douglas Jehl, "Clinton Says U.S. Will Deter Abuses by Haiti Police," *New York Times,* September 22, 1994, A1; John Kifner, "American Commanders Give Cédras a Warning," *New York Times,* September 22, 1994, A12; John Kifner, "U.S. Soldiers Begin Dismantling Elite Haitian Military Company," *New York Times,* September 23, 1994, A1; Peter Slevin and Martin Merzer, "A Show of Force in Haiti, U.S. Takes All Big Guns from Army," *Miami Herald,* September 23, 1994, A1, A14 (reprinting new rules of engagement).

A second incident occurred on September 30, when attachés killed a number of peaceful demonstrators commemorating the third anniversary of the coup. Susan Benesch et al., "Haiti March Turns Deadly: Attachés Fire on Crowd, Killing 4," *Miami Herald,* October 1, 1994, A1; John Kifner, "Pro-Junta Gunmen Fire on Rally in Haitian Capital," *New York Times,* October 1, 1994, sec. 1, p. 1; see also Michael R. Gordon, "The Decision Not to Be the Police Backfires," *New York Times,* October 1, 1994, sec. 1, p. 4; Garry Pierre-Pierre, "Village Mourns Marchers Mowed Down by Van," *New York Times,* October 11, 1994, A15.

108. Slevin and Merzer, "Show of Force." On September 21, 1994, the Clinton administration announced that U.S. troops would act both to deter abuses by the Haitian police and to disarm the Haitian military. Jehl, "Clinton Says U.S. Will Deter Abuses"; Kifner, "American Commanders Give Cédras a Warning." Within days, the U.S. forces had confiscated all of the Haitian military's heavy arsenal. Slevin and Merzer, "Show of Force."

109. Steven Greenhouse, "U.S. Forces to Widen Role in Curbing Haiti Violence," *New York Times,* October 2, 1994, sec. 1, p. 1.

110. John Kifner, "Hit or Miss, U.S. Presses Hunt for Arms in Haiti," *New York Times,* October 9, 1994, sec. 1, p. 3; John Kifner, "Searching for Pro-Aristide Guns, U.S. Raid Finds Dancers Instead," *New York Times,* October 3, 1994, A1; Peter Slevin, "Disarming Haiti," *Miami Herald,* October 3, 1994, A1.

111. Larry Rohter, "U.S. Troops Will Bar Legislators from Amnesty Session," *New York Times,* September 27, 1994, A17.

112. See Susan Benesch, "Haitian Senators Approve Amnesty," *Miami Herald,* October 8, 1994, A1; Larry Rohter, "Haitian Bill Doesn't Exempt Military from Prosecution," *New York Times,* October 8, 1994, sec. 1, p. 4; see also "Lower House Approves Amnesty Law," *Miami Herald,* October 7, 1994, A18; Larry Rohter, "Haiti's Military May Not Avoid Criminal Trials," *New York Times,* October 6, 1994, A1. On Aristide's position, see Steven Greenhouse, "Exiled President Urges Quick Disarming of Haitian Troops and Paramilitary Units," *New York Times,* September 21, 1994, A16.

113. Larry Rohter, "Military Leader in Haiti Resigns, Vowing to Leave," *New York Times,* October 11, 1994, A1; Peter Slevin, "Somber Cedras Steps Down to Chorus of Jeers," *Miami Herald,* October 11, 1994, A1. General Biamby, the army chief of staff, also retired. Rohter, "Military Leader Resigns"; Slevin, "Somber Cedras Steps Down." The other major figure in the military, Chief of Police Michel François, had fled to the Dominican Republic on October 4, 1994. Susan Benesch, "Dreaded Coup Leader First to Flee," *Miami Herald,* October 5, 1994, A1; Larry Rohter, "Haiti's Military Power Structure is Showing Signs of Falling Apart," *New York Times,* October 5, 1994, A1.

114. John Kifner, "Not Looking Back, Cedras Flies to Panama Exile," *New York Times,* October 14, 1994, A6.

115. See Susan Benesch, "Joy, Rage Hit Towns as Haiti Troops Flee," *Miami Herald,* September 28, 1994, A1 (mix of delight and rage in Haitian citizens led to mobs attacking paramilitary thugs); see also Rick Bragg, "G.I.'s Take Joy and Relief on the Road," *New York Times,* September 29, 1994, A16 (U.S. military leader says Gonaives just one of many cities that could explode because of festering hatred).

116. For example, Haitian police clubbed and fired on a crowd of civilians who were trailing two marine trucks; two people were killed. Eric Schmitt, "U.S. Soldiers Begin Dismantling Elite Haitian Military Company; Marines Tighten Security," *New York Times,* September 23, 1994, A12. Hai-

tian military supporters were blamed for the deaths of five Haitians who were killed when an explosion ripped through a democratic rally. Larry Rohter, "5 Haitians Killed As Explosion Rips Democratic Rally," *New York Times*, September 30, 1994, A1. Military supporters fired on pro-Aristide demonstrators, killing several. Yves Colon, "No One Was Prepared to Stop the Violence," *Miami Herald*, October 1, 1994, A20; Kifner, "Pro-Junta Gunmen Fire on Rally"; Susan Benesch et al., "Haitian March Turns Deadly, Attachés Fire On Crowd, Killing 4," *Miami Herald*, October 1, 1994, A1.

117.   Peter Slevin and Yves Colon, "Haitian Parliament Secured," *Miami Herald*, September 28, 1994, A1. Some authorities have repeatedly suggested that the warehouses were not raided by the poor but rather by the paramilitary forces.

118.   Susan Benesch, "Rural Towns Lack Even Basic Services, Soldiers Find," *Miami Herald*, September 30, 1994, A8.

119.   Michael R. Gordon, "U.S. Plans to Increase Force in Haiti," *New York Times*, September 30, 1994, A7.

120.   Cédras resigned on Monday, October 10, and de facto president Jonassaint resigned on Wednesday, October 12. "De facto President Resigns in Haiti," *Miami Herald*, October 13, 1994, A16. Cédras's departure from Haiti was delayed, however, until the United States agreed both to lease his Port-au-Prince mansion and seaside retreat and to give him access to his frozen bank accounts. Christopher Marquis, "U.S. Paid Cédras to Go Away," *Miami Herald*, October 14, 1994, A1.

121.   See Larry Rohter, "Joyous Haitians Decorate the Capital for Aristide," *New York Times*, October 15, 1994, A6.

122.   See Peter Slevin et al., "Let Us Live in Peace," *Miami Herald*, October 16, 1994, A1.

123.   "President Aristide Returns," *New York Times*, October 16, 1994, sec. 4, p. 14; Larry Rohter, "Aristide Can Speak, but Can the U.S. Hear?" *New York Times*, October 16, 1994, sec. 4, p. 5.

124.   John Kifner, "Aristide, in a Joyful Return, Urges Reconciliation in Haiti," *New York Times*, October 16, 1994, sec. 1, p. 1; Slevin et al., "Let Us Live in Peace."

In accordance with its earlier resolution, the Security Council lifted sanctions against Haiti. S.C. Res. 948, U.N. SCOR, 3437th mtg. para. 10, U.N. Doc. S/RES/948 (1994); see also "A New Seat of Power for Leader," *Miami Herald*, October 16, 1994, A19. In its resolution of September 29, 1994, it urged the OAS to lift its own sanctions at the appropriate time. See S.C. Res. 944, para. 6. The OAS lifted the ban on flights and financial transactions on October 12, 1994. Note from Dr. Antonio Quiroga, President of the Ad Hoc Meeting of Ministers of Foreign Affairs (Haiti), Requesting Rescindment of the Measures Concerning the Suspension of Commercial Flights and International Financial Transactions with Haiti, OEA/Ser.F/V/1, OAS Doc. MRE/INF. 53/94 (1994); see also "OAS Lifts Air, Finance Sanctions against Haiti," *Agencé Francé Pressé*, October 12, 1994 (available in LEXIS, News Library, AFP File). Two days later, it approved a lifting of all remaining sanctions against Haiti upon Aristide's return to office. Note from the President of the Ad Hoc Meeting of Ministers of Foreign Affairs (Haiti) Requesting the

Lifting of All Measures Imposed against Haiti as soon as the Constitutional President, Jean-Bertrand Aristide, Resumes Office, OEA/Ser.F/V/1, OAS Doc. MRE/INF. 54/94 (1994).

CHAPTER THREE

1. See Christopher Marquis, "Aristide Inspires Hope and Hatred," *Miami Herald*, October 15, 1994, A22.

2. For example, a few days before Aristide's return, a van allegedly driven by a paramilitary member ran through a pro-democracy demonstration and killed fourteen people. "Van Plows through March in Haitian Town, Killing 14," *New York Times*, October 10, 1994, A8. On Aristide's first full day back, paramilitary auxiliaries hacked to death two of his supporters. Larry Rohter, "2 Slain by Attaches on Aristide's First Full Day Back," *New York Times*, October 17, 1994, A3.

3. Douglas Farah, "Aristide Returns to Acclaim in Haiti; Crowds Sing, Dance as President Calls for Reconciliation," *Washington Post*, October 16, 1994, A12; see prologue.

4. At the Summit of the Americas, held in early December of 1994, Aristide made his pitch for economic investment in Haiti in the name of democracy. See Jane Bussey, "Haiti to Offer Incentives for Investment," *Miami Herald*, December 16, 1994, A22 (Aristide unveiled eight-point plan to attract foreign investment); see also Tony Pugh et al., "Development, Democracy Go Together, Aristide Says," *Miami Herald*, December 9, 1994, A25.

By mid-December, there were definite preludes to economic improvement. The United States signed an agreement with Haiti to revitalize its economy. "U.S. Signs Agreement to Help Haiti Revitalize Its Economy," *New York Times*, December 16, 1994, A5. The World Bank approved a $40 million credit to support an emergency economic recovery program. "World Bank Approves Emergency Loan," *Miami Herald*, December 21, 1994, A18. The U.S. Agency for International Development (USAID) announced a plan to plant millions of trees and preserve Haiti's topsoil. "Haiti," *Miami Herald*, December 20, 1994, A7. In April of 1995, the Inter-American Development Bank (IDB) granted $45 million to Haiti for road repairs and maintenance. "Haiti," *Miami Herald*, April 7, 1994, A24. The tourism industry received a shot in the arm as Royal Caribbean Cruise Lines announced it would resume sailing to Haiti in late January. Ted Reed, "Cruise Line Resumes Haiti Visits," *Miami Herald*, December 17, 1994, C1.

As of early February 1995, thirty-two Haitian companies that were not operating under military rule were back in business. See "U.S. Envoy Talks of Building Economy," *Miami Herald*, February 12, 1995, A23. Perhaps even more significant, small businesses are now starting up in even the worst slums. See Steve Komarow, "Pride is Back in Port-au-Prince, U.S. Troops Brim with Enthusiasm," *USA Today*, April 3, 1995, A6. In addition, electric power is available most of the day, and a few streets have been paved. Ibid.

5. See Susan Benesch, "Truth and Consequences: Haiti's Investigation of Atrocities Is Risky," *Miami Herald*, December 31, 1994, A1; "U.S. Envoy Talks of Building Economy," A23.

6.   See Larry Rohter, "After the Homecoming, the Hard Part," *New York Times,* October 16, 1994, A1; see also Peter Slevin, "Haiti's Rulers Struggle to Rebuild a Battered Nation, Step by Tiny Step," *Miami Herald,* February 5, 1995, A1; see also chapters 1 and 6.

7.   Tod Robberson, "Revered Ex-Exile 'More Than Just a President,'" *Washington Post,* October 16, 1994, A1.

8.   See Rohter, "After the Homecoming" (Haiti has high hopes and few resources); see also Steven Greenhouse, "Donors Urge Haiti to Tax the Rich," *New York Times,* October 30, 1994, sec. 1, p. 1 (as United States and World Bank attempt to round up $550 million in international aid planned for Haiti, they are urging Aristide to make sweeping changes in the way Haiti's government works, including collecting far more in taxes from the rich); John Kifner, "Nothing to Build On: Haiti Starting at Zero," *New York Times,* December 4, 1994, sec. 1, p. 1 (ambulance for the only public maternity hospital is rusting and without tires); Catherine S. Manegold, "Behind U.S. Shield, Aristide Copes with a Stripped Nation," *New York Times,* October 23, 1994, sec. 1, p. 1 (Aristide copes with a stripped nation—takes his first bath with a bucket and a cup); Catherine S. Manegold, "With Embargo Lifted, Haitians Scramble for Trade," *New York Times,* October 17, 1994, A3 (merchants gathering resources in an effort to restore Haiti's economy over time); Patrick May, "Tough Prognosis: Can Haitian Death House Be a Place of Healing?" *Miami Herald,* January 22, 1995, A1 (Haitian hospital widely known as a death house); Larry Rohter, "Over 100 Inmates Escape from Haiti's Main Prison," *New York Times,* November 1, 1994, A16 (100 inmates escape from Haitian prison, magnifying both fragility of Haiti's legal and justice system and disarray of local authorities); Peter Slevin, "Overhauling Justice, From Bad Judges to Pen Shortage," *Miami Herald,* October 18, 1994, A1 (Haiti desperately needs to overhaul justice system, including corrupt judges and medieval prison conditions).

9.   See Peter Slevin, "Rural Haiti on Hold," *Miami Herald,* October 24, 1994, A1.

10.   See chapter 1.

11.   For example, with over two thousand national and local posts to fill, Haiti was not able to hold its November elections until July because it would take months to ensure a free and fair vote, as there were no reliable voter-registration rolls, there was no security for voters, and there was even a shortage of paper on which to print ballots. Larry Rohter, "Aristide under Pressure to Set an Election Date," *New York Times,* November 13, 1994, sec. 1, p. 3.

12.   See John Kifner, "Aristide Vows to Include Wealthy in Haiti's New Cabinet," *New York Times,* October 20, 1994, A3 (Aristide states that Cabinet comprised of both rich and poor will best project the image of reconciliation); see also Susan Benesch, "Old Aristide Friend's New Challenge," *Miami Herald,* November 25, 1994, A1 (Aristide under heavy pressure to placate his old enemies by not choosing a prime minister from his inner circle).

13.   Many Haitians, impatient for a new government, were disappointed when Aristide failed to name a prime minister at his first press conference. See Susan Benesch, "Haitians Criticize Aristide's Lack of Action,"

Miami Herald, October 20, 1994, A19. In an apparent balancing act, Aristide named a moderate, Smarck Michel, as prime minister. Michel is a promoter of free-market ideas, and his pragmatic, pro-market philosophy makes him acceptable to the United States, international organizations, and the Haitian elites, see Benesch, "Old Aristide Friend's New Challenge," but not necessarily to the Haitian masses.

14. Susan Benesch, "Death Toll from Gordon in Haiti is 829 and Could Go Much Higher," *Miami Herald,* November 24, 1994, A24.

15. "Less Haste in Haiti," *Miami Herald,* October 28, 1994, A20.

16. See Michael R. Gordon, "The Decision Not to be the Police Backfires," *New York Times,* October 1, 1994, sec. 1, p. 4 (Haitian police fail to respond as members of FRAPH fire on crowd of Aristide supporters, killing at least eight).

17. See Susan Benesch, "Dreaded Coup Leader First to Flee," *Miami Herald,* October 5, 1994, A1 (military structure further weakened when the chief of police, Lieutenant Colonel Michel François, fled Haiti); see also Gordon, "Decision Not to be the Police."

18. See Susan Benesch, "30 Nations Help Haiti Create a New Force," *Miami Herald,* October 26, 1994, A4. The United States resorted to massive recruitment of civilians for the police force after many Haitian police fled or refused to work. See Eric Schmitt with John Kifner, "Training of Police in Haiti Hampered by Personnel Gap," *New York Times,* October 24, 1994, A1. Moreover, in response to public sentiment, Aristide dismissed many of the police who remained. See "Aristide Says He's Trying to Reform Army," *Miami Herald,* December 1, 1994, A24; see also "Time to Muster Out," *Miami Herald,* December 2, 1994, A32.

19. See Benesch, "30 Nations Help."

20. Larry Rohter, "Clinton, in Haiti, Marks the Withdrawal of G.I.'s," *New York Times,* April 1, 1995, sec. 1, p. 1.

21. Ibid.

22. The remaining U.S. troops were to be partly comprised of special "rapid-response" teams that are able to travel anywhere in the country on short notice. Paul Bedard, "U.S. Ready for Trouble in Haiti Takes Over Mission Today," *Washington Times,* March 31, 1995, A1.

23. See prologue, note 8.

24. See Andres Viglucci, "435 in Camps Sign Up for New Police Force," *Miami Herald,* October 3, 1994, A8; see also Eric Schmitt, "U.S. Scrambles for Recruits to Bring Order to the Streets of Haiti's Two Largest Cities," *New York Times,* October 7, 1994, A14.

25. "Haitians Jostle for Police Jobs," *Miami Herald,* January 6, 1995, A14.

26. "Aristide Inaugurates New Police Academy," *Miami Herald,* February 4, 1995, A25.

27. See Charles Maechling Jr., "Can't Haiti's Cops Just Fight Crime?" *New York Times,* November 29, 1994, A25.

28. See "U.S. Close to Shifting Haiti Role to U.N.," *New York Times,* January 15, 1995, A28.

29. See John F. Harris, "Clinton Cheers Haiti's '2nd Chance'; President,

on Visit, Puts U.S. Troops under U.N. Command," *Washington Post,* April 1, 1995, A1; Larry Rohter, "Uneasy Haitians Await U.S. Pullout," *New York Times,* January 27, 1995, A10; "Securing Haiti for Keeps," *Miami Herald,* February 28, 1995, A28; see also "Beware Complacency Over Haiti," *Post and Courier* (Charleston), March 27, 1995, A6; "No Haste in Leaving Haiti," *Miami Herald,* January 21, 1995, A24.

30. In the early stages of the occupation, the Clinton administration expanded the U.S. military's role in curbing violence, but it stopped short of authorizing the use of force to disarm the paramilitary aids. Steven Greenhouse, "U.S. Forces to Widen Role in Curbing Haiti Violence," *New York Times,* October 2, 1994, sec. 1, p. 1. Eventually, the U.S. forces stepped up the search for weapons among the paramilitary aids; overall, however, the efforts were never serious. See "U.S. Troops in Haiti Seize Arms Caches," *Miami Herald,* October 2, 1994, A16 (U.S. troops disarmed Haiti's naval base and seized private caches of arms); see also John Kifner, "U.S. Troops Conduct Arms Search in Haiti," *New York Times,* October 2, 1994, sec. 1, p. 20. The U.S. reticence is apparently due to the fear that possible American casualties will produce a political backlash at home. The American public's general disdain for getting U.S. troops bogged down in an unfriendly country without a clear mission has been aptly termed the "Somalia syndrome." "Less Haste in Haiti."

31. See Peter Slevin and Yves Colon, "Troops' Task: Disarm the Thugs," *Miami Herald,* September 23, 1994 A1; see also Kifner, "Aristide Vows."

32. Steven Greenhouse, "Haitian Premier Says Security is Still Fragile," *New York Times,* February 3, 1995, A5. Although the U.S. military forces stepped up efforts to seize arms from paramilitaries just before they were to be replaced by the MNF, in an effort to make Haiti more secure prior to their withdrawal, U.S. officials never announced any plan for a systematic and full-scale disarmament. See "U.S. Special Forces Hunting Haitian Paramilitary Cell," *Miami Herald,* October 22, 1994, A21; see also Larry Rohter, "U.S. Force Steps Up Haiti Arms Seizures," *New York Times,* February 27, 1995, A8.

33. See "No Haste," A24; see also Bob Shacochis, "Our Two Armies in Haiti," *New York Times,* January 8, 1995, sec. 4, p. 19 (U.S. troops have trouble distinguishing between friend and enemy). The flaws in the U.S. mission are particularly evident in rural areas. These areas are isolated by harsh terrain and are almost immune to even moderately paced change. Slow to receive supplies, news, U.S. military protection, and the Aristide-inspired aura of peace and reconciliation, the countryside was also slow to be rid of the section-chief rulers that oppressed the citizens prior to the U.S. occupation. See Garry Pierre-Pierre, "In the Hinterlands, a Maverick Waits," *New York Times,* October 7, 1994, A14 (even after the U.S. occupation, Haitian paramilitary forces in remote areas were planning to fight invading U.S. troops); see also Peter Slevin, "Rural Haiti," A1 (one week after Aristide's return, rural Haitians saw little change but were waiting for him to do something).

On October 29, 1994, Aristide held a news conference to announce that the rural section chiefs were no longer in charge. "Aristide Removes Rural

Bosses," *New York Times*, October 30, 1994, sec. 1, p. 10. Absent police en-
forcements, however, such an announcement was unlikely to have much
effect in rural areas; for example, in Petite Riviere de L'Artibonite, section
chief Jean Lacoste Edouard has ruled with an iron fist since 1986, outlasting
more than six military and civilian governments. See Larry Rohter, "In Rural Haiti, 'Section Chief' Rules Despite U.S. Presence," *New York Times*, October 31, 1994, A1. Moreover, months into the U.S. occupation, the grisly
violence continued. For example, in November, the deputy mayor of Mire-
balais, Cadet Damzal, was beheaded, spreading a clear message across Haiti
that the U.S. Special Forces cannot guarantee safety in Haiti's rural commu-
nities. "Beheading Sows Terror in Rural Haiti," *Miami Herald*, November 14,
1994, A10.

34. See "Beware Complacency Over Haiti"; Philip Smucker, "Haitians
Wary of Pre-Vote Violence," *Miami Herald*, March 20, 1995, A10.

35. See "Beware Complacency Over Haiti"; David LaGesse, "Climate
of Crime; Killings in Haiti Rise as U.S. Prepares to Pull Out," *Dallas Morning
News*, March 25, 1995, A1.

36. See "Beware Complacency Over Haiti"; LaGesse, "Climate of
Crime"; Smucker, "Haitians Wary of Violence."

37. See LaGesse, "Climate of Crime" (climate of violence definitely has
a political origin); see also "Haiti," *Miami Herald*, April 11, 1995, A6 (parliamentary elections have been pushed back by three weeks to June 25 because of pre-election violence); Sandra Marquez, "Fear Lingers as Haitian
Vote Nears," *Miami Herald*, March 28, 1995, A4.

38. The Bush administration consistently showed its disdain for Aristide. See Schnably, "Santiago Commitment," 511. Even public displays of
support were tainted "by obvious leaks of administration 'anger' and 'antip-
athy' toward Aristide." See French, "U.S. Presses Ousted Haitian Chief,"
sec. 1, p. 2. In early October 1991, a State Department spokesman's statement was interpreted as an indication of dubiety about Aristide's return,
when he commented that "the U.S. supported efforts by all sides to support
a solution that would contribute to constitutional democracy arrived at and
approved by all sectors of Haitian society through national dialogue." See
"U.S. Backs Haiti's Aristide, Wants Human Rights Improvements," *Reuter
News Service*, October 7, 1991 (available in LEXIS, TXTLNE Library, TXTLNE
File). U.S. officials also demanded that Aristide publicly disavow mob vio-
lence and agree to share power with the Parliament. See Clifford Krauss,
"In Policy Shift, U.S. Criticizes Haitian on Rights Abuses," *New York Times*,
October 7, 1991, A1.

The Clinton administration has also failed to show that it is committed
to Aristide as Haiti's leader. In 1993, it at best allowed, and at worst encouraged, the CIA to publish a false psychological profile of Aristide that depicted
him as a mentally unstable demagogue. The administration is also rumored
to have flirted with the idea of a "soft coup," favoring former Prime Minister
Malval over Aristide. See Schnably, "Santiago Commitment," 514; see also
chapter 2, note 2. After his forced resignation as Clinton's special adviser
on Haiti, Lawrence Pezzullo made clear his hostility toward Aristide. See

"Washington's Haiti Gamble: A Democratic Mission Impossible," *Miami Herald,* September 18, 1994, A1.

39.   Under the Bush administration, the CIA prepared a psychological profile of Aristide, falsely depicting him as mentally unstable. See Sciolino, "Haiti's Man of Destiny Awaiting His Hour," A1, A5. Specifically, the report stated that he suffered from nervous breakdowns and was disconnected from reality. Ibid. In addition, it was publicly revealed that the CIA attempted to sabotage Aristide's call for a boycott of the military's sham elections by attempting to funnel money to individual candidates. See Jim Mann, "CIA's Aid Plan Would Have Undercut Aristide in '87–'88," *Los Angeles Times,* October 31, 1993, A1. It was also revealed that Haitian military leaders had been on the CIA payroll "from the mid-1980s at least until the 1991 coup." See Weiner, "Key Haiti Leaders in CIA's Pay," A1. The United States acknowledged that Emmanuel Constant, the head of FRAPH, was still on the CIA payroll at the time he led the mob efforts to turn back the USS *Harlan County.* See Allan Nairn, "Behind Haiti's Paramilitaries," *Nation,* October 24, 1994, 458, 460–61; Allan Nairn, "He's Our S.O.B.," *Nation,* October 31, 1994, 481–82; Stephen Engelberg, "A Haitian Leader of Paramilitaries Was Paid by C.I.A.," *New York Times,* October 8, 1994, sec. 1, p. 1. It was never reported, by either the broadcast or print media, but it is common knowledge in Haiti, that Constant has a serious drug habit and that the CIA used his habit to induce him to follow its orders.

On December 3, 1995, Emmanuel Constant, the leader of the FRAPH, appeared as a guest on the television program *60 Minutes* and claimed that he had been a paid employee of the CIA in Haiti from 1991 to 1994. Secretary of State Warren Christopher tacitly acknowledged this arrangement. Constant's organization was in charge of the terror operation intended to keep Aristide from returning to Haiti. He claimed that the CIA encouraged him to provide damaging information about Aristide and that, out of this information, the CIA created a psychological profile that made out Aristide to be mentally unstable. *60 Minutes,* CBS television broadcast, December 3, 1995.

The charges that Aristide is mentally unstable are based on second-hand reports and information that has been supplied to U.S. intelligence offices by high-ranking members of the very same military that overthrew him. See Steven A. Holmes, "Administration is Fighting Itself on Haiti Policy," *New York Times,* October 23, 1993, 1; Garry Pierre-Pierre, "Terror of Duvalier Years is Haunting Haiti Again," *New York Times,* October 18, 1993, A6; World Council of Churches, Caribbean Conference of Churches, "Restore Our Stolen Vote!" 3 (1992); see also chapter 2, note 2. The CIA profile claims that in 1990, Aristide was treated by two psychiatrists in Montreal, Canada, for megalomania and manic-depressive illness.

The reports and the CIA profile have been totally discredited by the investigative reporter Christopher Marquis, a journalist for the *Miami Herald.* Marquis obtained the name of the hospital at which the CIA claimed Aristide had been treated. He then persuaded Aristide to write him a letter authorizing Marquis to request from this hospital, and three others in Montreal, all records regarding any psychiatric treatment Aristide may have received. All four hospitals certified they had no record of ever having treated Aristide for any psychological or other problems. Perusse, *Haitian Democracy Restored*, 8–9.

The CIA clearly had a different agenda from President Clinton. It subverted the president's policy. Ibid. For a more thorough description of CIA activities in Haiti, including Constant's role, see chapter 8, "Security and U.S. Involvement in Haiti."

40.   Both the United States and the UN/OAS joint envoy expressed their dislike of Aristide's unreasonableness during the negotiations. See, e.g., John Donnelly, "Talk, Signs of Uprising Stir in Troubled Haiti," *Miami Herald*, January 17, 1994, A1; Howard W. French, "U.S. Tells Aristide to Bend on Plan," *New York Times*, February 23, 1994, A1.

41.   See Schnably, "Santiago Commitment," 498.

42.   See "Military Chiefs Seem to OK Talks," *Miami Herald*, November 5, 1993, A18.

43.   See Kenneth Roth, "Haiti and Clinton," *New York Review of Books*, March 4, 1993, 54.

44.   See Christopher Marquis, "Aristide Ouster Surprised CIA, Officials Say," *Miami Herald*, December 15, 1993, A1. Note also that Senator Jesse Helms used the Lafontant murder accusation as part of his campaign to depict Aristide as a "psychopath." Christopher Marquis, "Aristide Calls Claims of Depression 'Garbage,'" *Miami Herald*, October 23, 1993, A1; see chapter 2, note 2; see also note 39 above.

45.   See Marquis, "Aristide Ouster."

46.   See Jonathan Power, "If the Crisis in Haiti is a Replay of 'The Comedians,' It Seems the Climax is yet to Come," *Chicago Tribune*, October 16, 1991, 19.

47.   See Howard W. French, "Haitian Townspeople Tell of New Fear of Violence," *New York Times*, March 1, 1993, A3.

48.   Kurzban, continuing interview; President Aristide, continuing interview.

49.   "The Aristide Government's Human Rights Record," *Haiti Observateur*, October 2–9, 1991, 24–25 (translated by National Coalition for Haitian Refugees et al.). More specifically, the necklacing charges are claims that Aristide was not doing enough to calm the masses intent on vigilante violence against former members of the Tonton Macoutes, Catholic Church officials, and other supporters of the Duvaliér regime. See Lee Hockstader, "President-Elect Condones Vigilantism in Haiti; Aristide Laments Attacks on Religious Sites," *Washington Post*, January 10, 1991, A14; Ron Howell, "Icon Abroad with Enemies at Home," *Newsday*, October 7, 1991, A25.

50.   See Schnably, "Santiago Commitment," 500–1.

51.   See Linda Diebel, "U.S. Appears to Double-Deal during Coup," *Toronto Star*, October 13, 1991, H2; Thomas L. Friedman, "The White House Refuses to Link Aristide's Return and Democracy," *New York Times*, October 7, 1991, A10; Christopher Marquis, "Embargo Has an Even Chance of Aiding Aristide, U.S. Says," *Miami Herald*, November 1, 1991, A29.

52. Douglas Jehl, "White House and Aristide Clash on Broadcasts to Haiti," *New York Times*, June 24, 1994, A4.

53. Paul Quinn-Judge, "U.S. Monitors Aristide's Calls, Hears Him Complain of Inaction," *Miami Herald*, September 9, 1994, A16.

54. See Elaine Sciolino, "Invasion of Haiti Would Be Limited, Clinton Aides Say," *New York Times*, September 12, 1994, A13. But cf. Christopher Marquis, "Administration Resists Pullout Date," *Miami Herald*, September 28, 1994, A21 (in a slight role reversal, Clinton administration opposed congressional motions, in both houses, to set deadlines for withdrawal of U.S. troops from Haiti).

55. Elaine Sciolino, "Aristide Adopts a New Role: From Robespierre to Gandhi," *New York Times*, September 18, 1994, A1.

56. See Engelberg, "Haitian Leader of Paramilitaries Was Paid by C.I.A.," A1. Although Constant made a sudden about-face by publicly promoting democracy, both the reality and the appearance of impropriety continued. John Kifner, "Haitians Ask of U.S. Links to Attachés," *New York Times*, October 6, 1994, A8. Constant was apparently surreptitiously allowed into the United States after Aristide's return to power. He was finally arrested by Immigration and Naturalization Service (INS) officers in June 1995. Several months after his arrest, after a deportation hearing, the administrative law judge declared him deportable. Lawyers for Constant appealed this decision. Presently, the Haitian government is attempting to extradite him so that he can stand trial for serious crimes. Lawyers for the Aristide government deposed him in July and again in August 1995. He refused to allow the depositions to be videotaped and denied any complicity in any crimes. See note 39 above. In June 1996, the U.S. government simply released him from custody, claiming that he presented too great a danger to Haitian democracy if returned to stand trial for committing serious crimes, such as murder and rape. See chapter 8, "Security and U.S. Involvement in Haiti."

57. See William Neikirk, "Clinton Hails Transfer of Duties in Haiti," *Chicago Tribune*, April 1, 1995, N2; Larry Rohter, "U.S. Suspicions Over Killing May Mar Clinton's Haiti Trip," *New York Times*, March 31, 1995, A1.

58. See chapter 8, "U.S. Politics: The Presidential Election and Political Murders."

59. "Helms Blasts Aristide, U.S. Role in Haiti," *Miami Herald*, March 10, 1995, A12.

60. See Ben Barber, "Slain Aristide Foe Foresaw Her Fate," *Washington Times*, March 30, 1995, A1.

61. See Wilentz, *Rainy Season*.

62. See Howard W. French, "Haitians Overwhelmingly Elect Populist Priest to the Presidency," *New York Times*, December 18, 1990, A1 (stating that Aristide's radicalism earned him the disdain of the United States, and noting that many U.S. officials hated him for blaming them for much of Haiti's economic woes); see also Wilentz, *Rainy Season*, 112, 330 (noting that Aristide made statements to the effect that, for example, Haitians want to leave for the United States because the United States has devastated Haiti,

and the American plan for Haiti is a dream for the United States and a nightmare for the Haitian people).

63. In keeping with this approach after he returned to the presidency, Aristide appointed another pro-business prime minister, Smarck Michel. See Susan Benesch, "Old Aristide Friend's New Challenge," A1.

64. For more on Aristide's economic plans after his return to power, see Jean-Bertrand Aristide, "Haiti Emerges, Eyes Blinking, In the Sunlight of Democracy," *New York Times*, October 16, 1994, sec. 1, p. 15; Don Bohning, "Aristide Blueprint Offers Broad Economic Reforms," *Miami Herald*, August 26, 1994, A24; Barbara Crossette, "Aristide, at U.N., Emphasizes Need for Conciliation," *New York Times*, October 5, 1994, A1, A9. For a detailed discussion and critique of this plan, see chapter 7.

65. The issue of privatization continues to be a controversial problem during Preval's term in office. See chapter 8, "The Economy."

66. See Benesch, "Old Aristide Friend's New Challenge" (amnesty is a very sensitive issue, as Aristide has promoted reconciliation to soothe his old enemies, while promising his supporters justice for state crimes during his exile).

67. See Susan Benesch, "Aristide's Cautious Approach Dismays Many Supporters," *Miami Herald*, December 9, 1994, A29. In early October, the Haitian Parliament authorized Aristide to exempt political crimes, leaving it to him to initiate investigations into human rights abuses. See Larry Rohter, "Haiti's Capital Throbs with New Life," *New York Times*, November 1, 1994, A16; see also Peter Slevin, "Aristide's Backers Come Out of Hiding," *Miami Herald*, October 7, 1994, A18.

68. Benesch, "Aristide's Cautious Approach."

69. "Presidential Proclamation" (on file with Irwin P. Stotzky).

70. See chapter 8, "Prosecutions: The Zimbabwe Trial," "Prosecutions: The Jean-Ronique Antoine and Robert Lecorps Trial," "Other Steps toward Justice," and prologue.

71. Susan Benesch, "Yearning for Justice, Haitians Put Courts to the Test," *Miami Herald*, December 31, 1994, A13.

72. For example, after a tentative judge in Milot mustered enough courage to issue arrest warrants against alleged government-sponsored human rights violators, a higher court refused to try the case, and turned those who were implicated in these crimes over to the Haitian military, which freed them. Ibid.

73. See "Clinton Grants Haitian Exiles Hearing at Sea."

74. Rachel L. Swarns, "Haitians Shun U.S. Effort to Lure Them Home," *Miami Herald*, January 5, 1995, A1.

75. "Forced Return of Camp Haitians Begins," *Miami Herald*, January 7, 1995, A20.

76. See Rachel L. Swarns, "Haitians Shun U.S. Effort."

77. Andres Viglucci, "INS Reverses Order for Deportations," *Miami Herald*, November 18, 1994, A14.

78. See "Haitian Kids Win Big," *Miami Herald*, November 24, 1994, A26; Andres Viglucci, "Free 230 Haitian Children, U.S. Told," *Miami Herald*, November 23, 1994, A1; see also Mireya Navarro, "Federal Judge Permits

Entry of Haitian-Refugee Children," *New York Times*, November 23, 1994, A14 (in October 1994, the Clinton administration began allowing unaccompanied Cuban children to enter the United States, and another 3,000 Cuban children are expected to be brought to the United States along with their families).

79. The HRC sought review by the U.S. Supreme Court. Andres Viglucci, "High Court Asked to Review Haitian Kids' Case," *Miami Herald*, April 4, 1995, B3. The Court, however, refused to hear the case. Haitian Refugee Center v. Christopher, 43 F.3d 1412 (11th Cir.), *cert. denied*, 115 S. Ct. 2578 (1995).

CHAPTER FOUR

1. See, e.g., *Enciclopedia jurídica española* (Barcelona: Francisco Seix, 1910); Aquilino Iglesia Ferreirós, *La creación del derecho: Una historia del derecho español—Antología de textos* (Barcelona: Signo, 1991); Visigoths, *Fuero juzgo: O libro de los jueces* (Valladolid: Editorial Lex Nova, 1980); Claudio Sanchez-Albornoz, *Estudios sobre las institutiónes medievales españolas* (Mexico: Universidad Nacional Autonoma de Mexico, Instituto de Investigaciones Historicas, 1965); E. N. van Kleffens, *Hispanic Law until the End of the Middle Ages* (Edinburgh: Edinburgh University Press, 1968).

2. See, e.g., William A. Morris, *The Medieval English Sheriff to 1300* (Manchester: Manchester University Press; New York: Longmans Green, 1927); Benjamin Thorpe, *Diplomatarium Anglicum Aevi Saxonici* (London: Macmillan, 1865).

3. The Declaration of Independence (U.S., 1776); "Canadian Bill of Rights; Constitutional Act of 1982, pt. I," in *The Canadian Charter of Rights, Annotated* (Aurora, Ontario: Canada Law Book, 1982).

4. See, e.g., "Declaration of The Rights of Man and of the Citizen" (France, 1789), quoted in Edward Lawson, ed., *Encyclopedia of Human Rights*, 2d ed. (New York: Taylor and Francis, 1996), 529.

5. See, e.g., Edmund J. Osmańcyzk, ed., *The Encyclopedia of the United Nations and International Relations* (New York: Taylor Francis, 1990), 402.

6. See chapter 8, "What to Do about Massive Human Rights Abuses," "Prosecutions: The Zimbabwe Trial," "Prosecutions: The Jean-Ronique Antoine and Robert Lecorps Trial," "Continuing Security Concerns."

7. The search for solutions to this dilemma is one of the main reasons for writing this book. While theoretical, the book has an objective that is essentially practical: it aims to contribute to the respect for human rights by applying a theoretical discussion to the transition to democracy in Haiti, and to analyze ideas and processes adverse to that transition.

CHAPTER FIVE

1. See Carlos S. Nino, *The Constitution of Deliberative Democracy* (New Haven: Yale University Press, 1996).

2. I first met Carlos Santiago Nino in 1987 at the Yale Law School, where I was spending the year as a scholar-in-residence. Owen Fiss introduced us because he thought that we had mutual scholarly and political interests. At that time, Carlos was presidential adviser to President Alfonsín

of Argentina. I spent 1991–92 in Buenos Aires, Argentina, on a Fulbright Scholarship, working at the Center for Institutional Studies (Centro de Estudios Institucionales). Carlos was the director of the center. Carlos visited me in Miami often, when delivering papers and lectures. I have taken advantage of similar trips to Argentina to visit him. We have collaborated on several conferences and papers. See, e.g., Irwin P. Stotzky and Carlos S. Nino, "The Difficulties of the Transition Process," in *Transition to Democracy in Latin America: The Role of the Judiciary*, edited by Irwin P. Stotzky (Boulder, Colo.: Westview Press, 1993), 3; see also Carlos S. Nino, "Transition to Democracy, Corporatism and Constitutional Reform in Latin America," *University of Miami Law Review* 44 (1989): 129–64; Irwin P. Stotzky, "Carlos S. Nino: Public Intellectual," *University of Miami Inter-American Law Review* 25 (1994): 349–50; Irwin P. Stotzky, "The Fragile Bloom of Democracy," *University of Miami Law Review* 44 (1989): 105–28. Carlos died suddenly on August 29, 1993, while on a trip to LaPaz to work on the reform of the Bolivian Constitution. His work, however, lives on.

3.   In general, constitutional lawyers are more likely than the others to ascribe to democracy both an explanatory and a justificatory import.

4.   See Joseph A. Schumpeter, *Capitalism, Socialism, and Democracy*, 5th ed. (London: Allen and Unwin, 1976).

5.   See Robert A. Dahl, *A Preface to Democratic Theory* (Chicago: University of Chicago Press, 1956).

6.   See Anthony Downs, *An Economic Theory of Democracy* (New York: Harper, 1957).

7.   See Crawford B. MacPherson, *The Life and Times of Liberal Democracy* (Oxford and New York: Oxford University Press, 1977).

8.   See Jürgen Habermas, *Communication and the Evolution of Society*, translated by Thomas McCarthy (Boston: Beacon Press, 1979).

9.   See Cass R. Sunstein, "Interest Groups in American Public Law," *Stanford Law Review* 38 (1985): 29–87.

10.   See Bruce Ackerman, *We the People* (Cambridge: Harvard University Press, Belknap Press, 1991).

11.   See Giovanni Sartori, *The Theory of Democracy Revisited, Part 1: The Contemporary Debate* (Chatham, N.J.: Chatham House Publishers, 1987), 241.

12.   At least in theory, this is the role that political parties play.

13.   For a complex discussion of these dimensions of constitutionalism and their relationship to democracy, see Nino, *Constitution*.

14.   For a thorough description and analysis of the variety of different conceptions of democracy, see ibid., 67–106. For a complicated exegis of Nino's epistemic theory, see ibid., 107–43.

15.   Carlos S. Nino, *Etica y Derechos Humanos* (The ethics of human rights), 2d ed. (Barcelona: Editorial Ariel, 1989), 368.

16.   There are also strong theoretical challenges to such a position. Indeed, the epistemic vision of democracy differs from both the stronger and weaker versions of Habermas's theory of communicative action. This theory, unlike Habermas's, does not conceive of consensus, even when reached under ideal conditions, as constitutive of just solutions. To a proponent of this view, the collective enterprise of discussion is not seen as the exclusive

way of attaining those just solutions. Rather, this process of discussion is seen as the most reliable method in practice. This position is also contrary to Rawls's position that individual reflection is the best method for reaching morally correct solutions. See, e.g., Habermas, *Communication;* John Rawls, *A Theory of Justice* (Cambridge: Harvard University Press, Belknap Press, 1971).

17. In addition to Carlos Nino's epistemic theory, the conception of a democratic order sketched out in this section of the book is strongly influenced by the writings of John Rawls. See Rawls, *Theory;* John Rawls, "Kantian Constructivism in Moral Theory," *Journal of Philosophy* 57 (1988): 515–72. This is obviously a very brief description of the democratic order.

18. It is clear, therefore, that I agree with Carlos Nino on some of these points. See Nino, "Transition to Democracy"; see also Stotzky, "Fragile Bloom."

19. See chapter 6, "The Absence of Material Deprivation: A First Step toward Democracy."

CHAPTER SIX

1. A small contingent of the UN peace-keeping force (1,000 to 1,500 troops) remains in Haiti. U.S. troops, however, are not part of that force. See Bohning, "Sigh of Relief."

2. For a discussion of extensions of the mandate, see prologue, note 8.

3. There are few, if any, wealthy regions in Haiti. Certain areas of Petionville, a wealthy suburb of Port-au-Prince, are exceptions to this proposition.

4. For a general discussion of the Aristide government's economic program, including privatization, see chapter 7. For a discussion of the Preval government's plans for privatization and how they differ from total privatization, see chapter 8, "The Economy."

5. Paul W. Kahn, "Independence and Responsibility in the Judicial Role," in *Transition to Democracy in Latin America: The Role of the Judiciary,* edited by Irwin P. Stotzky (Boulder, Colo.: Westview Press, 1993) 79–81.

6. Indeed, the very question of whether certain Latin American and European nations remain in the transition toward democracy or have already completed the journey is one that requires both empirical corroboration and conceptual clarification. This is an extremely difficult task. It has rarely been carried out successfully. For an analysis of my justifications for a democracy, see chapters 4 and 5.

7. Every nation that attempts to make the transition from authoritarianism to democracy faces economic, political, and social crises. Haiti, however, may have among the most serious of these problems compared with other nations attempting the transition.

8. Crises of this magnitude would surely and unavoidably lead to the destruction of any nascent democratic system. Yet, even in the midst of these crises, the brutal dictatorship in Haiti appeared to grow stronger with each passing day. This clearly showed the force of the repression in Haiti—the climate of terror—and its intractable staying power.

9. See Larry Rohter, "Haiti Is a Land without a Country," *New York Times,* August 14, 1994, E3. The state of education, a key to any kind of

development, is one of the major reasons that Haiti remains one of the poorest countries in the world. It is not only a question of denying access to education for most Haitians. The teachers remain wholly inadequate to the task. For example, in December 1996 and January 1997, Haiti's approximately twelve hundred grade-school teachers took a simple test. Almost all of them failed. Only four hundred could alphabetize a list of words; only forty-one could arrange fractions by size. Most of the teachers have only a sixth-grade education. Under the current system, that is what qualifies them to teach up to grade six. This ignorance is reflected, of course, in the students. More than half of the children between six and twelve cannot read. In addition, of the approximately seventy-five thousand students who make it to their senior year in high school, only 15 percent pass final exams to graduate. Moreover, classes are extremely overcrowded—some have more than two hundred students—and most classrooms do not have benches, chalk boards or even doors. Michael Norton, "Teacher Strike Highlights Education Crisis in Haiti," *Miami Herald,* January 13, 1997, A8.

10.   Indeed, before the restoration of the Aristide government, the military leaders appeared to be taking over the economic monopolies of the nation, which were traditionally controlled by the economic elites. See, e.g., Howard W. French, "Power Means Brutality; Practice Makes Perfect," *New York Times,* October 17, 1993, sec. 4, p. 1.

11.   See chapter 1, "A Historical Vision: The Origins of Dictatorship," "The First Steps toward Democracy."

12.   The concept of corporatism refers to two distinct situations. In the traditional sense, corporatism refers to the control exercised by the state over organizations and interest groups. The more technical meaning, usually used in the political arena, refers to the contrary phenomena: these same organizations and interest groups acquire considerable influence over, and exert persistent pressure against, state decision makers. See James M. Malloy, ed., *Authoritarianism and Corporatism in Latin America* (Pittsburgh: University of Pittsburgh Press, 1977), passim.

13.   Most of the information about the civil society has been gleaned from extensive continuing interviews with Cathy Maternowska, President Jean-Bertrand Aristide, and Jean Jean-Pierre, from extensive discussions with Léon-François Hoffmann, and through the writings of all of these people and others, particularly Michel-Rolph Trouillot, too numerous to list.

14.   See, e.g., Alan Cowell, "Aristide Has Long Posed Problem for Vatican," *New York Times,* October 28, 1993, A16. But see " 'Friendship and Solidarity' Visit by Aristide," *European Report,* October 30, 1991, 5.

15.   See Aristide and Wargny, *Autobiography.* For a thorough discussion of the Catholic Church and its role in Haiti, see Ann Green, *The Catholic Church in Haiti: Political and Social Change* (East Lansing: Michigan State University Press, 1993).

16.   Papa Doc created a reign of terror that constantly attacked and decimated the civil society. After Baby Doc's downfall, however, the civil society slowly increased its power. By 1991, a vastly reinvigorated civil society existed.

17.   French, "Power Means Brutality."

18.   Indeed, directly after the 1990 election, President Aristide called in the prominent families of Haiti to discuss their refusal to pay taxes. He told them that he would not impose taxes retroactively, even though they owed incredibly large sums of money. He stated that they would not have to pay taxes for the many years they refused to pay before his election. Nevertheless, they would have to pay taxes in the future. The elites responded by telling Aristide that he would not be in office long enough to collect their taxes. Less than a month later, he was ousted from office by a military coup. President Aristide, continuing interview.

19.   For a comprehensive look at the role of the judiciary and the rule of law in the transition to democracy, see Irwin P. Stotzky, ed., *Transition to Democracy in Latin America: The Role of the Judiciary* (Boulder, Colo.: Westview Press, 1993).

20.   Lawyers Committee, *Paper Laws,* 1–2.

21.   Constitution de la République d'Haiti (Republic of Haiti).

22.   Haiti's court system is based on the Napoleonic Code in effect in France almost two hundred years ago.

23.   For example, Haiti ratified the American Convention on Human Rights on September 14, 1977, through a declaration signed by Jean-Claude Duvaliér.

24.   Philippe Texier, *Advisory Services in the Field of Human Rights,* E/CN.4/1989/40, para. 89 (February 6, 1989).

25.   Ibid., para. 48.

26.   See *Analysis of the Haitian Justice System with Recommendations to Improve the Administration of Justice in Haiti,* Working Group on the Haitian Justice System of the OAS/UN International Civilian Mission to Haiti (MICIVIH), March 17, 1994.

27.   Although President Aristide set in motion the forces to professionalize the police, and President Preval continues this process, it would be inaccurate to claim that the National Police are as of yet professionals.

28.   Carlos S. Nino used this term in describing this phenomenon in Argentina. See Carlos S. Nino, *Un País al Margen de la Ley* (Buenos Aires: Emece Editores, 1992), passim.

29.   See Laurence H. Tribe, *American Constitutional Law,* 2d ed. (Mineola, N.Y.: Foundation Press, 1988), 666–67; Irwin P. Stotzky and Alan C. Swan, "Due Process Methodology and Prisoner Exchange Treaties: Confronting an Uncertain Calculus," *Minnesota Law Review* 62 (1978): 733–812.

30.   *American Journal of International Law* 65 (1971): 679–702 (official document).

CHAPTER SEVEN

1.   See "Strategy of Social and Economic Reconstruction," 1994 (on file with Irwin P. Stotzky) (hereafter cited as Aristide Plan), 1.

2.   Ibid., 2.

3.   By the start of Preval's term, Parliament was almost too strong; it fought the executive branch of government on almost every issue.

4.   Aristide Plan, 3.

5.   Ibid.

6. Indeed, it is often stated publicly, and discussed in depth privately, that the Haitian army has become a marching band. This change is a remarkable achievement.

7. President Aristide initially asked Michael Ratner and me to organize a team of lawyers, investigators, and students to work on these cases. In line with this request, we hired several lawyers and experienced human rights investigators. Investigations and prosecutions started shortly after Aristide's return, and continue into Preval's term.

8. For a discussion of the Zimbabwe trial, see chapter 8, "Prosecutions: The Zimbabwe Trial." On the other hand, those tried for the murder of Guy Malary were acquitted. This trial exposed the weaknesses in the administration of justice. For a discussion of the Malary case, see chapter 8, "Prosecutions: The Jean-Ronique Antoine and Robert Lecorps Trial."

9. Aristide Plan, 4.

10. Ibid., 5.

11. Ibid.

12. Ibid., 6

13. Disagreement over privatization plans led to the resignation of Prime Minister Smarck Michel, a strong advocate for total privatization. Under President Preval, a lively debate on this question took place in Haiti. The plan was finally adopted by Parliament, but only after significant changes were made to it. See chapter 8, "The Economy."

14. This appears to be the same model that led Mexico into financial collapse by undermining the production of small farmers, building export industries on exploited labor, and concentrating wealth and resources in the hands of the very few.

15. *Emergency Economic Recovery Program, Inter-American Development Bank, Report of the Joint Mission* (November 7–20, 1994), Annex I (January 3, 1995).

16. For a more thorough discussion of the privatization issue, see chapter 8, "The Economy."

CHAPTER EIGHT

1. President Aristide appointed a National Truth and Justice Commission to investigate human rights abuses and to write a report. He also proceeded with the prosecutions. See prologue, note 13; this chapter, "Prosecutions: The Zimbabwe Trial," "Prosecutions: The Jean-Ronique Antoine and Robert Lecorps Trial," and "Other Steps toward Justice." The Preval government is continuing these investigations and prosecutions.

2. Immanuel Kant, *The Metaphysics of Morals,* translated by Mary Gregor (Cambridge: Cambridge University Press, 1991), 140–45. The connection between punishment and solidarity with the victim has become apparent in the last two decades in the numerous countries that have overcome dictatorial regimes and have begun the transition to democracy. In the mid-1980s in Argentina, for example, the Alfonsín government attempted to prosecute the generals who caused mass disappearances of perhaps thirty thousand people. The victims' families themselves insisted on prosecution as a means of vindicating their dignity as citizens. The American version of

these concerns is the series of trials in which women, gays and lesbians, blacks, and Jews have expected solidarity from the rest of society. If society refuses to respond to these concerns, the argument goes, all members of society become complicitous to some degree, however minor, in the crimes committed against the victims.

3. See Jaime Malamud-Goti, *Game without End: State Terror and the Politics of Justice* (Norman: University of Oklahoma Press, 1996).

4. See Carlos S. Nino, *Radical Evil on Trial* (New Haven: Yale University Press, 1996).

5. For example, the defenses raised by the perpetrators of these crimes, such as self-defense, necessity, and so forth, raise these questions.

6. Bruce Ackerman, *The Future of Liberal Revolution* (New Haven: Yale University Press, 1992).

7. There are, of course, other moral, political, and legal concerns that, while central to human rights trials in general, are less pressing in Haiti. See Irwin P. Stotzky, "Haiti: Searching for Alternatives," in *Impunity and Human Rights in International Law and Practice*, edited by Naomi-Roht-Arriaza (New York: Oxford University Press, 1995), 185–97.

8. The negotiations leading to a possible amnesty were a major issue in Aristide's reinstatement to office. See chapter 2.

9. Under Article 147 of the Haitian Constitution, any Haitian president, including Presidents Aristide and Preval, "may grant amnesty only for political matters as stipulated by law."

10. I obtained the information about the Zimbabwe trial from interviews with, and reports from, several participants in the trial, including the prosecutors and judge, and from other international observers of the trial. The astute observations and notes of Richard Harvey shaped my discussion of the Zimbabwe trial. Katie Orenstein's views were also very instructive.

11. *In absentia* convictions are almost always criticized by human rights activists. In the conditions that face Haiti, however, these convictions have both positive and negative aspects. *In absentia* prosecutions can be used as a draconian tool by authoritarian regimes. They do not allow the person charged with a crime to defend himself or herself; only one side of the story is told. On the other hand, under a democratic regime, those charged with crimes are free to return and defend themselves. Moreover, there is often no way, other than an *in absentia* prosecution, for the Haitian government to prosecute those who are responsible for massive numbers of murders and the torture of thousands of people. In Haiti, one convicted *in absentia* has five years in which to return to face his or her charges. If he or she does return, the *in absentia* conviction becomes invalid, and he or she has the same rights to a fair trial as one who had not been so tried. After five years, however, the *in absentia* conviction becomes permanent. Jean-Joseph Exumé, continuing interview by author, March 10, 1995, to November 1, 1995 (Exumé is the former minister of justice of the Republic of Haiti).

12. For a detailed report on the assassination of Antoine Izméry, see OAS/UN Report.

13. Under "Jury Selection" below, I offer a few comments on aspects of the selection process.

14. This part of the discussion is based on reports from several observers at the trial, particularly Richard Harvey.

15. Paragraph 3 reads in pertinent part:

In the determination of any criminal charge against him, everyone shall be entitled to the following minimal guarantees, in full equality:

(b) To have adequate time and facilities for the preparation of his defence and to communicate with counsel of his own choosing; . . .

(d) To be tried in his presence, and to defend himself in person or through legal assistance of his own choosing; to be informed, if he does not have legal assistance, of this right; and to have legal assistance, assigned to him, in any case where the interests of justice so require, and without payment by him in any such case if he does not have sufficient means to pay for it; . . .

(f) To have the free assistance of an interpreter if he cannot understand or speak the language used in court; [and]

(g) Not to be compelled to testify against himself or to confess guilt.

International Covenant on Civil and Political Rights, adopted by General Assembly December 16, 1966, art. 14, para. 3 (hereafter cited as ICCPR); Manfred Nowak, ed., *U.N. Covenant on Civil and Political Rights: CCPR Commentary* (Kehl, Germany; Arlington, Va.: N. P. Engel, 1993).

16. Article 14(3)(a) of the ICCPR requires this, also mandating that the accused be informed "promptly." From interviews of the *doyen* and Zimbabwe conducted by members of the team of international lawyers, and from what I have learned of the pretrial proceedings before the *juge d'instruction,* this requirement seems substantially to have been met. The minister of justice received the indictment on July 7, 1995. Zimbabwe appeared before the *doyen* on August 12, 1995, who fully informed him of the charges against him and of the August 18, 1995, trial date.

17. The government hid this witness for two months to protect him before he testified. The international group of lawyers had been the first to discover him and to devise a plan for his protection.

18. See ICCPR. This right is, of course, a universally recognized due process requirement.

19. Certainly Massac is right and, under Article 14(3)(f) of the ICCPR, if any proceedings are conducted in French, there should be an interpreter for Creole-speaking defendants like Zimbabwe. See ICCPR.

20. I have outlined many of these concerns in the text of this section of the book.

21. *Standard Minimum Rules for the Treatment of Prisoners,* adopted August 30, 1955, *First U.N. Congress on the Prevention of Crime and the Treatment of Offenders,* U.N. Doc. A/CONF/611, Annex I, E.S.C. Res. 663C, 24 U.N. ESCOR, Supp. No. 1, at 11, U.N. Doc. E/3048 (1957), *amended,* E.S.C. Res. 2076, 62 U.N. ESCOR, Supp. No. 1, at 35, U.N. Doc. E/5988 (1977).

22. ICCPR, art. 8, para. 3(a), (b).

23. "2 Defendants Go on Trial in '93 Malary Slaying," *Miami Herald,* July 23, 1996, A7.

24. Paul v. Avril, 901 F. Supp. 330 (S.D. Fla. 1994).

25. "Le Meurtre de Guy Malary Perpétré par des Tueurs Professionnels (Guy Malary's Murder Perpetrated by Professional Killers)," *Haiti Observateur*, October 20–27, 1993, 10.

26. *Frontline*, "Showdown in Haiti," WGBH-TV/PBS television broadcast, November 9, 1993 (transcript).

27. Ibid., 12.

28. John Donnelly and Harold Maass, "Aristide Aide Assassinated: Haiti Justice Minister Was a Leading Figure in Democracy Effort," *Miami Herald*, October 15, 1993, A1.

29. The Anti-Gang Service was a specialized unit of the military police in Port-au-Prince, which shared its offices with the headquarters of the military police under Lieutenant Colonel François.

30. UN/Secretary-General Report, p. 5, para. 11.

31. See "2 Are Acquitted in Death of a Haitian Minister," *New York Times*, July 25, 1996, A5; "Jury Acquits 2 Men in '93 Assassination," *Miami Herald*, July 25, 1996, A15.

32. Reed Brody, telephone interview by author, July 24, 1996 (Brody is an attorney and criminal investigator for the Haitian government); Katie Orenstein, telephone interview by author, July 24, 1996 (Orenstein is a criminal investigator for the Haitian government).

Corruption remains endemic to the administration of justice. For example, on July 26, 1996, a provincial district attorney claimed that he was in hiding out of fear of being killed because of a report he submitted to President Preval's minister of justice, Pierre Max Antoine, detailing the corruption of political, judicial, and police officials. The report accuses a judge, a mayor, and police officers of taking bribes to allow hundreds of boat people to set out for Miami illegally. "Haitian Prosecutor in Hiding: He Made Bribery Accusations," *Miami Herald*, July 26, 1996, A17. The report claims that approximately 545 men, women, and children paid up to $3,000 each for a chance to get to Miami on a boat that could not comfortably have carried sixty people. The official accomplices were paid varying amounts up to $6,700. The boat owner organized the trip and paid bribes to the magistrate, mayor, and police chief of St. Louis du Nord to make sure that the boat would leave Haiti. Ibid.

33. Camille LeBlanc, continuing interview by author, October to December 1995.

34. I am in continuous contact with a variety of officials and other sources in Haiti and the United States, as well as with international sources. Much of the information in the remaining sections of the book has been obtained from these personal sources. There is another issue of some importance in describing the sources of information: documents do not exist for much of this information, which is based, instead, on personal knowledge. I have been directly involved in many of the events I describe. Furthermore, many of the sources of information cannot be revealed for security reasons.

35. Under this formula, the political system of the United States appears to be in deep trouble. Indeed, if the degree and scope of citizen participation

in elections are the criteria for judging the vitality of a democracy, the United States ranks among the least democratic states of those holding free elections. See Walter Dean Burnham, *The Current Crisis in American Politics* (New York: Oxford University Press, 1982), passim; Joshua Cohen and Joel Rogers, *On Democracy* (New York: Penguin Books, 1983). Further complicating this problem is the lack of equality of participation. The working-class voter turnout in the United States, for example, is approximately 30 percent lower than middle-class turnout. Burnham, *Current Crisis;* Cohen and Rogers, *On Democracy.* Perhaps even more disturbing is the fact that blacks vote substantially less often than whites. In the 1992 presidential election, however, black voter participation increased as compared with white voter participation—from approximately 20 percent less than white voter turnout to approximately 10 percent less. For statistical information about the 1992 presidential election, see U.S. Department of Commerce, Bureau of the Census, *Population Characteristics: Voting and Registration in the Election of November 1992,* Current Population Reporter, Series P-20, No. 466, p. v (table A) (April 1993). There are, of course, a host of other factors that indicate that the American democratic system suffers from serious maladies. These factors include, inter alia, serious problems with the American economy and the standard of living, wealth and income distribution inequities, and defense and foreign policy misadventures during the past five decades. Haiti is not the only nation that must periodically assess its development as a democracy.

36. Pollworkers and CEP members, interview by author, Port-au-Prince, Haiti, June 27, 1995; see Don Bohning, "Vote-Weary Shun Haiti's Election," *Miami Herald,* September 18, 1995, A10.

37. Invited by the government of Haiti to help monitor the elections, the OAS had an observer team in the field for months, and nearly three hundred observers throughout the country on election day.

38. *Final Report of the OAS Election Observation Mission on Legislative and Municipal Elections Held in Haiti (Report on the June 25, 1995 Elections),* OEA/Ser.G/CP/Doc. 2703/96 Add. 1 Corr. 2, March 5, 1996, at 25 (hereafter cited as *Final Report on the June 25 Elections*); Jean Jean-Pierre, continuing interview by author, December 1994 to November 1996 (Jean-Pierre is a journalist for the *Village Voice*). Much of the information in this section of the book was obtained from interviews with, and notes of, Jean Jean-Pierre.

39. Ibid.

40. The Independent Electoral Commission administered South Africa's elections in 1994. Gay McDougall observed Haiti's elections as a member of the nine-person American Inter-Organizational Observer Mission co-ordinated by TransAfrica.

41. *Legislative and Municipal Elections in Haiti: Hearing on S-381-28.1 before the Subcomm. on Western Hemisphere and Peace Corps Affairs,* 104th Cong., 1st Sess. 41 (oral), 44 (written) (1995) (statement of Gay J. McDougall, Executive Director, International Human Rights Law Group) (hereafter cited as *Elections Hearing*).

42. Jean-Pierre, continuing interview; see also *Final Report on the June 25 Elections,* 23–25.

43.   Jean-Pierre, continuing interview; see *Final Report on the June 25 Elections,* 23–25.

44.   Jean-Pierre, continuing interview.

45.   Ibid.

46.   Ibid.

47.   See International Republican Institute, *Haiti, IRI Assessment of the June 25, August 13, and September 17, 1995 Legislative and Municipal Elections in Haiti* (1995) (hereafter cited as *IRI Report*). The IRI has consistently objected to almost every action taken by the Aristide government. IRI is clearly not an objective organization. Its intent appears to have been blatantly political and partisan—to embarrass the Clinton administration for supporting the return of the democratically elected president (Aristide) so that he could finish his term in office.

48.   *Irregularities Mar Electoral Process: Statement by Rep. Porter Goss (R-FL), Delegation Chairman,* News Release, International Republican Institute, June 26, 1995, at 3.

49.   Ibid.

50.   "Haiti Finds a Voice," *Washington Post,* June 27, 1995, A16.

51.   Robert A. Pastor, *Mission to Haiti #3: Elections For Parliament and Municipalities, June 23–26, 1995* (July 17, 1995) (unpublished report, Council of Freely Elected Heads of Government, The Carter Center, Atlanta, Georgia) (hereafter cited as Pastor Report). This report should be taken more seriously than the IRI report because it is clearly from a more objective source than the one issued by the IRI. Indeed, Pastor has traditionally been more supportive about progressive change in Haiti than some other groups. He has generally supported any positive steps toward democracy in Haiti, including Aristide's reinstatement to office. Nevertheless, many Haitians are highly critical of him. They see him as Carter's man in Haiti and, therefore, biased against the progressive forces in Haiti. Jean-Pierre, continuing interview.

52.   Ibid., preface, acknowledgments.

53.   Ibid., 19.

54.   Ibid., "Executive Summary."

55.   Ibid., 17.

56.   Ibid., 7.

57.   Pastor Report, 20.

58.   Pastor Report, "Executive Summary."

59.   For a discussion of the complementary elections, see this chapter, "Elections."

60.   Pastor Report, 17.

61.   "Decree of President Jean-Bertrand Aristide," June 30, 1995 (unpublished); President Aristide, continuing interview.

62.   Pastor Report, 21–23.

63.   President Aristide, continuing interview.

64.   National Democratic Institute for International Affairs, *Report of the NDI Survey Mission to Haiti: October 30–November 5, 1994,* at 8–9.

65.   Ibid., 21.

66.   Pastor Report, 21–23. The change in composition of the electoral

panel was slow in coming. Beset by internal dissension, however, Haiti's nine-member electoral panel was to be replaced by a new one that will be in charge of organizing the next election. On October 18, 1996, the Preval government announced that the three branches of government—Parliament, the Supreme Court, and the Executive—had until October 30, 1996, to choose three panel members each. "New Electoral Panel to Replace Current One," *Miami Herald*, October 19, 1996, A16. The three branches of government met that deadline and, on November 6, 1996, the government formally appointed the nine-member provisional electoral panel. "New Electoral Board Named by Government," *Miami Herald*, November 7, 1996, A26.

67.   For example, according to the CEP list, in two areas where complementary elections had taken place because of the cancellation of the vote on June 25, 1995, the breakdown of candidates per party was as follows: (1) (in Limbe) FNCD, 4; FULNH, 1; KONAKOM, 7; Lavalas, 7; PAIN, 3; PANPRA, 7; RDNP, 1; UPAN, 4; PROP, 1; and (2) (in Dondon) FNCD, 1; CONACOM, 1; Lavalas, 4; PANPRA, 3; RDNP, 1; UPD, 1; GMRN, 1; RDC, 1; Independent, 2. According to Robert Pastor, the most significant of these parties, other than Lavalas, are: FNCD (Front National pour la Convergence Democratique), a coalition of groups that originally supported Aristide; CONACOM (Komite Nasyonal Kongre Mouvman Demokratik), originally part of the coalition that elected Aristide, but later remained apart from the FNCD and Lavalas to present its own candidates; PAIN (Parti Agricole Industriel National), a center-right party supported mainly from the south because of the legacy of Louis Dejoie, who ran against Duvaliér in 1957; PANPRA (Parti National Progressiste Revolutionnaire Haïtien), a Social Democratic group that opposed the FNCD in 1990, but separated itself from MIDH (Movement pour l'Instauration de la Democratie en Haïti) (another significant party, which boycotted the 1995 election), denouncing the coup in 1991; and RDNP (Rassemblement des Democrates Nationaux Progressistes). Pastor Report, appendix 2. For a description of these as well as other political parties and coalitions of Haiti, see Pastor Report, appendix 2. For an analysis of the complementary elections, see this chapter, "Elections."

68.   Continuing interviews with various Haitian officials, international observers, and Haitian citizens, conducted by author both before and after the June 25, 1995, election.

69.   Ibid.

70.   *IRI Report.*

71.   Ibid.

72.   Don Bohning, "Haiti Elections Reflect Growing Power of Aristide," *Miami Herald*, September 17, 1995, A20; see Bohning, "Vote-Weary Shun Haiti's Election."

73.   Bohning, "Haiti Elections Reflect Growing Power of Aristide"; see Tim Johnson and Don Bohning, "What Will Aristide Do for His Third Act?" *Miami Herald*, December 17, 1995, A1; "Haiti," *Miami Herald*, November 25, 1995, A24.

74.   Continuing interviews with various Haitian officials, international

observers, and Haitian citizens, conducted by author, October 1994 to July 1996.

75. See Julia Preston, "Haitians Vote Peacefully in 2d Round," *New York Times*, September 18, 1995, A4.

76. Jean-Pierre, continuing interview.

77. Approximately five de facto governments existed between the fall of Baby Doc in 1986 and the election of Aristide in 1990. The Nerette-Honorat government was one of these regimes. Jean-Pierre, continuing interview.

78. "Preval Is Declared Winner of Election," *New York Times*, December 24, 1995, sec. 1, p. 3.

79. Larry Rohter, "A Haitian's Iffy Mandate," *New York Times*, December 24, 1995, sec. 4, p. 2.

80. Ibid.

81. Douglas Farah, "Haiti Gives Preval Wide Vote Margin; Turnout Estimated at under One-Third," *Washington Post*, December 19, 1995, A25.

82. Don Bohning and Tim Johnson, "Low Turnout Stirs Debate on Haitian Vote," *Miami Herald*, December 19, 1995, A15.

83. "Who Will Rule Haiti?" *New York Times*, December 20, 1995, A20.

84. Ibid.

85. Don Bohning, "Haiti Bound for Uncertainty as Power Shifts from Aristide," *Miami Herald*, February 5, 1996, A8.

86. Ibid.

87. Douglas Farah, "Aristide's 'Twin' On Center Stage; Likely Successor Preval Emerges from Wings," *Washington Post*, December 17, 1995, A33.

88. Ibid.

89. Ibid.

90. Ibid. This statement, however, seems a bit too facile. Aristide has shown an increasing sophistication on these issues. My experience with him demonstrates that he is very knowledgeable on a wide range of issues. He is acutely sensitive to nuances in human behavior and in social organization. He is not to be underestimated in his intelligence and know-how.

91. See prologue, note 8. The hope is that, with more time, the National Police Force will have more people trained so that the UN peace-keeping forces will be able to leave Haiti. For a detailed discussion of the moves toward police reform, see Robert Maguire, *Demilitarizing Public Order in a Predatory State: The Case of Haiti*, North South Agenda Papers 17 (December 1995): 1–12.

92. *Report of the Secretary-General on the United Nations Mission in Haiti*, U.N. Doc. S/1994/828 (July 15, 1994).

93. See this chapter, "Security and U.S. Involvement in Haiti," "Continuing Security Concerns."

94. When the United States first sent troops into Haiti, one of the goals was to disarm Haitian military and paramilitary forces. Indeed, U.S. officials publicly proclaimed this to be one of their goals. But they have been inconsistent in their approach to this issue. For example, Stanley Schrager of the U.S. embassy in Haiti discussed the situation on weapons in Haiti at that time:

It's difficult to say how many guns are still out there, and the United States has not engaged itself in an active policy of disarmament. I think we felt that that was not our role. However, we're clearly reducing the number of weapons in that society, and clearly, in my opinion, reducing the capacity for violence. We've confiscated over 12,000 weapons already. . . .

[G]iven the fact that we are not engaging in an active disarmament plan, we do follow up leads and reports and we continue to disarm police and military units around the country, as well as attempting to reduce the weapons in the hands of these paramilitary organizations like FRAPH.

USIA Foreign Press Center Briefing, Federal News Service, November 15, 1994, at 7 (available in LEXIS, Legis Library, FEDNEW File) (statement of Stanley Schrager, Public Affairs Officer, U.S. Embassy in Haiti).

Other official pronouncements made the same claim. For example, on October 20, 1994, Christine Shelly, in a State Department briefing, said:

[W]e're working on three main things. The first is dismantling Haiti's illegal paramilitary structure. The second is to do everything that we possibly can to get the guns off the street. And, third, to create and do everything we can to contribute to the stable and secure environment in Haiti. . . .

[T]he MNF has also conducted 35 sizable company-sized operations on the arms caches since October 1st. I'm told that of those 35 raids that they've had, approximately 15 of those did not produce any direct and immediate weapons result, but 20 of those raids produced weapons and/or detainees associated with the weapons.

State Department Regular Briefing, Federal News Service, October 20, 1994, at 16–17 (available in LEXIS, Legis Library, FEDNEW File) (statement of Christine Shelly).

95.   Larry Rohter, "Haitian Leader's Angry Words Set Off New Wave of Violence," *New York Times,* November 19, 1995, sec. 1, p. 1.

96.   These concerns continued into the Preval term. See this chapter, "Continuing Security Concerns."

97.   Ibid.

98.   Historically, there have been incidents, of course, in which the Haitian people have taken the law into their own hands. See chapter 3. In addition, in several different actions, certain parts of the U.S. government continue to oppose democratic reforms in Haiti and to support members of the de facto coup regime. See this chapter, "Security and U.S. Involvement in Haiti."

99.   Douglas Farah, "Haiti's Nascent Prospects Turn Suddenly Bleak; Killing of Aristide Friend, Fiery Presidential Speech, New Street Violence Increase Tension," *Washington Post,* November 26, 1995, A1.

100.   Ibid.

101.   Jean-Pierre, continuing interview.

102.   Ibid.

103.   This is, of course, just the kind of lawless action that cannot be tolerated if the rule of law is to become part of the future of Haitian society. But, unless the Haitian government can enforce the law, vigilante action cannot always be condemned; nor can it be stopped. Haitian history will repeat itself endlessly until the rule of law is incorporated in the minds of the Haitian people and is thus enforceable.

104.   There have long been reports by reliable informants that Avril has prospered in the illicit drug trade and has strong personal contacts with several Colombian drug lords.

105.   Douglas Farah, "U.S.-Haitian Relations Deteriorate; Disarmament Dispute, Contact with Ex-Ruler Infuriate Aristide," *Washington Post,* November 29, 1995, A1.

106.   Ibid.

107.   Paul v. Avril, 901 F. Supp. 330, 335 (S.D. Fla. 1994).

108.   Ibid.

109.   President Jean-Bertrand Aristide, "Address at the Port-au-Prince Cathedral," November 11, 1995 (transcript, on file with Irwin P. Stotzky).

110.   S. Res. 940, 49th Sess., U.N. Doc. S/RES/940 (July 31, 1994).

111.   Rohter, "Haitian Leader's Angry Words." For some unknown reason, the international press criticized his speech, claiming it called for vigilante action. These articles failed to report that President Aristide did not tell the Haitian people to invade the homes of the elites, but rather to help the legal authorities in searching for weapons.

112.   President Jean-Bertrand Aristide, "Address at Cathedral."

113.   "Aristide Critics See Intimidation in Street Violence," *New York Times,* November 16, 1995, A8.

114.   Cap-Haïtien, located in the far northeast corner of Haiti, is the second largest city in the country after Port-au-Prince.

115.   Rohter, "Haitian Leader's Angry Words."

116.   Press report (on file with Irwin P. Stotzky).

117.   This quote is taken from the notes of a participant at the conference. Because of security concerns, his name cannot be revealed. This statement is, of course, an affirmation of the importance of deliberative democracy.

118.   For an example of such a misinterpretation, see "Aristide Raises Doubt about Vote," *Miami Herald,* November 25, 1995, A24.

119.   "Violence in Haiti Claims Three Lives," *Miami Herald,* November 24, 1995, A26.

120.   "Mr. Aristide's Deadly Rhetoric," *New York Times,* November 26, 1995, sec. 4, p. 10.

121.   These incidents, of course, reflect the continuing attempts by certain U.S. government agencies to portray Aristide as an authoritarian, not a democratic, leader, and to undermine the movement toward democracy.

122.   Some of the photos are "trophy photos" of FRAPH victims that U.S. Captain J. B. Shattuck described as "bodies, all mutilated." Allan Nairn, "Haiti under Cloak," *Nation,* February 26, 1996, 4.

123.   Farah, "U.S.-Haitian Relations."

124.   Ibid.

125. Letter from members of the U.S. Congress to President Clinton, 1995 (on file with Irwin P. Stotzky).

126. Ibid.

127. Letter from representatives of nongovernmental groups to President Clinton, 1995 (on file with Irwin P. Stotzky).

128. Jim Lobe, *U.S.-Haiti: Rights Group Voices Concern Over U.S.-Held Documents*, Inter Press Service, February 28, 1996. The New York–based Human Rights Watch stated that Washington's "refusal to return the seized documents on acceptable terms represents a concrete impediment to ending impunity for political violence." The rights group stated further that the immediate return of the documents to the Preval government was "consistent with a policy that places top priority on establishing the rule of law in Haiti." The group's appeal follows protracted negotiations between the U.S. and Haitian governments over the return of the approximately 150,000 pages of documents that U.S. soldiers seized from FRAPH and the Haitian army. Ibid.

129. This information is taken from private negotiations between the U.S. government and the Haitian government. On September 26, 1996, U.S. officials claimed that thousands of pages of these documents would soon be returned to Haiti. They also claimed that some of these documents—the "nonsensitive" ones—had been sent to Haiti in January 1996. "Haiti," *Miami Herald*, September 27, 1996, A13. Haitian officials, however, have no knowledge of ever receiving these documents and are simply not inclined to receive documents that have been heavily censored to exclude any reference to U.S. involvement with the coup regime and paramilitary forces. In addition, these officials refuse to receive these documents because of the conditions imposed by the U.S. government on the use that can be made of them.

130. Larry Rohter, "Cables Show U.S. Deception on Violence in Haiti," *New York Times*, February 6, 1996, A8.

131. Ibid.

132. Ibid.

133. Ibid.

134. *60 Minutes.*

135. Ibid. Constant claims that he started working for the CIA in 1992, but was in close contact well before that with officials of the Pentagon's Defense Intelligence Agency (DIA). Lobe, "U.S.-Haiti: Concern."

136. Haitian officials claim that, for at least one year, they told U.S. officials of Constant's whereabouts in the United States, and that the United States failed to act on this information. It is not clear why U.S. officials finally arrested Constant and attempted to deport him.

137. Tim Weiner, "Haitian Ex-Paramilitary Leader Confirms C.I.A. Relationship," *New York Times*, December 3, 1995, sec. 1, p. 6. See chapter 3.

138. Weiner, "Haitian Leader Confirms C.I.A. Relationship."

139. Ibid.

140. Nairn, "Haiti under Cloak."

141. Ibid.

142. Ibid. Allan Nairn, reporting in the *Nation*, "revealed that the [CIA]

and the [DIA] helped Constant set up FRAPH to 'balance the Aristide movement.' (Another historical note: Constant told Nairn that the CIA station chief and the DIA station chief were inside the headquarters of the coup leaders when Aristide was overthrown.)." "The Haiti Model; Cynical U.S. Policy," *Progressive* 58(12) (December 1994): 8.

143.   President Aristide, continuing interview.

144.   Maria Myers, "U.S. Frees Haitian Suspected of Atrocities," *Miami Herald*, July 28, 1996, A14.

145.   Tim Weiner, "C.I.A. Report Said Haitian Agent May have Helped Plan Killing," *New York Times*, October 13, 1996, Y7. An intelligence official familiar with the report claims that this passage is attributable to a "fairly reliable" source. Ibid.

146.   This accusation was attributed to an "untested" source, the intelligence official said. A December 1995 CIA report on the murder did not mention Mr. Constant. According to the same intelligence official, this suggests that the "untested" source was not reliable. Ibid. Given the CIA actions described in the text, this explanation lacks any credibility.

Mr. Constant seems to be enjoying his freedom. On November 2, 1996, he was seen celebrating at a club in Queens, New York. The club, Imagine, was holding a celebration to honor a Voodoo holiday called Zede. The holiday celebrates the spirit of the dead in the Voodoo religion. Several Haitians who were at the club were sickened by the sight of Mr. Constant and his five-person entourage ("posse"). There was a small altercation between Constant and several of the Haitians who were not members of his party. It seems bizarre that one who has caused so many deaths should celebrate the spirit of the dead. Jean-Pierre, continuing interview.

147.   Douglas Farah and Dana Priest, "Haiti Says U.S. Troops May Have Helped Foes," *Washington Post*, December 8, 1995, A43.

148.   James Ridgeway and Jean Jean-Pierre, "Selling Out the President: As Elections Near, Aristide Faces Attacks from All Sides," *Village Voice*, December 5, 1995, 21.

149.   Ibid.

150.   Farah and Priest, "U.S. Troops May Have Helped Foes."

151.   Ibid.

152.   I interviewed Mr. Morissaint several times. This discussion is taken from the extensive notes I took during these interviews. See also Allan Nairn, "Our Payroll, Haitian Hit," *Nation*, October 9, 1995, 373–74; James Ridgeway and Jean Jean-Pierre, "Federal Bureau of Obfuscation: Aristide Investigates Crimes the U.S. Would Prefer Left Unsolved," *Village Voice*, October 10, 1995, 23. In October 1995, "[t]he U.S. weekly, the *Nation*, disclosed . . . . that Haitian gunman Marcel Morissaint worked with U.S. intelligence while serving as an attache under former police chief Lt. Col. Michel Francois, one of the leaders of the 1991 coup that deposed Aristide." Yvette Collymore, *Haiti-U.S.: Aristide a Political Punching Bag on Key Anniversary*, Inter Press Service, October 13, 1995; see also "Haiti Accuses U.S. of Helping Suspected Assassin," *Miami Herald*, September 23, 1995, A20 (U.S. officials accused of helping Morissaint escape from prison).

153.   I later discovered that the chief prosecutor in Port-au-Prince, Bru-

tus, had signed the papers authorizing Morissaint's release. Brutus claimed that he did not know that Morissaint was being held on other serious charges. Brutus, however, was the official who had sought and obtained an arrest warrant for Morissaint on those other serious charges. He is the same man who prosecuted Gérard Gustave (Zimbabwe) for the murder of Antoine Izméry, and Jean-Ronique Antoine and Robert Lecorps for the murder of Guy Malary. See this chapter, "Prosecutions: The Zimbabwe Trial," "Prosecutions: The Jean-Ronique Antoine and Robert Lecorps Trial."

154.   Nairn, "Haiti under Cloak," 73.

155.   Indictment, United States v. Joseph Michel François (No. 97-6007, S.D. Fla). François is fighting extradition. It remains uncertain whether he will ever stand trial for these crimes.

156.   Interviews with anonymous U.S. Justice Department officials; Jean-Pierre, continuing interview.

157.   Ibid.

158.   A convicted member of the Medellin cocaine cartel, Gabriel Taboada, told a Senate Foreign Relations Subcommittee in April 1994 that the shipments were protected by the Haitian military and that François protected the drugs in Haiti and then allowed the drugs to continue to the United States.

In addition, despite being identified by the U.S. Treasury Department in 1993 as a drug trafficker and as one of forty-one senior military and police officials who obstructed the restoration of democracy in Haiti, Marc Valme was granted political asylum in 1994 by the U.S. government. David Lyons, "U.S. Gave Asylum to Drug Trafficker," *Miami Herald*, March 18, 1997, B1.

159.   U.S. Justice Department, International Criminal Investigative Training Assistance Program in Haiti (ICITAP), interviews by author, November 1994, June 1995; see also Human Rights Watch/Americas and National Coalition for Haitian Refugees, "Haiti: Security Compromised: Recycled Haitian Soldiers on the Police Front Line," 7(3) (March 1995).

160.   USAID officials believed that many of the FAD'H members would retire because of their advanced age. USAID, *Briefing Paper: Demobilization and Reintegration Program*, September 1, 1994; Johanna Mendelson Forman, *Beyond the Mountains, More Mountains: Demobilizing the Haitian Army*, North South Agenda Papers (forthcoming 1996).

161.   The Haitian Parliament refused to confirm his appointment. This shows that Parliament is becoming a separate, independent institution, which is a very positive sign for democracy. Michael Norton, "Police Debate Tests Haitian Democracy," *Miami Herald*, January 27, 1996, A18. On March 5, 1996, the Haitian Senate confirmed Preval's nominee, Pierre Denize, as the new National Police chief. Denize is the first civilian to serve in this position in the 192 years of Haitian independence. "Civilian Is Confirmed as New Police Chief," *Miami Herald*, March 6, 1996, A15.

162.   Larry Rohter, "Support Is Waning for Haiti's U.S.-Trained Police," *New York Times*, December 24, 1995, sec. 1, p. 3. Indeed, the approximately 5,300-member force has been widely accused of resorting to the harsh practices of its predecessors. But these accusations are not wholly accurate. A report by the UN Civilian Mission in Haiti, issued on August 2, 1996, gives

a more positive, but mixed, review of the National Police. According to the report, the police force has shot and killed twenty-six and wounded approximately fifty civilians between July 1995 and May 1996. OAS/UN International Civilian Mission in Haiti, *The Haitian National Police and Human Rights*, July 1996, at 2 (summary in English) (report in French) (hereafter cited as OAS/UN Police Report). In isolated cases, "it seems that the police deliberately killed or wounded people, or shot at suspects whom they had already wounded." These killings and woundings occurred in about fifty incidents when police used their weapons. Furthermore, allegations of police misconduct have increased from eleven in 1995 to eighty-six in 1996. Nevertheless, the report concluded that "respect for human rights by the National Police is quite satisfactory and its behavior is encouraging." The report also found that most National Police officers are doing an effective job, despite inexperience and lack of equipment. Most important, the phenomenon of massive and systematic violations of human rights that typified de facto rule has disappeared. "A Mixed Review for Haiti's Police," *Miami Herald*, August 3, 1996, A17; see OAS/UN Police Report, 1–3 (summary in English), 43–44 (conclusions in French).

Human rights groups have been particularly critical of the Haitian National Police. In a report issued on January 22, 1997, a coalition of human rights groups claims that in the approximately eighteen months since its deployment, members of the 5,300-member U.S.-trained force have committed serious abuses, including torture and summary executions. See Human Rights Watch/Americas, National Coalition for Haitian Refugees, and Washington Office on Latin America, "Haiti: The Human Rights Record of the Haitian National Police," 9(1)(B) (January 1997).

According to this report, since the force began operations in July 1995, agents and police have killed at least forty-six civilians. While a minority died when police used deadly force in legitimate self-defense, the report claims that most suffered extrajudicial executions or the excessive unjustified use of lethal force by the police.

The report recognizes the extreme difficulty in reforming the police. It also points out that violence against civilians is not government policy. But it cautions that the failure to address these issues promptly risks institutionalizing abusive practices and undermining the credibility and legitimacy of the new police force. The human rights groups warn that the startling number of human rights abuses—eighty-six cases of abuse and torture of detainees were reported to the police inspector general's office in 1996—raises serious concerns about the training and leadership of the police force. They call for strictly enforced discipline and the aggressive prosecution of police who torture and kill.

The report acknowledges the difficulty in creating the first civilian, professional police force in Haiti's nearly 200-year history as an independent nation, given the country's traditions and limited resources. Contributing to the police abuses are slow progress in key areas of institutional development and a lack of leadership resulting from lagging recruitment efforts and disputes over the background of officer candidates. The force has also faced severe logistical and resource constraints, problems attributed in part to a timetable for police reform that was shortened because of domestic pressure in the United States. Further challenges faced by the police leadership include shortages of basic equipment, a weak and corrupt judicial system lacking qualified personnel and basic materials, and poor police-community relations.

In conclusion, the report notes that

> Haiti's repressive history created widespread mistrust of security forces and profound skepticism about the possibility of creating a professional police force. Ending police abuse and establishing accountability, as well [as] improving understanding of the role of the police in a democracy, are vital steps toward overcoming this legacy. Police authorities so far have shown a desire to end impunity and work with the population to tackle these challenges. If they succeed, they will establish a solid foundation for human rights and the rule of law in Haiti.

Ibid., 39. The U.S. Department of State's annual human rights report makes similar claims. See U.S. Department of State, *Haiti Country Report on Human Rights Practices for 1996* (January 30, 1997-[cited 3 February 1997]), available from http://www.state.gov/www/issues/human rights/1996 hrp report/ haiti.html; INTERNET.

163.   "Key Lawmaker OKs Releasing Frozen Funds," *Miami Herald*, January 13, 1996, A19.

164.   Christopher Marquis, "Canadians to Follow U.S. Forces in Haiti," *Miami Herald*, January 25, 1996, A16.

165.   Ibid.

166.   Ibid.

167.   "U.N. Says Peacekeepers Will Remain in Haiti," *New York Times*, January 11, 1996, A3.

168.   Interviews with members representing a federation of peasant development groups in northern Haiti, conducted by author, November 1994.

169.   President Aristide, continuing interview.

170.   Having already reduced the size of the Haitian army to 1,500 men, President Aristide purged the entire senior officer corp in February. Furthermore, he transferred FAD'H headquarters to his newly formed Ministry of Women's Affairs. Larry Rohter, "Aristide Weakens Army and Makes it Dependent on Him," *New York Times*, January 15, 1995, sec. 1, p. 8; Larry Rohter, "Aristide Forces Retirement of Haiti's Top Military Officers," *New York Times*, February 22, 1995, A4. Nevertheless, disbanding the army has not alleviated the problem with the army. See this chapter, "Continuing Security Concerns."

171.   Susan Benesch, "Haitian Army Trades Truncheons for Trumpets," *Miami Herald*, June 12, 1995, A1.

172.   See this chapter, "Prosecutions: The Zimbabwe Trial."

173.   John M. Goshko, "Haitian Paramilitary Leader Arrested by INS in New York," *Washington Post*, May 13, 1995, 9; "Haitian Says He's Political Candidate; Ex-Paramilitary Chief Fights U.S. Deportation," *Washington Post*, August 26, 1995, A22; Garry Pierre-Pierre, "Haitian Paramilitary Leader Ar-

rested in New York," *House Chronicle,* May 13, 1995, A26; Garry Pierre-Pierre, "Haitians' Sigh of Relief," *New York Times,* sec. 1, p. 31.

174. See this chapter, "Other Steps toward Justice."

175. Convention against Torture and Other Cruel, Inhuman, or Degrading Treatment or Punishment, February 4, 1985, art. 7, paras. 1,2,5, S. Treaty Doc. No. 100-20, 23 I.L.M. 1027 (entered into force June 26, 1987).

176. Kurzban, continuing interview.

177. Douglas Farah, "Aristide Confirms He Will Step Down; Haitian Links Boat People to Aid Cutoff," *Washington Post,* December 1, 1995, A29.

178. Ibid. Indeed, the privatization issue has caused great debate in Haiti. As of August 1996, the issue remained unresolved, although it appeared that Parliament would soon pass the necessary legislation that would, in some form, privatize the nine state-run enterprises and thus lead to hundreds of millions of foreign aid dollars.

The economic plans, particularly the privatization plan, however, have not met with universal acclaim from the Haitian people. Almost from the beginning of the debate about privatization, there has been strong opposition. As the outlines of the plan have unfolded and the possibly negative effects of privatization have become increasingly clear, opposition to it has increased, culminating in a series of national strikes. The most serious events occurred on January 16, 1997. On that day, protesters burned tires and threw stones in towns and cities across Haiti. They called for Prime Minister Rosny Smarth to resign, and for President Preval to suspend negotiations with international lending institutions and end austerity measures.

In Port-au-Prince, in the largest of antigovernment strikes, demonstrators set piles of tires on fire, blocking main intersections with these smoking barricades. Shops remained closed, parents kept their children home from school, and no public transportation was running. The Anti–International Monetary Fund Committee organized the strike one day after a man lost his right hand to an exploding tear-gas canister fired by police who were attempting to break up a peaceful street demonstration.

More than one hundred and sixty grass-roots groups participated in the strike. These organizations attribute inflation and unemployment to the government's efforts to collect unpaid taxes, cut spending, privatize state-run enterprises, and streamline the bloated bureaucracy—prerequisites to receiving the foreign loans that have kept the government economically viable. Approximately 7,000 out of 43,000 government employees are expected to lose their jobs as a result of the austerity measures. "Protests Erupt Across Haiti As Leaders Push Austerity," *New York Times,* January 17, 1997, A3; "Violence, Protests Spread in Haiti," *New York Times,* January 17, 1997, A25. On June 9, 1997, capitulating to these strikes and violent protests, Rosny Smarth resigned. The move came less than one week before a scheduled runoff election for the Haitian Senate, in which Mr. Smarth's stewardship was virtually the only issue. His resignation may further jeopardize the privitization reforms. Don Bohning, "Haitian Premier Quits under Pressure," *Miami Herald,* June 10, 1997, A20.

179. "Haitian Candidate Promises Reforms—But at His Pace," *Miami Herald,* December 12, 1995, A15.

180.   Sandra Marquez Garcia, "On the Road to Reform, Haiti Is Walking Gingerly," *Miami Herald,* June 11, 1996, A14.

181.   "Haiti," *Miami Herald,* September 26, 1996, A20.

182.   "Haiti," *Miami Herald,* August 19, 1996, A10.

183.   "Privatization Measure Passed by Legislature," *Miami Herald,* September 7, 1996, 10A.

184.   Don Bohning, "Economic-Reform Laws Set Stage For Rebuilding Haiti," *Miami Herald,* October 21, 1996, A8. See this chapter, "The Economy."

185.   Don Bohning, "Haiti, Land of Opportunity—So They Hope," *Miami Herald,* January 1, 1996, A10.

186.   Ibid.

187.   Ibid.

188.   Ibid.

189.   Farah, "Aristide Confirms He Will Step Down."

190.   Jean-Pierre, continuing interview.

191.   Ibid. Privatization has a number of risks. The experiences of Latin American nations with privatization are mixed. Since the 1980s, when many Latin American nations began selling off government-owned companies to the private sector, bloated bureaucracies have become leaner, and overall economic statistics have improved. Unemployment and corruption scandals, however, have increased dramatically. Andres Oppenheimer and Katherine Ellison, "Awaiting Broader Shift to Private Enterprise, Latin America Frets Over Pitfalls of the Past," *Miami Herald,* August 17, 1996, A1.

192.   This source must remain anonymous.

193.   This source must remain anonymous.

194.   Jean-Pierre, continuing interview.

195.   In particular, the Mevs family has long competed with the Brandt family for preeminence in Haitian affairs. Both families have had lobbyists in Washington for some time. Some knowledgeable Haitian experts have told me that these families have been lobbying Washington politicians and contributing to their campaign funds since the 1950s. Part of the Haitian lore surrounds the enmity between these two families. However, they apparently are now working together to attract international support for their projects. Jean-Pierre, continuing interview.

196.   The Foreign Ministry must approve these activities. The problem with this phenomenon is the nearly impossible task of separating the business from the diplomatic activities.

197.   This source must remain anonymous.

198.   Jean-Pierre, continuing interview; Don Bohning, "Haiti Wages Losing Battle against Smugglers," *Miami Herald,* February 17, 1997.

199.   According to several high-ranking Haitian government officials, the country pays approximately $100 million each year to buy imported rice from the United States, much of it from American Rice, Inc., a subsidiary of ERLY Industries, a Los Angeles–based conglomerate with a history of controversy in dealing with USAID. In 1992, American Rice approached Prime Minister Marc Bazin; it soon thereafter established supply routes to Haiti. That company also became involved in processing local rice. American

Rice established enough of a foothold in the Haitian political scene that, in January 1995, it thought it worth the trouble of flying five congressional staffers to Haiti. Apparently, the trip was organized by the State Department, and the U.S. embassy helped arrange a busy schedule that included a 45-minute meeting with President Aristide. After the trip was exposed by the U.S. media, the Republican members of the trip claimed they had repaid the costs. Jean-Pierre, continuing interview.

200. For example, J. Brian Atwood, director of USAID, which has seen its Haiti budget cut back from $235 million in fiscal year 1995 to $85 million in fiscal year 1996, clearly made this point. He claimed that Haiti could become a U.S. political football. As Atwood put it: "It's clear that important members of Congress don't want us to succeed in Haiti. I think that's regrettable." Christopher Marquis, "Release Aid, Haitian Leader Urges on Visit to U.S.," *Miami Herald,* March 21, 1996, A22.

201. Foreign Operations, Export Financing, and Related Programs Appropriations Act, Pub. L. No. 104-107, sec. 583, 110 Stat. 752 (1996) (hereafter cited as Limitation on Assistance for Haiti).

202. The original version of the Dole Amendment reads as follows:

(Purpose: To limit the availability of funds for the Government of Haiti until certain human rights conditions are met, and for other purposes)

At the end of the last committee amendment, insert the following:

Sec.   . Limitation on Assistance for Haiti.

(a) Limitation.—None of the funds appropriated or otherwise made available by this Act or any other Act may be furnished to the Government of Haiti until the President determines and reports in writing to the Congress that—

(1) the government of Haiti has conducted or is conducting a thorough and professional investigation into, and prosecution of those responsible for the murder of Mireille Durocher de Bertin on March 28, 1995, and other possible cases of political or extra-judicial killings, including the 20 cases of "commando-style executions" cited by the United Nations/Organization of American States International Civilian Mission in Haiti on September 12, 1995;

(2)(A) the police and security forces of Haiti are not assassinating or abducting civilians, are not engaging in other acts of violence directed at civilians, and are controlling such activities by elements subject to the control of those forces; or

(B) the government of Haiti is investigating effectively the members within its police and security forces engaged in acts of violence against civilians, and has put in place effective policies to deter and punish such activities in the future.

(3) the Government of Haiti has actively sought and encouraged a law enforcement service from outside Haiti to assist and monitor investigators of the Government of Haiti in their investigation of the murders cited in section   (1) above; and

(4)(A) the Government of Haiti has cooperated fully and in a timely fashion with U.S. Federal Bureau of Investigation efforts to investigate the murder of Mireille Durocher de Bertin, including providing access to Haitian government employees in a manner which facilitates prosecution of those responsible for her murder; or

(B) the Government of Haiti has not cooperated fully and in a timely fashion with U.S. Federal Bureau of Investigation efforts to investigate the murder of Mireille Durocher de Bertin, including providing access to Haitian government employees in a manner which facilitates prosecution of those responsible for her murder, in which case the President shall submit a detailed accounting of the areas of non-cooperation and his assessment of all the reasons for such non-cooperation by the government of Haiti.

(b) Report.—Not later than 60 days after enactment of this section, the President shall report to the appropriate committees of Congress, based on information available to him, on the identity or identities of those responsible for the murder and any subsequent coverup, and on the status of the Government of Haiti's investigation of:

(1) the murder of American citizen Richard Andre Emmanuel on February 13, 1991;

(2) the murders of Bastian Desrosiers, Stevenson Desrosiers, Jacques Nelio, Pierre Schiller and Louis Walky on July 26, 1991;

(3) the murder of Reverend Sylvio Claude on September 17, 1991;

(4) the murder of Roger Lafontant on September 29, 1991;

(5) the murder of Antoine Izmery on September 11, 1993; and

(6) the murder of Minister of Justice Guy Malary on October 14, 1993.

(c) Humanitarian Assistance.—Nothing in this section shall be construed to restrict the provision of humanitarian or electoral assistance to the Haitian people by nongovernmental or private voluntary organizations.

(d) Waiver.—The President may waive the requirements of this section if he determines and certifies to the appropriate committees of Congress that it is necessary to facilitate the safe and timely withdrawal of American forces from Haiti.

141 Cong. Rec. S14,070-71 (daily ed. September 21, 1995).

203. Ibid., sec. a(1).

204. The United States, of course, did not send the FBI to investigate human rights abuses during the coup period. This may have been on the assumption that the coup leaders would refuse U.S. investigators entry to Haiti, but it may also have been because the United States had ties to the coup leaders and did not wish those ties to be publicly exposed.

205. This information is based on first-hand knowledge and thorough interviews of people who must necessarily remain anonymous.

206. Colin Granderson and other members of the MICIVIH, continuing interview by author, Port-au-Prince, Haiti, October 1994 to June 1996.

207. Sandra Marquez Garcia, "Haiti May Soon Lose Millions in U.S. Aid," *Miami Herald,* April 4, 1996, A17.

208. Limitation on Assistance for Haiti. The president has delegated his functions under this provision to the secretary of state. Letter from Acting Secretary of State to Congress, February 6, 1996 (on file with Irwin P. Stotzky).

209. See this chapter, "Other Steps toward Justice."

210. Letter from Acting Secretary of State. The only assistance within the scope of Section 583(a) that the Clinton administration provided during the period that the U.S. peace-keeping forces were withdrawing, was assistance to the Special Investigation Unit and the Haitian National Police.

211. Staff of House Comm. on International Relations, 104th Cong., 2d Sess., Report of Congressional Staff Delegation to Haiti (1996).

212. The report also claims that the investigation of the killings has been "severely compromised" by the Haitian government's employment of three American lawyers whose Miami firm is representing people suspected of being involved with the killings. See ibid., 6; 141 Cong. Rec. S14,070-71 (daily ed. September 21, 1995) (statement of Sen. Dole). This is a total distortion of reality. To begin with, there have been approximately five American lawyers investigating that case. I am one of those attorneys, and I do not work at any firm. I am a law professor. The other lawyers are not Miami lawyers and have no offices in Miami. The lawyers who are representing Haitian government officials work at their own private firms. The lawyers and investigators who are working with the Special Investigative Unit have not shared any information with the lawyers representing Haitian government officials in the FBI investigation of the de Bertin murder.

213. See this chapter, "Other Steps toward Justice."

214. Continuing interviews with several anonymous sources, conducted by author.

215. For example, one of Senator Helms's staff members was part of the delegation that drafted the report. Helms, of course, knowingly spread false information about Aristide, saying that he was psychotic and used psychotropic medication. See chapter 3. Other staff members who were part of this delegation include those of then Senator Dole and Congressmen Callahan (Alabama), Combest (Texas), Gilman (New York), and Livingston (Louisiana). None of these people necessarily wishes to see democracy succeed in Haiti, at least not during President Clinton's term in office.

216. Majority Staff of House Comm. on International Relations, 104th Cong., 2d Sess., *Haiti Quagmire: Clinton Administration Actions & Political Killings* (1996); Christopher Marquis, "Report: U.S. Let Aristide Stall Probe," *Miami Herald,* October 23, 1996, A1.

217. Ibid.

218. Letter from Lee H. Hamilton, Representative from Indiana, to Virginia Templeton, Reference Librarian, University of Miami Law School, October 23, 1996 (on file with Irwin P. Stotzky).

219.   Marquis, "U.S. Let Aristide Stall Probe." Hamilton, in a news release issued on October 22, 1996, more directly refuted the charges. The
release states in pertinent part:

A Republican staffer of the International Relations Committee has
released his report on Haiti today. I have three concerns about the
serious charges contained in this report.

First, these charges are not new. The Republicans have raised them
before, in four full committee hearings, in numerous subcommittee
hearings, and in the press. However, the staff has never been able to
substantiate the very serious allegations that the Clinton Administration covered up execution-style murders in Haiti. They simply repeat
the charges over and over.

The Administration could not cover up these killings, which occurred in broad daylight, if there was a desire to do so. In fact the
opposite is true. At every opportunity the Administration pressed the
Haitian authorities to deal—for the first time in Haitian history—
justly and swiftly with political violence.

The Administration has also been cooperative in dealing with the
Committee's investigation of Haiti. It is worth noting that this report
was written partly on the basis of more than 1000 documents and
numerous briefings provided to the International Relations Committee by various agencies of the Executive Branch.

Second, I am concerned about the way this Republican staff investigation was conducted. It was a partisan investigation that brought
forth a partisan result.

The State Department has responded to 14 document requests related to Haiti over the past year. All of the requests have come from
Republican members of Congress. The staff report is also based in part
on a Republican staff trip to Haiti earlier this year. In a departure from
long-standing Committee practice, my request to allow Democratic
staff to participate in that key trip was denied. Nor did Republican staff
allow Democrats to review in advance or provide dissenting views to
the report being issued today. This, too, is a break with Committee
practice.

Finally, I strongly disagree with the report's conclusion that the
Administration policy in Haiti is a failure. No one can argue that Haiti's
transition from dictatorship to democracy is complete, but no one can
deny that Haiti has made progress.

Haiti has had two free and fair elections. Haiti is no longer ruled by
a military regime that committed in excess of 3000 political murders.
Haitians are no longer fleeing their country by the hundreds, seeking
refuge in the United States. Haiti remains a fragile country: its democratic institutions are new and weak. But Haiti has begun economic
reforms in order to create, for the first time in Haitian history, a viable,
independent and open economy.

House Comm. on International Relations, 104th Cong., 2d Sess., *Hamilton
Praises Clinton Record on Haiti*, News Release, 1996.

220.   Leslie Casimir, "Ex-Miami Cop Killed in Haiti," *Miami Herald*, August 31, 1996, B1.

221.   "Slaying of Officer Is Haiti's Eighth in Recent Months," *Miami Herald*, August 14, 1996, A7.

222.   "Mob Kills 7 Suspects after Mayor's Murder," *Miami Herald*, June 1, 1996, A18.

223.   Ibid.

224.   "Haiti," *Miami Herald*, July 25, 1996, A15.

225.   Christopher Marquis, "Troops Sent to Haiti in Wake of Threats," *Miami Herald*, August 2, 1996, A1.

226.   Larry Rohter, "Haiti Jittery after Gunmen Stage Attack on Police Site," *New York Times*, August 20, 1996, A4; Nicole Volpe, "U.N. Troops, Police Battle Attackers in Haiti," *Miami Herald*, August 20, 1996, A8; Jean-Pierre, continuing interview.

227.   Rohter, "Haiti Jittery"; Volpe, "Police Battle Attackers."

228.   "Haiti," *Miami Herald*, August 21, 1996, A11.

229.   Jean-Pierre, continuing interview.

230.   Don Bohning and Christopher Marquis, "Security Unit Blamed in Haiti Deaths," *Miami Herald*, September 7, 1996, A1.

231.   Kurzban, continuing interview; Jean-Pierre, continuing interview.

232.   Kurzban, continuing interview; Jean-Pierre, continuing interview; continuing interview with anonymous sources.

233.   Bohning and Marquis, "Security Unit Blamed."

234.   See this chapter, "U.S. Politics: The Presidential Election."

235.   Christopher Marquis, "U.S. Lawmaker Wants Haiti Killings Probed," *Miami Herald*, September 11, 1996, A13.

236.   See this chapter, "U.S. Politics: The Presidential Election."

237.   Ibid.

238.   Christopher Marquis and Sandra Marquez Garcia, "Aristide Says Corruption, Chaos Tainting Preval's Government," *Miami Herald*, September 20, 1996, A14.

239.   Kurzban, continuing interview.

240.   Larry Rohter, "Pressed by U.S., Haitian President Begins Purge of Guards," *New York Times*, September 16, 1996, A6.

241.   Ibid.

242.   Christopher Marquis, "U.S. Rushes Security Agents to Haiti," *Miami Herald*, September 14, 1996, A1; Jean-Pierre, continuing interview.

243.   Marquis, "U.S. Rushes Agents to Haiti"; Jean-Pierre, continuing interview. Several sources claim that the suspected members of the security unit are simply scapegoats.

244.   Kurzban, continuing interview.

245.   "U.S. Recruits Police for Training Program," *Miami Herald*, October 3, 1996, A19.

246.   Larry Rohter, "U.S. Is Asking Police to Join A U.N. Force Helping Haiti," *New York Times*, October 2, 1996, A5.

247.   "Marines Fly to Haiti in a Show of Force," *New York Times*, August

22, 1996, A7; "U.S. Marines Arrive to Train at Tense Time," *Miami Herald,* August 22, 1996, A20.

248. "Haiti's Journalists Targets Again," *Miami Herald,* August 23, 1996, A14.

249. Jean-Pierre, continuing interview.

250. "Homemade Explosive Found on Main Street," *Miami Herald,* September 1, 1996, A22.

251. "Anti-Aristide Vandalism Reported at Car Wash," *Miami Herald,* September 14, 1996, A15.

252. "Ex-Congressman from Rightist Group Arrested," *Miami Herald,* September 9, 1996, 10A. After being held for more than two months, judges ordered the government to release Deus Jean-François because it could not provide evidence to justify holding him. Deus Jean-François is among approximately fifty people arrested since April 1996 for allegedly attempting to subvert the government or illegally possessing firearms. "Former Legislator Freed after 2 Months in Jail," *Miami Herald,* November 23, 1996, A21.

253. "Gunmen Attack, Kill 3 Near Haiti's Presidential Palace," *Miami Herald,* August 5, 1996, A8. These problems are exacerbated by the incompetence of the police and corruption of state officials. A recent incident makes the point. On December 26, 1996, gunmen held two customs inspectors hostage in the customs house of Cap-Haïtien, Haiti's main northern port, while the police stood idly by and refused to rescue them. The two inspectors had traveled from Port-au-Prince to examine merchandise from a cargo ship owned by Haitian businessman William Bove. Armed men blocked the office and refused to allow the inspectors out until they signed a release order for the unidentified merchandise. Under threat of serious physical harm, they signed the release order. Neither police nor port authority security officers would intervene. This incident reflects the difficulties the government faces in trying to reform customs procedures and the port authority, which generates the largest share of Haiti's meager tax revenues. For example, in November 1996, customs receipts from Haiti's fifteen customs houses amounted to almost $14 million, but the twelve provincial customs houses brought in only $2.5 million. "Gunmen in Haiti Seize a Shipload of Contraband," *Miami Herald,* December 26, 1996, A19.

254. "Haitian Plot Foiled by Arrests of Ex-Soldiers," *New York Times,* October 1, 1996, A7.

255. Catherine Orenstein, "Haitian Coup Leaders Get Away with Murder," *Miami Herald,* October 7, 1996, A13.

256. "Alleged Haiti Coup Plotters Arrested," *Miami Herald,* September 30, 1996, A8.

257. Sandra Marquez Garcia, "Haitian Dilemma: Pay Ex-Soldiers or Risk Unrest," *Miami Herald,* November 6, 1996, A13; Larry Rohter, "Haiti's 'Little Kings' Again Terrorize the Populace," *New York Times,* August 25, 1996, sec. 1, p. 3.

258. Garcia, "Haitian Dilemma"; Rohter, "Haiti's 'Little Kings.'"

259. Garcia, "Haitian Dilemma"; Rohter, "Haiti's 'Little Kings.'"

260. Garcia, "Haitian Dilemma"; Rohter, "Haiti's 'Little Kings.'"

261. Jean-Pierre, continuing interview.

262. "70 Shacks Razed in Haiti as Drug-Gang War Intensifies," *Miami Herald*, February 1997, A15.

263. Don Bohning, "Violence in Haiti has White House Biting its Nails," *Miami Herald*, August 26, 1996, A6.

264. "U.N. Votes to Extend Civilian Force 6 Months," *Miami Herald*, August 30, 1996, A14. On November 13, 1996, President Preval formally asked the UN to extend its peace-keeping mission through July 1996 to give Haiti's National Police Force more time and more training. "President Asks U.N. to Extend Its Mission," *Miami Herald*, November 14, 1996, A26. On December 5, 1996, the UN Security Council renewed the UN peace-keeping mission in Haiti for a maximum of eight months before it is shut down entirely at the insistence of Russia and China. In a 15–0 vote, the Security Council agreed to extend the mission until May 31, 1997, subject to renewal for another two months until July 31, 1997, as President Preval has requested. "Haiti," *Miami Herald*, December 6, 1996, A24; "U.N. Security Council Extends Mission in Haiti until May 31," *New York Times*, December 6, 1996, A5. Indeed, it is clear that the Haitian police need more training. They seem to be involved in numerous serious incidents. The Haitian people still do not trust them, and with good reason. On November 11, 1996, for example, hundreds of enraged people burned down a courthouse and police station in the town of Anse-a-Galets on Gonaive Island. The people were furious because the police had burst into a video club searching for a man who had had a dispute with a policeman over the weekend. According to witnesses, the police needlessly killed an acquaintance of this man. CIVPOL officers arrived by helicopter and helped evacuate the Haitian police from the town. "Angry Mob Attacks Police in Haiti," *Miami Herald*, November 13, 1996, A10. Members of the rescuing UN force were newly recruited Haitian-American police officers. Sandra Marquez Garcia, "Haitian-American Cops Play Vital Peacekeeping Role," *Miami Herald*, January 2, 1997, A8. Moreover, police seem unable or unwilling to stop crime. On December 13, 1996, twelve people died in a gun battle and stoning between a gang of robbers, and residents of Croix-de-Bouquets, a suburb of Port-au-Prince. The incident began when gunmen burglarized a home and killed the homeowners. Confronted by neighbors, the gunmen opened fire into a crowd. Residents captured one of them and stoned him to death. After the killings a crowd set fire to a pile of tires on an area highway to protest the lack of police protection. "Gun Battle Leaves 12 Dead," *Miami Herald*, December 14, 1996, A18.

In addition, corruption makes justice unlikely, and the Haitian people, therefore, do not trust the legal system. This has terrible effects on all aspects of Haitian life, including the economy. For example, the suspicious release from prison of a bank official accused of embezzlement has raised doubts about the government's ability to attract desperately needed foreign investment. The alleged embezzler, Faustin Marcellin, was chief of Promobank's check-clearing division. Promobank is one of Haiti's leading commercial banks. On October 4, 1996, a bank official accused him of embezzling $700,000. Marcellin signed a confession and was imprisoned pending an investigation. On December 9, 1996, he was released from the National Penitentiary and has since disappeared. So has the money. The special judicial commission that ordered his release later claimed that the release was a mistake. Marcellin's brother-in-law, attorney Kely Tabuteau, is a high-ranking official for a USAID-financed private company that gives legal assistance to the Justice Ministry, including the special commission that released Marcellin. "Jailed Banker's Release Imperils Haiti Investments," *Miami Herald*, December 16, 1996, A10.

265.   Larry Rohter, "An Extended Stay in Haiti," *New York Times*, September 17, 1996, A4.

266.   Kurzban, continuing interview; Jean-Pierre, continuing interview.

267.   President Aristide, continuing interview. Another serious problem confronts the Preval government—the return of former prominent Duvaliérists to Haiti. For example, Ernest Bennett, Jean-Claude Duvaliér's former father-in-law, and two of his sons recently returned to Haiti. Moreover, a ten-year constitutional ban keeping Duvaliérists from running for office expires in March 1997, when elections for local councils and a third of the Senate are scheduled. After Duvaliér's ouster in a popular uprising in 1986, the Bennetts fled Haiti, fearing for their lives. The Aristide government confiscated the Bennett family properties for misappropriation of state funds, but no prosecutions followed. The issue is whether the Preval government will now prosecute Bennett and other returning Duvaliérists for a wide variety of criminal acts committed during the Duvaliér era. Michael Norton, "Haiti's Democracy Tested with Return of Duvalier Ally," *Miami Herald*, January 8, 1997, A13.

268.   Sandra Marquez Garcia and Don Bohning, "Haitian Security Shake-Up Strengthens Preval's Grip," *Miami Herald*, September 16, 1996, A6. More recently, Aristide opponents have claimed that Aristide is working to destabilize President Preval's government. Senator Paul Denis, a member of the Haitian Senate investigating alleged corruption during Aristide's administration, has claimed that Aristide is orchestrating a disruption campaign by creating a new movement called the Lavalas Family. "Ex-President Accused of Disruption Scheme," *Miami Herald*, January 2, 1997, A8.

269.   Christopher Marquis and Sandra Marquez Garcia, "Aristide Says Corruption Tainting Government."

270.   Ibid.

271.   Kurzban, continuing interview.

CONCLUSION

1.   The National Labor Relations Act and the labor law regime in the United States comprise an interesting model for the civil society in Haiti.

2.   While the problems I have addressed in this book concerning the conditions of national life may well be worse in Haiti than almost anywhere else, political instability, health and environmental problems, and economic and social restructuring are problems that confront every nation struggling toward democracy. Indeed, these problems can be overcome only with the help of the international community. Even more importantly, these problems must necessarily be addressed in the first instance by the people of

each particular nation undergoing this transformation. Success depends crucially on the inculcation of democratic values into the hearts and minds of people. Ultimately, of course, democratic values must become part of the everyday actions of the people within each nation.

A number of countries besides the United States, such as Argentina, Trinidad, and Tobago, took leading roles in the MNF, which restored the democratically elected government to Haiti, and in the UNMIH, which succeeded the MNF. These countries and others in the hemisphere initially worked with the United States through the OAS in calling for a trade embargo of Haiti, launching an intense diplomatic initiative in the hope of peacefully solving Haiti's political crisis, and sending the MICIVIH and the Inter-American Commission on Human Rights to bear witness to Haiti's appalling human rights situation during the coup period.

The international community took these unprecedented measures in Haiti because it was in the self-interest of every democratically elected government in the region to do so. The message that came out of this effort was for the hemisphere at large. It said: "The days of dictators and coups are over. The days of committing massive human rights abuses with impunity are over." Anyone contemplating the overthrow of a democratically elected government anywhere in the region can now expect a strong, united hemispheric response. Coups simply will not be allowed to succeed. Thus, the international community's success in helping the population to reverse the coup in Haiti is a success for the policy of supporting democracy in the world at large.

3. See "Aristide Launches a New Movement," *Miami Herald,* November 4, 1996, A12; "Aristide to Unveil New Political Movement," *Miami Herald,* October 31, 1996, A22.

Index

Abellard, Lt. Cesar, 174
Ackerman, Bruce, 63
Adrien, Father Antoine, 122, 126
agriculture, 19–20, 26, 110, 190–91,
    268–69n. 199
Alfonsín, Raúl, 252–53n. 2
American Convention on Human
    Rights, 100, 251n. 23
American Rice, Inc., 268–69n. 199
Americas Watch, 226–27n. 29
amnesty: Constitution on, 32, 33,
    253n. 9; criticism of, 226–27n. 29;
    debate on, 40, 49–50; influence on,
    47; language on, 225n. 8; and nego-
    tiations, 32, 39; role of, 118–20
Anti-Gang Unit, 138, 173–74
Anti-International Monetary Fund Com-
    mittee, 267n. 178
Antoine, Jean-Ronique. *See* Antoine
    and Lecorps trial
Antoine, Pierre Max, 255n. 32
Antoine and Lecorps trial: background of,
    135–38, 263–64n. 153; events of, 138–
    39; jurors for, 135, 138; verdict in, 135
Argentina: human rights violations in,
    252–53n. 2; in MNF, 276–77n. 2
Aristide, Jean-Bertrand: accusations
    against, 195, 200, 204; alliances of,
    159, 161, 163; and amnesty, 32, 49–
    50; appointments by, 43, 136; back-
    ground of, 159; characterizations of,
    45–47, 211–12; conferences orga-
    nized by, 36, 165; criticism by, 206–
    7; economic policies of, 48–49, 87,
    183; election of, 18, 27–28, 105–6,
    158; and electoral impartiality, 150–
    52; exile of, 6; on foreign troops, 206;

and human rights issues, 252n. 1; mil-
    itary policies of, 7, 10, 28–29, 179–
    80; negotiations by, 31–33, 35–37; of-
    fice and living quarters of, 9, 213n. 3;
    opposition to, 30, 166, 168–69, 192,
    195–97, 222–24n. 2, 242–43n. 38,
    257n. 47, 271n. 215; plots against,
    198, 215n. 11, 243–44n. 39; prob-
    lems for, 42–43, 49–50; on reconcilia-
    tion and justice, 7–8; reinstatement
    of, ix–x, 1–8, 33, 41, 42, 90, 221–
    22n. 54; security for, 9, 199–200;
    staff of, 156, 198, 213n. 2, 214n. 7;
    tax policy of, 217–18n. 12, 251n. 18;
    term of office for, 154–55, 165; U.S.
    relations with, 45, 48–49, 206; vio-
    lence condemned by, 47, 164. *See also*
    Aristide Plan; presidency
Aristide Foundation for Democracy,
    211–12
Aristide Plan: deficiencies in, 109, 111–
    13; on economic reconstruction,
    109–13; goals of, 106; implementa-
    tion of, 108–9; on social reconstruc-
    tion, 106–9
Armand, Sgt. Andre Pierre, 215n. 11
armed forces: Aristide's policies on, 7,
    10, 28–29, 179–80; changes for, 85;
    control over, 88, 90, 106; corporat-
    ism of, 88; destabilization efforts by,
    197–207; discontent of disbanded,
    203–5; documents from, 166–68;
    professionalization of, 107. *See also*
    disarmament; Forces Armées d'Haïti
    (FAD'H); foreign troops; Haitian Na-
    tional Police (old); paramilitary; Ton-
    ton Macoutes